MORAL PLURALISM AND LEGAL NEUTRALITY

LAW AND PHILOSOPHY LIBRARY

VOLUME 9

WOJCIECH SADURSKI
Department of Jurisprudence,
University of Sydney

MORAL PLURALISM AND LEGAL NEUTRALITY

KLUWER ACADEMIC PUBLISHERS
DORDRECHT / BOSTON / LONDON

Library of Congress Cataloging in Publication Data

Sadurski, Wojciech, 1950-
Moral pluralism and legal neutrality / Wojciech Sadurski.
p. cm. -- (Law and philosophy library)
Includes bibliographical references.
ISBN 0-7923-0565-5 (U.S.)
1. Law and ethics. I. Title. II. Series.
BJ55.S55 1990
340'.112--dc20 89-28102

ISBN 0-7923-0565-5

Published by Kluwer Academic Publishers,
P.O. Box 17, 3300 AA Dordrecht, The Netherlands.

Kluwer Academic Publishers incorporates
the publishing programmes of
D. Reidel, Martinus Nijhoff, Dr W. Junk and MTP Press.

Sold and distributed in the U.S.A. and Canada
by Kluwer Academic Publishers,
101 Philip Drive, Norwell, MA 02061, U.S.A.

In all other countries, sold and distributed
by Kluwer Academic Publishers Group,
P.O. Box 322, 3300 AH Dordrecht, The Netherlands.

Printed on acid-free paper

Printed in the Netherlands

TABLE OF CONTENTS

ACKNOWLEDGEMENTS

This book was completed in 1988-89, during my study leave from the Department of Jurisprudence, University of Sydney, when I was a Fellow at the Netherlands Institute for Advanced Study in the Humanities and Social Sciences. I am grateful to the Institute and its staff for their hospitality and help. I also thank the University of Sydney, and in particular my friends from the Department of Jurisprudence, Alice Tay and Alex Ziegert, for their continuous support and encouragement.

Several friends and colleagues commented on drafts of papers which I wrote during the work on the book. In particular I would like to thank Jack Donnelly, Mary Gergen, Martin Krygier, Peter Kwan, Grant Lamond, Sarah McNaughton, David Mason, Philip Pettit and Stuart Scheingold.

Some parts of this book are based on material (which is here considerably revised and extended) previously published in *Oxford Journal of Legal Studies* vol. 7 (1987) pp. 258-278, *Virginia Law Review* vol. 73 (1987) pp. 339-397, *Law & Philosophy* vol. 7 (1988) pp. 35-66 and 351-374, and *Philosophical Investigations* vol. 12 (1989) pp. 33-51. I gratefully acknowledge the permission given by the publishers and editors of these journals for the use of these articles in the present revised version.

PREFACE

It is a commonplace that law and morality intersect and interpenetrate in all the areas of legal decision-making; that in order to make sense of constitutional, statutory or common-law questions, judges and other legal decision-makers must first resolve certain philosophical issues which include moral judgments of right and wrong. This is particularly evident with regard to constitutional interpretation, especially when constitutions give a mandate for the protection of the substantive norms and values entrenched as constitutional rights. In these situations, as a leading contemporary legal philosopher observed, the "Constitution fuses legal and moral issues, by making the validity of a law depend on an answer to complex moral problems".[1] But the need for substantive value elucidation is not confined, of course, only to constitutional interpretation under Bills of Rights.

This, however, immediately raises a dilemma stemming from the moral diversity and pluralism of modern liberal societies. How can law remain sensitive to this pluralism and yet provide clear answers to the problems which call for a legal resolution? Sharply conflicting values in modern societies clash in the debates over the death penalty, abortion, homosexuality, separation of state and religion, the scope of the freedom of the press, or affirmative action. It would often be difficult to discern a broader consensus within which these clashes of values operate, unless this consensus were described in such vague terms as to render it practically meaningless. To take just one example: In a recent exchange about affirmative action, one of the discussants argued convincingly that the disagreement about race-conscious preferential treatment represents a clash of fundamental values, not the conflict occurring in the context of an overriding commitment to racial equality shared by all the participants in the debate.[2]

How *does* contemporary law respond to this fundamental dilemma, and how *should* it respond? These two questions are taken up, subsequently, in the two parts of this book. The first part focuses on the diagnosis of the problem; the second, on prescription. The main goal of the first part of the book is to outline legal and philosophical dimensions of the dilemma raised for law by the moral pluralism of liberal societies. The three chapters of this Part have an ascending order of generality. I begin in the first chapter with the time-honoured method of legal analysis: a study of two actual cases. I will show how an attempt to satisfy conflicting moral demands is reflected at the level of judicial rhetoric, and how we can learn, from the study of judicial rhetoric, about the constraints imposed upon the judges by dominant conventional moralities, even when the judges take decisions which seem to go against the grain of the prevailing community standards. But since this conclusion, to avoid the charge of groundlessness, can be inferred only from a detailed analysis of the structure of judicial rhetoric in my selected case-studies, the reader will have to bear a rather detailed (the impatient will say: tedious) textual discussion of these cases, before more general conclusions will be drawn.

These conclusions will lead to a more direct treatment of the place of conventional moralities in judicial reasoning in Chapter 2. I will open my discussion by contrasting two conflicting theories about the role of community standards in judicial decisions, and having disposed of the "non-majoritarians" argument that the appeal to majority values by judges is undemocratic and illegitimate, I will reflect upon the question of how such an appeal is possible. I will look at a representative sample of methods by which the courts and legal scholars (proponents of the "majoritarian" theory of judicial review) try to resolve the conflict between an avowed fidelity to community standards and the actual moral pluralism in a society. Scepticism about the possibility of finding unambiguous guidance for the courts in actual conventional moral norms will lead me to raise, in Chapter 3, a number of more general philosophical issues about the existence of a deeper consensus behind the observable moral disagreements. In the process, I will review some of the recent philosophical responses to the basic dilemma described in earlier chapters: these responses stipulate "common understandings" or "shared meanings" of important social goods, or postulate the attitude of moral relativism by arguing about the agreement-based morality.

After this diagnosis of the problem, and a review of unsatisfactory answers to the dilemma posed in this book, Part II will contain a more positive discussion: it will focus on the once popular and recently much criticised postulate of law's neutrality between competing conceptions of the good. Chapter 4 provides a general account of this ideal against the background of fundamental presuppositions underlying a characteristically liberal discourse about the substance of fundamental liberty-rights. The contours of anti-perfectionist, neutralist conceptions are drawn in connection with the harm principle, the idea of "priority of the right over the good", and most fundamentally, in this moral constellation, the principle of equal moral agency. It will be argued that this set of interrelated ideas, implicit in the typically liberal rejection of legal paternalism and legal moralism, gives weight to a coherent liberal program which provides not only for a substantial protection of individual liberties, but also for regulative and redistributive functions of the state.

The remaining chapters develop the ideas outlined in Chapter 4 which is central to the argument in this book, with respect to two selected key issues of law and legal philosophy. Chapter 5 discusses the ideal of liberal neutrality in its application to the jurisprudence of the equal protection of the laws, and more specifically to the issue that superficially may seem to be incompatible with neutrality, namely to the special judicial protection of powerless minorities. The key argument which makes it possible to reconcile the ideal of neutrality with special protection lies in the rejection of the operative force of the analysis of "prejudice" against these minorities, and in the grounding of such protection in the objective social characteristics of powerless groups. Chapter 6 considers the theory of criminal punishment from an anti-perfectionist point of view: it argues for a specific retributivist account of criminal punishment, having its moral sources in the general principle of the equal moral agency of individuals. In Chapter 7, I discuss what has traditionally been seen as a rather evident area of application of a concept of state neutrality, namely the area of the relationship between the state and religion. I show how a neutral legal framework helps us to resolve a number of "hard cases" of conflicting demands deriving from the principles of free exercise of religion and of the non-establishment of religion by the state, as well as to handle the perplexing problem of the legal definition of "religion". In general, the message of the second part of this book is that the principle of neutrality towards competing substantive conceptions of the good — a principle in itself not neutral because derived from strongly normative liberal value judgments — provides the best normative framework for resolving the fundamental dilemma of the search for moral clarity of law in a morally non-consensual society.

PART ONE

MORAL PLURALISM AND LAW

CHAPTER 1

JUDICIAL RESPONSES TO MORAL PLURALISM (I): THE RHETORIC OF REASSURANCE

There are two styles of judicial argumentation in the opinions of the appellate courts[1] that may be distinguished for the purposes of this Chapter. The first provides a useful contrasting background: it consists in a straightforward, cumulative reasoning, in which argument unfolds in a linear way: one argument is piled upon another and each points in the same direction. Perhaps the simplest way of distinguishing this strategy is to suggest an easy practical test: after reading the first sentence, or the first paragraph, or the first page, of the judge's opinion, do we already know what the conclusion will be? For instance, when we read the first sentence of the Section I.A of Justice Marshall's opinion in *Bakke*:[2] "Three hundred and fifty years ago, the Negro was dragged to this country in chains to be sold into slavery",[3] we already sense the flavour of the opinion and, even if we had omitted the very first paragraph in which he anticipates his conclusion, we can easily guess what the conclusion will be. If we still have doubts, they will be easily dispelled by the second sentence: "Uprooted from his homeland and thrust into bondage for forced labor, the slave was deprived of all legal rights".[4] We already know how it will end, although the case is not about the Blacks, and much less about slavery. Rather, it is about the claim of a white applicant to a Medical School, that a preferential admissions program in favour of black people and other minority groups denies him equal protection of the laws. But we read the judges' opinions with the political context of the case in our minds, and we know that more conservative judges are likely to disagree with the policy of preferential admissions; hence they will have little interest in mentioning, let alone emphasizing, the past or present discrimination against Blacks. In contrast, those judges who have taken a political option in favour of preferential admissions, will be likely to support their positions with dramatic descriptions of the Blacks' misfortune in order to create a predisposition in the audience, for a more compassionate and generous attitude towards the disadvantaged racial groups. When, therefore, Justice Marshall begins his argument with the invocation of "chains" and "slavery" and "forced labor", he sets the tone for the remainder of his opinion. We can recognize that he belongs to a particular camp, and it easy to guess what the conclusion will be.

Marshall's opening shots locate the case in a broader context, and this is the context of the history of racial discrimination in the United States. Contextualism works here to the detriment of Alan Bakke, and favours the Court's upholding of the legality of preferential admissions. In contrast, decontextualizing *Bakke* reduces the chances of the University's winning the legal battle in defence of its admissions process and improves the prospects for Alan Bakke: if the context of racial discrimination in the United States is deemed irrelevant, it is hard to see how the University might lawfully exclude Bakke while admitting black applicants with significantly lower scores. Now read the opinion of Mr. Justice Stevens. The first two sentences of Section I of his opinion are: "This is not a class action. The controversy is between two specific litigants".[5] Although nothing is said yet about the merits of the case, we already know that the stage is set for the inevitable conclusion. Everything between "This is not a class action" and the final phrase: "The University's special admissions program violated Title VI of the Civil Rights Act of 1964 by excluding Bakke from the Medical School because of his race"[6] is a steady, gradual, linear, straightforward movement in a perfectly predictable direction.

Now in a sense both Marshall and Stevens are right: the litigation is between two specific parties and at the same time it is in context. As with any judicial procedure, it concerns a specific claim by one litigant against another; and as with any litigation, it is part of the broader social setting. Emphasizing one or another of these two aspects therefore serves as a rhetorical technique for supporting one or another fundamental value judgment about the rightness of preferential quotas, and of winning the adherence of the audience to these value judgments. It is a rhetorical technique which is, as it were, transparent because it reveals immediately the substantive goals it serves.

1. CONVOLUTED RHETORICAL STYLE: TWO CASES

The straightforward usage of judicial rhetoric is, naturally, the most frequent and typical, and the example given above may be supplemented by hundreds of others. But what is really puzzling is the opposite situation, in which the rhetoric used by a judge seems to ground a conclusion opposite to the one ultimately reached. There are judicial opinions in which a conclusion is reached in a roundabout, even convoluted way, but not all these are of relevance here. Neither am I interested in those cases in which the conclusion is simply not warranted by the arguments. But I am interested in the mode of argumentation in which the whole logic of reasoning seems to point in one direction, until there comes a twist in an argument, a sort of about-face, an unexpected reversal, and the conclusion reached is the opposite of that we expected on the basis of the opening remarks by the judge. I will illustrate this strategy by two examples taken from the practice of the highest courts in the United States and Australia.

a) Paris Adult Theatre

In *Paris Adult Theatre I v. Slaton*[7] the United States Supreme Court considered the constitutionality of pornography prohibition, and more particularly, the privacy-based challenge by the owners of an adult movie theatre to a civil provision allowing injunctive relief against the presentation of obscene materials. Before briefly summarizing the Supreme Court's conflicting opinions, it will be useful for me to describe the context of the Court's attitude to pornography at that time, especially since the judges in *Paris Adult Theatre* made extensive use of two particular precedents: *Griswold v. Connecticut*[8] and *Stanley v. Georgia.*[9] Although *Griswold* was concerned with a quite different matter, namely with the sale of contraceptive devices, it was relevant to *Paris Adult Theatre* because it announced emphatically the existence of a constitutional right to privacy. The Court decided to strike down the Connecticut anti-contraception statutes on the basis that they unconstitutionally intruded upon the right of marital privacy. The Court did not, however, determine the nature of that right and did not specify its contents; rather, it extrapolated the right to privacy from the penumbral radiations of existing constitutional guarantees and asserted that "[v]arious guarantees in the [Bill of Rights] create zones of privacy".[10] *Stanley* confirmed and consolidated the privacy argument, focusing on the area of obscenity control, and emphasizing the privacy of the home. The defendant was convicted under Georgia law for the possession of obscene materials. Since it had been an established principle that obscenity is not protected by constitutional guarantees,[11] Georgia claimed that it could freely exercise police power to control what it regarded as offensive. The Court rejected this contention stating that the regulation of obscenity should not reach into the privacy of the individual's home.

In this context came *Paris Adult Theatre:* the right of privacy had already been firmly (if quite recently) established, and its ambit had been determined so as to embrace the right of persons to possess, read or watch obscene materials in their homes. The reversal of the theatre owner's appeal would mean that this right was strictly confined to the boundaries of a private house only: this would in turn suggest that the genuine rationale of the right to privacy as affirmed in *Stanley* was that its exercise does not offend any unwilling persons. The adoption of such an analysis would rationalize the conclusion that offensiveness to public morals may be a justifying basis for legal prohibition and, consequently, that where there is no likelihood of such an effect, there are no ground for regulation. *Paris Adult Theater,* in this theoretical perspective, would therefore be distinguished from *Stanley* on the basis of the distinction between private home and public theatre. A judge who takes this line of interpretation of *Stanley* would thereby commit himself to the view that the law may legitimately enforce dominant public morality or prevent offence to others.[12]

In contrast, a judge who wished to protect the theatre owner's right to exhibit pornographic movies, and the individuals' right to watch obscene movies of their own choice, would disregard the relevance of the distinction between public and private activity, and interpret *Stanley* from a different angle: a decisive rationale in protecting the right to have obscene materials would be that every adult individual has a right to do what he wants with his time and money as long as he harms nobody. From this theoretical perspective, *Stanley* and *Paris Adult Theater* turn out to be analogous, and the principle in the former case should be applicable to the latter. In both these cases the readers and viewers are adult and mature individuals who acquired the materials (or tickets to the cinema) in a voluntary manner and whose action does not harm anyone. This line of argument, therefore, commits a judge to Mill's principle that harm to others is the only legitimate basis for a State interference with a person's liberty. So, not surprisingly, we might speculate that judges favouring the affirmation of the Georgia Supreme Court decision would take a philosophical line close to that identified in jurisprudence textbooks with the Stephen/Devlin approach to legal enforcement of morals, while the judges willing to reverse the anti-pornography decision would argue along Mill/Hart lines.

But, equipped with these expectations, we are in for a surprise. Chief Justice Burger, who delivered the majority judgment, opened his argument (after having stated the facts) with a categorical rejection of the theory that "obscene, pornographic films acquire constitutional immunity from state regulation simply because they are exhibited for consenting adults only".[13] This sounds illiberal but we quickly realize that the grounds for this rejection are not moralistic at all, but are instead firmly connected with Mill's harm principle (without mentioning it explicitly). The basis for a state regulation of obscene materials is that there are "legitimate state interests at stake in stemming the tide of commercialized obscenity" and these include, in particular, "the interest of the public in the quality of life and the total community environment, the tone of commerce in the great city centers, and, possibly, the public safety itself".[14]

What comes next in Burger's opinion is an elaboration of the theme set by this statement, an elaboration aimed at showing that "exposure to obscene material adversely affects men and women or their society".[15] Note that these are *other* men and women whose interests are at stake, not those who are the active consumers of the obscene materials. Burger is at pains to show that obscenity necessarily affects adversely those who do not wish to be so affected.[16] Both the language and the spirit of the argument is, therefore, unequivocally grounded in the arguments about harm to others, and to society as a whole. But, as if to dispel any remaining doubts, Burger asserts:

> The issue ... goes beyond whether someone, or even the majority, considers the conduct depicted as "wrong" or "sinful". The States have the power to make a morally neutral judgment that public exhiition of obscene material, or commerce in such material, has a tendency to injure the community as a whole...[17]

The last phrase clearly shows the influence of Mill's view on Burger's argument. Pornography control is represented as based on a "morally neutral judgment" about injury to the community, and the appeals to judgments about the behaviour being "wrong" or "sinful" are explicitly rejected as irrelevant. The final conclusion (the upholding of the ban on pornographic films) comes therefore as a result of the judgment about the harm to the community.

Now consider the dissenting opinion by Justice Brennan. This is a very lengthy opinion, most of which is devoted to a rather technical analysis of the test of protected expression, and to the demonstration of the vagueness of the existing standards which distinguish between protected and unprotected speech. Although Brennan criticizes the existing standards on these grounds, he rejects at the same time a radically liberal view that "the First Amendment bars the suppression of any sexually oriented expression".[18] He refers to the *Stanley* case to support the rejection of thought control, but then immediately produces this crucial passage:

> That is not to say, of course, that a State must remain utterly indifferent to — and take no action bearing on — the morality of the community. The traditional description of state police power does embrace the regulation of morals as well as the health, safety and general welfare of citizenry. ... And much legislation — compulsory public education

laws, civil rights laws, even the abolition of capital punishment — is grounded, at least in part, on a concern with the morality of the community.[19]

This is a very powerful and rather orthodox statement of the community's right to enforce its dominant morality. States must not remain "indifferent to ... the morality of the community": this proposition clearly goes far beyond Mill's harm principle, especially when coupled with the examples of legitimate State intervention given by Brennan. The example of "compulsory public education laws" is very significant in this context. The Mill/Hart philosophy may accept this interference with individual freedom precisely because the agents coerced are not mature adult individuals. By equating other cases of regulating morality with compulsory education, Brennan implicitly rejects the moral relevance of the child/adult distinction which is of such an importance for the liberal tradition as far as the legitimate interference with individual freedom is concerned. In doing so, Brennan quite firmly establishes his philosophical perspective on *Paris Adult Theater* as being outside the Mill/Hart liberal tradition.

At this point there is a twist in Brennan's reasoning. Having established the states' right to legislate with regard to the morality of the community, Brennan continues:

But the State's interest in regulating morality by suppressing obscenity, while often asserted, remains essentially unfocused and ill defined. And, since the attempt to curtail unprotected speech necessarily spills over into the area of protected speech, the effort to serve this speculative interest through the suppression of obscene material must tread heavily on rights protected by the First Amendment.[20]

The contrast between the moral weight of Brennan's commitment to the regulation of morality on one hand, and the relative insignificance of his reasons for rejecting the suppression of obscene material on the other hand, is striking. And yet these latter grounds are those which substantiate the final conclusion about the invalidity of Georgia action. Overall, there is an ironic symmetry between Burger's and Brennan's opinions. Burger asserts a serious and significant principle, that of the right of the State to make *neutral* judgments about what is harmful to a community, but he grounds his final decision on the assertion which he himself calls "unprovable" and which is, in any event, extremely weak: the connection between obscenity and danger to public safety, the adverse impact on the unwilling public etc.[21] Brennan asserts an important and fundamental principle, that of the State's right to regulate the morality of the community, but his conclusion is based on grounds which are evidently weak, namely that suppressing obscenity is "unfocused", ill defined, and tends to spill over into the other areas. All these are purely contingent, practical matters which may be remedied by sharp legislation and proper enforcement, and which are in any case incomparably less important than the basic philosophical principle adopted by Brennan. The general outcome of *Paris Adult Theater* is therefore that a Mill/Hart judge upholds the suppression of pornography and a Devlinite invalidates it! One feels that if Burger and Brennan swapped their philosophical luggage, they would be much more comfortable in their arguments.

b) Gerhardy

Gerhardy v. Brown[22] was the first, and so far, the only, reverse-discrimination case before the Australian High Court. The Justices were asked to determine whether a particular piece of state legislation, drawing a distinction on racial ground for the benefit of a disadvantaged group, was constitutional and valid. The legislation in question was s. 19(1) of the South Australian *Pitjantjatjara Land Rights Act* of 1981, which made it an offence for a non-member of the Pitjantjatjara tribe to enter the Pitjantjatjara land, a large area in South Australia, without the permission of a corporate body representing the Pitjantjatjara people.

I will not summarize and discuss the High Court's decision in detail[23] but will only try to reconstruct the scheme of a "convoluted" rhetoric in the Judges' decision. All the judges with one exception found that the exclusion-from-land provision was prima facie discriminatory.[24] None of them seriously considered whether a distinction aimed at protection of an otherwise disadvantaged minority is equally discriminatory as an invidious distinction. In other words, they implicitly adopted a theory of "colour-blindness" according to which any racial distinction, irrespective of its invidious or benign character, is discriminatory by the sole virtue of the fact that it classifies citizens on the basis of race.

The opinion of Chief Justice Gibbs is very significant from this point of view. As "a critical question in the case"[25] he considers whether the exclusion-from-land provision is affected by s. 10(1) of the *Racial Discrimination Act* which provides that if, by reason of a provision of a particular law, persons of a particular race do not enjoy a right enjoyed by persons of another race, or enjoy such a right to a less extent, then, by force of s. 10, the first-mentioned persons shall enjoy that right to the same extent as those other persons. Peculiarly, s. 10 does not render a discriminatory provision void, but only confers upon everyone the same rights as those conferred upon a particular race. In practice, applying s. 10 to the exclusion-of-the-land provision would render this measure inoperative. The result would be identical, therefore, to a straightforward invalidation of the challenged provision.

There are various ways, identified by Gibbs, to avoid this conclusion, and hence, to avoid invalidation of the exclusion-from-the land provision with the help of this particular legal device, but he rejects all of them, one by one. The first would be to say that the *Pitjantjatjara Land Rights Act* does not disadvantage "persons of a particular race" but rather all persons other than those belonging to "a particular race" while "persons of a particular race", that is, Pitjantjatjara people, benefit from the distinction.[26] The lack of fit between the statutory notion of "persons of a particular race" and those who are in fact disadvantaged by the provision, would render s. 10 inapplicable to this situation, and hence incapable of affecting s. 19 of the *Pitjantjatjara Land Rights Act*. Such a defense of the measure in question would therefore distinguish between the "positive" or "benign" discrimination, aimed at benefiting a particular race, and an invidious one. But Gibbs rejects this with argument resorting to a time-honoured "parade of horribles" strategy: "On this suggested construction, it would be possible, for example, for the law of a State effectively to provide that only persons of the white races might use certain public facilities, for such a law would disadvantage, not persons of a particular race, but persons of many races. It is absurd to think that this result was intended...".[27] Although the concept of "colour blindness" is not used here expressly, it is clear that the aim of this analogy is to equate the discrimination in favour of a particular group, considered as disadvantaged, with a discrimination against such a group. This philosophy offers little prospects for upholding the exclusion-from-land regulation.

Two other possible defences of this regulation are also rejected by Gibbs. One concerns the classification in question being based allegedly not on racial criteria, but rather on the criteria of "traditional ownership" of land,[28] and the other that the rights in question do not belong to the "field of public life", but are purely private, and as such are not affected by the operation of s. 10(1) of the *Racial Discrimination Act*.[29] What is interesting is that in refuting both these arguments, Gibbs uses the same "parade of horribles" strategy, in which benign and invidious classifications are effectively equated. As to the former, he says that he "see[s] no distinction" between the law in question and a hypothetical law which would provide as follows: "white men and women who are the traditional owners of land in a particular town have unrestricted rights of access to that town: no-one else may enter it without their permission".[30] As to the latter defence, he answers that to analogize the restriction-from-the land with the ordinary, private-law privileges of the landowner won't do: "the vast area of the lands is enough in itself to falsify the analogy. If the vesting of the ownership of lands in a corporation were enough to justify the exclusion of persons from those lands on the grounds of race, it would be easy indeed to introduce a system of apartheid without contravening the Convention or the *Racial Discrimination Act*".[31] Hence, a measure aimed at a protection of a disadvantaged minority is criticized using an analogy to a hypothetical situation of white racism or even apartheid: particular interpretations of the benefits for the Blacks are rejected by showing how obnoxious would be the acceptance of similar benefits for the Whites. All these hypothetical examples have a clear rhetorical function: it is to convey the message, without stating it openly, that there is no substantive difference between the racially-conscious benefits for a disadvantaged minority and for the dominant race. Implied conclusion: racial classifications in favour of, and against, a disadvantaged minority must either stand or fall together. It is perhaps hard to find a more characteristic case of judicial "colour blindness" philosophy.

We reached a point in our description of the judgment (and this description applies to all other opinions in Gerhardy as well, with the exception of Justice Dawson for reasons explained above)[32] where, *as a matter of a fundamental, philosophical principle,* it has been established that considerations of the "discriminatory" nature of an act do not incorporate the criteria of invidiousness, but only the formal issue of whether a classification is based on racial grounds. This is what "colour-blindness" is all about: racial classifications, benign or invidious, are discriminatory alike. And at this point comes the twist, a sudden turnaround, *lex ex machina* reversing miraculously the whole course of the argument which seemed to lead inevitably to the conclusion about the illegality of exclusion-from-the-land clauses. The name of the trick: "special measures". Having mobilized all his guns against s. 19 of the *Pitjantjatjara Land Rights Act,* Gibbs asks a question "whether s. 19 may be justified as a special measure to which Art. 1(4) of the [International] Convention [on the Elimination of All Forms of Racial Discrimination] applies".[33] Art. 1(4) provides that special measures taken for the sole purpose of securing adequate advancement of certain racial or ethnic groups requiring protection necessary to ensure them equal enjoyment of human rights and fundamental freedoms shall not be deemed racial discrimination, provided that such measures do not lead to the maintenance of separate rights for different racial groups and that they shall not be continued after their objectives have been achieved. To the question of whether s. 19 answers this description of "special measures" Gibbs, at the very end of his opinion, gives an affirmative answer, and this permits him to uphold the *Land Rights Act.*[34] And similarly with every other judge (again, with the exception of Dawson). The general structure of all the opinions in *Gerhardy* is exactly the same: they first establish the conflict between the exclusion-from-the-land clause and the prohibition of racial discrimination; subsequently they validate the former as a "special measure".

But the problem with this reasoning is that the *Land Rights Act* hardly fits the description of "special measures" in the International Convention. There are at least three reasons for this. First, Art. 1(4), to which the judges refer in their analysis of "special measures", contains two provisos restricting the use of the "special measures" defence: in order to be legal, these measures must not maintain separate rights for different racial groups *and* they must not be continued after their objectives have been achieved. Note that the wording of art. 1(4) suggests that these are two independent conditions, each of which has to be satisfied in order to validate "special measures". Clearly, the literal application of these two requirements must invalidate the exclusion-from-the-land provision which does introduce separate rights (with respect to the entry to the land) for the Pitjantjatjaras and non-Pitjantjatjaras.

Secondly, the way in which "special measures" are described both in Arts. 1(4) and 2(2) of the Convention clearly suggests that they are seen as temporary, transitory means to an end the achievement of which will make them unnecessary in the future. There is an immediate contrast between "the air of temporariness" of this description and the "air of permanence" of the *Land Rights Act* with its exclusion-from-the-land provision, the aim of which is to protect the separate identity of a particular social group. There is nothing to suggest that the legislator envisages the repeal of the Act at a certain stage.

Thirdly, and most importantly, there is a contrast between the legitimate ends of "special measures", described by the Convention as "adequate advancement of certain racial or ethnic groups ... to ensure to such groups equal enjoyment ... of human rights and fundamental freedoms"[35] and the aims of the *Land Rights Act* which consist in the protection and preservation of Pitjantjatjara culture. The Judges of the High Court describe the aims of the Act in terms of "protection",[36] "preservation"[37] and even "restoration"[38] seemingly without realizing that the Convention defines the goals of the "special measures" in a totally different way. The Convention uses the language of "advancement" which suggests upgrading the situation of a particular disadvantaged group, raising it to a norm already enjoyed by the rest of society. But this is not what the *Land Rights Act* is about: the claim of the Pitjantjatjaras is not to be helped in "advancement" but simply to be left alone.

Now to all these three objections one may perhaps reply that they are inconclusive and somewhat formalistic. As to the first point made above, one may argue that to take literally two provisos of Art. 1(4) would be so rigourous as to make it virtually impossible to validate any serious compensatory programme of preferences. This cannot have been the intention of the drafters of the *Land Rights Act;* hence the appeal by the judges to the temporal sequence of Art. 2(2) seems justified. Second, "the air of permanence" of the *Land Rights Act* can also be accommodated in the "special measures" definition. After all, whether the Act becomes permanent is a matter for the future. And third, the aim of "restoration" may be interpreted in terms of "advancement". The ultimate umpires of what is good for a group — of what advances its interests — are the members of the group itself: if they want simply to be left alone, so be it. All this is right, and with some stretch of imagination we may perhaps be able to interpret the Act to make it comply with the "special measures" provisions. But now let us pause for a moment and consider what was the aim of engaging in this entire exercise in the first place. It was to defend the Act on the basis of a strict interpretation of a concrete legal provision, rather than with reference to the substantive moral values with all their vagueness and indeterminacy. Yet such a strict argument is unavailable with regard to "special measures". They can do the job only if we stretch the meaning of the "special measures" provisos very widely.

An alternative available strategy was to argue that exclusion-from-the-land is not discriminatory in the first place, not even *prima facie* discriminatory, because it lacks the attributes of invidiousness or arbitrariness.[39] This would require a sound philosophical argument about the nature of discrimination, and a substantive assessment of the classification in question. But the Court has chosen an opposite strategy: on the basis of a principled, if misguided, philosophical argument concerning colour blindness it has undermined the legitimacy of the regulation in question, only to validate it hastily on the basis of an argument of "special measures" which evidently doesn't hold water in this particular case.

2. THE STRATEGY OF REASSURANCE

The puzzle to be solved is this: why did the judges, in the decisions discussed above, prefer to reach their conclusions in such a zig-zag, roundabout fashion, rather than going to the point by the shortest way? In *Paris Adult Theater* we have seen that Chief Justice Burger first considered the anti-enforcement-of-morality arguments, and then concluded, with the help of the argument about alleged social harm, that the prohibition of pornography was legal. In a dissenting opinion, which forms a mirror image of the majority opinion, Justice Brennan accepted the principle of the state's right to legislate with regard to morality, but decided that he would invalidate the suppression of obscene materials, because of the risk that obscenity control might be unfocused and might spill over into other areas of expression. In *Gerhardy* the judges accepted the colour-blind theory of discrimination, but upheld the positive-discrimination provision in the *Land Rights Act* as a "special measure".

In all three opinions (we may, for the purposes of our analysis treat *Gerhardy* as a single opinion, and Burger's and Brennan's opinions in *Paris Adult Theater* as two distinct opinions) the pattern is identical: the fundamental, principled arguments incline the decision in one direction, but a "cancelling factor" appears, which suspends the force of the major arguments and results in the final decision being opposite to that suggested by the main argument. In all three opinions there is a clear imbalance between the weight of the principled, philosophical argument (in Burger's opinion in *Paris Adult Theater:* neutrality of State towards enforcing morality; in Brennan's opinion in *Paris Adult Theater:* community's right to enforce its dominant morality; in *Gerhardy:* the principle of colour-blindness) on the one hand, and on the other hand, the weight of the "cancelling factor" (in Burger's opinion: harm produced by pornography; in Brennan's opinion: difficulties in focussing clearly on the suppression of obscenity; in *Gerhardy:* application of "special measures" clauses). The weakness of these cancelling factors is more obvious in the context of the decisions than when asserted in an abstract fashion. Standing alone, they may appear as heavy as the arguments they are meant to cancel, but — as I have tried to demonstrate above — they are clearly unsatisfactory in the way they are used in the context of the three opinions. The assumptions about the harm produced by pornography are, in Burger's own words, "unprovable"; the objections to legislating morality in Brennan's version are related solely to the contingencies of the legislative drafting; the relevance of "special measures" provisions to the *Pitjantjatjara Land Rights*

Act is highly doubtful.

Why then did the judges adopt this strange manner of argumentation? There is one hypothesis that can be briefly considered (and rejected) at the outset. It would suggest that the structure of judicial argument represents an ordinary weighing and balancing of all competing arguments, with the final conclusion coming as an outcome of this process of weighing and balancing. In controversial cases there are prima facie reasonable arguments which point in different directions: honesty requires canvassing the merits of all these competing arguments and counter-arguments, and the more seriously we consider the arguments of our opponents, the more convinced we may feel about the conclusion. A refinement of this hypothesis would characterize the three opinions as cases of the "devil's advocate" strategy of argumentation: you try to give the best possible account of the arguments you disagree with, and if, after a proper deliberation, they do not withstand the test of counter-arguments, the latter prevail.

But the immediate response to this hypothesis, both in its straightforward, "balancing and weighing" version, and in its "devil's advocate" version, is that the strategies of the three opinions discussed above simply do not fit any of these descriptions. For one thing, the force of the arguments against any of the three conclusions reached is evidently stronger than the arguments in their favour: any balancing of the competing considerations would have to produce a result contrary to that achieved. The ordinary, routine weighing of the arguments cannot substantiate the result in any of the three cases. If, in turn, they are taken to exemplify the "devil's advocate" strategy, then the outcome would be really perverse: the devil actually wins the case. Burger as an advocate of moral neutrality clearly sounds more convincing than Burger censoring pornography; Brennan favouring enforcement of morality wins points against Brennan lamenting the "unfocused" nature of suppressing pornography; Gibbs *et. al.* postulating colour-blindness defeat Gibbs recognizing land rights as "special measures". If they really chose their convoluted strategies only to appreciate the arguments opposite to their own, then in the course of this exercise they all actually crossed the lines and became allies of their hypothetical opponents.

The "weighing and balancing" version of this explanation presupposes a judge who approaches a case to be decided with a *tabula rasa* state of mind: he or she is seen as a person who, without any preconceptions, bias or result-oriented intentions, compiles all possible arguments in favour and against any particular substantive outcome. But the view of a judge who is initially absolutely neutral as to the outcome of the decision can only be suspect. This is not to suggest that typically judicial arguments should be seen as merely *ex post* rationalizations of the choices already made, but rather that the very manner in which a judge conceptualizes the legal aspects of a hard case, selects, presents and assesses various arguments and doctrines, is to some degree already an effect of his own substantive values and intentions. When the facts and legal arguments are presented to him, he must meet them with a kind of censoring device which gauges the arguments against his previous ideas and beliefs. Some information and interpretations are ignored; others — which bolster an already firm opinion — are accepted more readily than is warranted by their merits. A realistic picture of the mental processes of a judge (and in particuar, of an appellate judge in a hard case) resembles probably something like a "reflective equilibrium":[40] the rules, principles and doctrines are selected in order to match initial value-judgments about a given legal issue (value judgments held prior to the deliberation of this given case), but these value judgments are subsequently subject to refinement, modification and sometimes rejection under the pressure of the realization of particular rules, principles and doctrines which seem to "control" a given issue.

This first hypothesis therefore fails, which is no surprising since, apart from anything else, it proposes finding an explanation for a particular mode of judicial rhetoric within the structure of argumentative discourse itself. This would make sense if judicial opinions were indeed exercises in intellectualism; if the best way to understand them was confined, as it were, to the very functioning of the argumentative modes. But this is a perspective which badly distorts the genuine nature of judicial decisions for it ignores a key aspect of them, namely their political role. Now judicial decisions *can* be analyzed as, among other things, theoretical arguments and pieces of reasoning, but there is surely much more to them than this. Judges not only think, reason, argue; they also decide about other people's lives. They participate in policy-making in that they determine, along with other political agencies, the distribution of benefits and burdens in their societies. They play an important, sometimes crucial, role in allocating the valuable assets of society: wealth, power, rights and liberty. The outcomes of judicial decisions may determine whether some people, or groups of people, will have access (and how much) to the scarce desired goods in a society, and what use of these goods they will be permitted to make. And, of course, courts also decide, or participate in deciding, about the distribution of unpleasant things: taxes, fines, duty to serve in the army, deprivation of liberty and life. Their utterances have meaning as constituting the discourse, but also as constituting part of the continuous flow of decisions about authoritative allocation of values in a society. In the memorable words of A. A. Leff, a trial "is like a game of chess in which, when the King is mated, a real king dies".[41] Real kings, queens, knights etc. die, and they also lose or regain liberty, acquire or lose wealth, obtain or are deprived of control over their children, get jobs or lose them, are made happy or miserable, when judges hand down their decisions. And judges do much more than that: it may well happen that as a result of their decisions universities are required to admit a certain proportion of minority applicants, fire brigades are prohibited from requiring a high school diploma from the candidates for a firefighter's job, local authorities are prohibited from constructing dams in some places, hospitals are told how to treat the mentally ill, doctors are allowed (or not) to conduct abortions, food producers are forced to follow set standards for food handling, and so on and so forth. The courts uphold, modify or nullify the authoritative acts made by the other political agencies, notably the legislatures and the executive branch. In a word, courts are in the business of policy-making.

This may be a banal proposition (though certainly not for all),[42] but it is only when we appreciate this political dimension of judicial decision-making, that shall we be able to make sense of the roundabout strategies of judicial rhetoric. For the Court not only determines the allocation of values in a community, it is also conditioned, within limits, by the community. The judges espouse, discuss and enforce values, but so do their communities. To what extent the judges are value-innovators rather than merely echoing conventional morality, is a matter that can be rationally discussed only with regard to particular historical and social circumstances. But, as political agents within concrete socio-political settings, they are never fully immune to the values shared by those who constitute dominant social forces in their societies. And there is a legion of legal scholars (some of whom will be discussed in Chapter 2) who explain why they *must not* be immune to these values.

This complex relationship between the Court and the dominant morality helps to throw a light on the "puzzle" we identified earlier in this Chapter. Moreover, understanding the causes of this puzzle helps in turn to appreciate better the nature of this relationship. The assumption here is that the judicial reasoning belongs to the domain of "rhetoric" in a non-pejorative, Perelmanian sense of the word,[43] that is, to the realm of argumentation rather than demonstration, and that its aims are basically to convince and persuade the audience — "to elicit or increase the adherence of the members of an audience to theses that are presented for their consent"[44] — rather than to demonstrate the validity of its conclusions through formally logical means. Moreover, if the rhetorical modes are adapted to a particular audience, then the puzzles in the rhetoric may perhaps be explained by information about the audience, or, more particularly by the rapport between the audience and the "rhetor". What must be kept in mind for our purposes is that, first, as any student of rhetoric will say, it is a prerequisite of any successful rhetorical activity, indeed of any communication, that there be at least some basic shared ideas, beliefs, experiences etc. between the communicator and her audience;[45] second, that the specificity of the relations between the highest appellate courts and their audiences (as compared to any rhetorical situation as such) is that these relations are moulded by the combination of authority (for, in democratic societies, the highest appellate courts enjoy a high degree of moral legitimacy) and power (for the rulings are enforceable by coercion). And if this particular social situation shapes rhetorics, then unusual rhetorics may reveal something important about this social situation.

Here is a proposed explanation of the roundabout strategy of judicial argumentation: in making the decision which may be unpopular among the dominant social forces of the community, and which conflicts with socially dominant attitudes, the Court at the same time affirms its allegiance to these dominant forces and to their shared values. It does so by endorsing a philosophy which is accepted by its traditional clientele: a coalition of politically and economically dominant social groups, though the specific outcome of an individual decision risks unpopularity.[46] But on balance the decision will be palatable because, apart from the particular ruling on a particular matter, there is also a broader hidden message: this is a message of reassurance that the Court stands firmly by the rules of the dominant social morality, though for some contingent reasons it had to decide in this particular way. This hidden message, if it is to be heard by those to whom it is addressed, must be powerful enough to outweigh the possible disappointment of a majority with a particular outcome of the decision. That is why the weight of the "principled" arguments in our examples was so much heavier than the reasons given for the decisions. The predictably unpopular decisions come therefore in a package, and a possible conflict with the dominant values is immediately moderated, or nullified, by the philosophy endorsed by the Court. Ultimately, the "puzzle" of the roundabout strategy can be explained not by the methods and aims of argumentation, but by the political context in which the Court operates.

Let us now reconsider, from the perspective of this hypothesis, judicial strategies in the cases discussed above. *Gerhardy* is an easier case, for it is a unanimous verdict. A practical, particular outcome is that a protective measure for Aboriginals has been upheld: non-Pitjantjatjaras are prohibited from entering upon the Pitjantjatjara land. Morally speaking, it is a decent and commendable decision: it recognizes that something positive has to be done to mitigate "the effects which almost two centuries of alien settlement have had on the lives of the Australian Aboriginals".[47] The decision upholding the special land-rights arrangements in one of the States can be seen, and applauded, as an attempt to undo some of these effects and to permit one of the Aboriginal groups to preserve and develop its own culture in relative isolation from unwanted contacts with other ethnic groups. But the degree of approval for such measures in Australian society as a whole is very limited. The majority of Australians do think that special land rights for Aborigines are unfair and discriminate against Whites, and the majority do think that Aboriginals should have the same legal access (no less but no more) to acquiring land as any other Australian citizen. The history of past discrimination against Aboriginals, or special spiritual relationship between Aboriginals and their land, or distance between the common-law regime of real property and traditional Aboriginal customary arrangements, do not convince the majority of Australians that special treatment in this regard is justified. This is clearly indicated by opinion polls: in a poll conducted in 1983, 78% respondents maintained that Aborigines should have the same land rights as other Australians, while only 13% believed that Aborigines "should have more land rights" (a synonym for the land rights legislation) than other Australians.[48] This corresponds to an overwhelming rejection of the very principle of preferential treatment for Aboriginals.[49]

The Court, while deciding about the legality of a preferential measure in *Gerhardy,* has of course been aware of this general public mood, and could have anticipated that its affirmative decision would be received with great displeasure. Moreover, the Court had good reasons to expect this reaction, especially when we realize that in its composition it overwhelmingly represents this same traditional Australian elite which is most vehemently opposed to the land-rights legislation. Support for Aboriginal land rights could be seen therefore as an act of dissension from its own class, a manifestation of moral apostasy, a betrayal of its own group. In order to neutralize this effect, and at the same time to weaken the legal impact of its own decision, the Court chooses to represent it as an almost insignificant incident, an act determined by merely contingent factors and not by the deep structure of its own argument. The Court reassures its traditional clientele — people of its own ilk — in the continued validity of the "colour-blindness" philosophy: preferences for Aboriginals are, as a general rule, equally suspect and unlawful as discrimination against Blacks. Alas, it just so happened (the Court further implies) that in this particular case there was no way the Court could strike down a particular preferential measure: the existence of "special measures" clauses (the Court suggests) forced it to validate the South Australian Act. There is nothing, however, which suggests that the principle of legality of preferences for Aboriginals is thereby announced by the Court; on the contrary, special effort is made to ensure that no such principle is stated and that, as a general rule, the "benign" character of a racial classification does not rescue it against the charge of discrimination.

Paris Adult Theater, at first sight, does not lend itself easily to the same analysis for we have here two opposed opinions.[50] In order to apply the hypothesis about the "strategy of reassurance", we would have to imagine two judges sending their messages in cross-directions. In this perspective, Chief Justice Burger gives satisfaction to the critics of obscenity by upholding the injunction against the owners of the "adult" theatre, and at the same time reassures the liberal and tolerant section of the general public that he is committed to the principle of the moral neutrality of law and to restricting legal coercion to harm prevention. Justice Brennan does exactly the opposite: he proposes invalidating the anti-obscenity state regulation, but at the same time he reassures the general public of his belief in the community's right to protect its morality through legal means. This overall picture does not seem to fit the hypothesis about the political role of the Court which is to reassure the majority about the Court's commitment to conventional morality while making a specific decision likely to be unpopular with that majority.

But the puzzle disappears when we realize the degree of social support for the alternatives in *Paris Adult Theater.* In *Gerhardy* the High Court spoke with one voice, and its "hidden message" sent to the majority was uniform for the simple reason that the majority itself was almost uniform. This is illustrated by the degree of social opposition to the Aboriginal land rights in Australia. But the attitudes of the American public towards the regulation of obscenity in the early 1970's came nowhere near such a quasi-consensus. Indeed, the statistics available indicate that the division of opinion in American society about the ban on obscenity oscillated around the fifty-fifty mark.[51] This explains the structure of *Paris Adult Theater:* the messages here are sent in opposite directions, that is both to those who support and to those who oppose the legal regulation of pornography, for neither the majority judges nor the dissenting minority want to antagonize a significant portion of public opinion.

Another way of expressing the same hypothesis about the strategy of reassurance (with regard to both cases discussed above) is to employ the conceptual framework of a theory of political influence and mass communication, and more particularly, a theory about a "strain toward consistency" in the situation of cognitive dissonance.[52] The theory postulates that there is a tendency to reduce dissonance, whenever one occurs, between these three components of the "influence situation": a person's own opinion about a given issue, his judgment of the position taken by the source of an influence, and his evaluation of this source. Now if we apply this theory to the situations studied above, and further extrapolate it from an individual to a societal scale, the particular dissonance may arise when a source which is generally evaluated positively (the High Court in Australia, the Supreme Court in the United States) endorses a generally unpopular position.[53] Now theoretically the strain towards consistency may take various forms: according to the "weakest link" hypothesis, the least resistant cognitive element is most likely to change.[54] One such mechanism would be the change of opinion, especially when an audience holds weak convictions about a particular matter, and its respect for the source of the dissonant influence is high. In the cases of *Paris Adult Theater* and *Gerhardy* such an occurrence is unlikely: in *Paris Adult Theater,* because of the highly emotive nature of convictions, beliefs and taboos related to sexual mores; in *Gerhardy,* because of the vested interests of the Australian economic elite which perceives in the Aboriginal land rights a threat to the existing structure of land ownership and to the expansion of the mining industry etc. Another way out of the cognitive dissonance is the "source reevaluation": there is always a possibility of a partial withdrawal of the community's confidence in the Court. This is, however, only a very limited possibility: both the persistence of the traditional political mythology in both countries, which elevates the judiciary to the highest ranks of national pride and honour, and the obvious fact that both these courts have usually served faithfully the politically and economically dominant groups in their societies, makes any massive "no confidence vote" on the part of public opinion very unlikely. But there are at least two other modes of reducing the cognitive dissonance: disbelief that a given communicator has taken the dissonant position, and the distortion of that position. The convoluted, zig-zag rhetorics employed in the judgments seem to lend themselves well to this latter strategy. It has been suggested that the public generally perceives greater agreement between its views and the positions taken by a popular source of influence than in fact exist.[55] The Courts may facilitate such a reinterpretation of its own positions by deliberately conveying contradictory or inconsistent messages to different sections of the audience. In effect, those who trust the Court highly, but at the same time are reluctant to change their own opinions even if they conflict with those endorsed by the Court, will find it easy to read their own views into the Court's decision. They will be able to maintain their high evaluation of the Court not by changing their own opinions about the substance of the controversial rulings, but by manipulating their perceptions of the Courts' positions so that the Court's view conforms more closely to their own. The opponents of the Aboriginal land rights will read *Gerhardy* as an affirmation of the general prohibition of "positive discrimination" and a rejection of the proposed theory justifying "benign discrimination" as generally valid. The opponents of the legal control of obscenity will read Burger's opinion as an endorsement of the liberal principle of moral neutrality of the State and of the "harm principle" restricting the State's role to harm prevention. The proponents of legal prosecution of pornographers will read Brennan's opinion in *Paris Adult Theater* as a reassurance about the legitimacy of State's defence of prevailing moral standards. By sending its messages in cross-directions, the Court deliberately facilitates the distortion, or reinterpretation, of its own positions and helps the general public to achieve a cognitive consistency without risking the loss of its own reputation and prestige.

It may be prudent at this point to consider two possible objections to my hypothesis. First, it may perhaps be argued that the evidential material used in this Chapter is dramatically thin: the analysis of two cases hardly warrants any broader hypothesis. I certainly do not make any claim as to the frequency or representativeness of this strategy (though I believe that, at closer analysis, a number of other decisions would exhibit a similar rhetorical pattern); however, what is puzzling is not how frequently or rarely the convoluted, zig-zag strategy has been followed, but rather that it has been employed at all. None of the opinions studied above can be easily dismissed as an instance of the pathology of legal reasoning: both are extremely important in their legal systems and in their respective areas of law. *Paris Adult Theater* belongs to the canon of landmark cases in privacy and obscenity-control law; *Gerhardy* (though it is too early to say to what extent it will become a landmark) is the very first case on "positive discrimination" in Australia. Neither can be dismissed as showing the lack of proper attention by their authors: both belong to the lengthiest decisions in their field.

Second, the discussion of two cases handed down by the courts belonging to two different, and in many respects dissimilar, legal systems may be said to be methodologically flawed. True, there are many differences between the

Supreme Court of the United States and the High Court of Australia but these differences do not touch the present point. Both these Courts exercise the power of judicial review within the context of written constitutions and federalism; both (regardless of the legalistic rhetoric, so prevalent in Australia) inevitably give effect to substantive value judgments in assessing the constitutionality of legislation. From this point of view, the similarities between the High Court of Australia and the Supreme Court of the United States are closer than, say, similarities between either of these courts and the House of Lords in England where there exists no power to invalidate the acts of Parliament on grounds of being unconstitutional.

At this stage we may ask: what exactly is it that the "strategy of reassurance" hypothesis tells us about the two Courts? Does it go beyond exposure of a particular rhetorical device used in order to mitigate the unpopularity of some of its controversial decisions? More specifically, does this particular rhetorical mode reveal anything about the position and self-perception of the Courts apart from the rather banal truth that, when they feel they have to disappoint their basic constituencies, they try to mitigate the pain? I believe that there is here a message for the theory of judicial review in general, but I can now only begin to sketch this message, which will receive more detailed treatment in the next Chapter of this book.

There are two opposing views as to the relations between the Court's standards of judicial review and the standards of conventional morality. There are — on the one hand — those who believe that it is the duty of a court to appeal to the prevailing moral standards of the community while reviewing the constitutionality of legislation; in the words of one of the exponents of this theory, the role of the Court is "to translate conventional morality into legal principle".[56] On the other hand, there are those who believe that the assumption of such a role would turn out to be inconsistent with the division of roles between the legislature and the Court: if a role of the Court is (among other things) to protect minorities against possible oppression by the majority, then the Court's deference to popular opinion would render this task impossible. If the Court is to protect the minority, then it cannot appeal to the majority when reviewing an act which is already supported by the majority (since the legislature in a democratic state expresses the prevailing social standards).[57]

Leaving aside for the moment the theoretical merits and demerits of this latter position, the "strategy of reassurance" indicates how uneasy the Courts are when they are called upon to protect minorities (or to endorse unpopular values) as against the dominant social morality. This is not a normative statement; it is too early in the course of our argument to suggest that it is either good or bad. All it shows is how firm is the umbilical cord which connects the highest courts to the dominant social standards: even in some of these cases where the decision runs counter to the conventional morality, a special device is employed to reassure the majority that the Court will respond to its claims.

But, of course, there are frequent situations where the courts employ the standards of conventional morality not in a roundabout way, as described above, but openly and unabashedly. The "how" and the "why" of this explicit resort to conventional morality will be discussed in Chapter 2.

CHAPTER 2

JUDICIAL RESPONSES TO MORAL PLURALISM (II): CONVENTIONAL MORALITY IN JUDICIAL DECISIONS

In the last paragraphs of the previous Chapter we alluded to the theoretical controversy between those who believe that the courts must give effect to community moral standards in their decisions (especially in the "hard cases", where the outcome is not controlled uncontroversially by the valid legal rules) and those who deny the legitimacy of such an appeal to conventional morality. It is now time to consider the arguments of both advocates and opponents of the judicial appeal to conventional morality in greater detail. The best example of the latter position is provided by the argument by John Hart Ely:

> There are two possible reasons one might look to consensus to give content to the Constitution's open-ended provisions. One *might* say one was seeking to protect the rights of the majority by ensuring that legislation truly reflect popular values. If that were the purpose, however, the legislative process would plainly be better suited than the judicial. This leaves the other possible reason for the reference, to protect the rights of individuals and minority groups against the actions of the majority.... Now think again about the consensus and the message will come clear: it makes no sense to employ the value judgments of the majority as the vehicle for protecting minorities from the value judgments of the majority.[1]

Ely's argument against the consensus-based judicial review is two-fold: first, that there is no moral consensus to be discovered in contemporary American society (and even if it were, it would not be reliably dicoverable by the courts) and, second, that it would be anti-democratic for the courts to exercise the review of legislative acts on behalf of conventional morality or moral consensus. As to the former prong of Ely's anti-consensus argument, this will be largely taken up in Sections 2-4 of this Chapter. I wish to begin my argument with the latter objection. On the face of it, it sounds utterly convincing: if a function of the courts is to protect individual rights and minority interests, then obviously this cannot be done by appeal to majoritarian values. Further, to the argument that representative institutions are often only imperfectly democratic, Ely replies sensibly that the proper response should be to make them more democratic, rather that try to turn the courts into representative bodies.[2]

This very powerful argument has been repeatedly endorsed by judges of the highest courts on both sides of the Atlantic. Judges have declared that "in a democratic society legislatures, not courts, are constituted to respond to the will and consequently the moral values of the people";[3] that "[t]he assessment of popular opinion is essentially a legislative, not a judicial, function",[4] and that the judicial functions "do not involve adjusting the common law to what are thought to be the social norms of the time".[5] Even when the proponents of these views do not agree with Ely's proposed grounds for judicial review, they join him in rejecting any obligation to follow society's current beliefs, reserving this responsive function to the legislature.

But the theory attacked by Ely is also supported by substantial arguments, and most importantly by appeal to the basic precepts of the democratic creed: unelected and unrepresentative judges should display proper deference to the majority will and refrain from substituting their own, personal value judgments for commonly held beliefs and generally accepted standards. Judicial review cannot be aimed at overturning the popular will expressed in duly enacted laws. What constitutes pornography and hence is not protected by the guarantee of "freedom of expression"; whether the death penalty is "cruel and unusual"; whether the right to privacy is so broad as to include a woman's right to terminate her pregnancy — these and similar questions must not be decided in isolation from, much less against, the standards accepted by the general public. In interpreting these, and similar, morally laden notions and standards, courts frequently refer to generally shared community values. This is the main thrust of the conventional morality theory of judicial review.

These two opposing theories of judicial review will serve as a point of departure in our discussion of the role of "conventional morality" in determining judicial standards. It should be observed that much of the attack against consensus-based judicial decisions is related specifically to those occasions when the courts exercise the power of judicial review. This is not surprising: it is in the context of judicial review that the possibility of confrontation between the judiciary and the legislatures raises the issue of institutional competence in its most dramatic form. However, the message of the discussion in this Chapter is broader than merely with respect to judicial review: if the conventional-morality appeals are seen not so much as illegitimate (the issue which, as we will argue, cannot really be settled by Ely's argument about institutional competence) but also as impossible, then there is lesson in it for the theory of judicial decision writ large, and not merely for the theory of judicial review.

For the sake of simplicity, the term "majoritarians" will be used to refer to those who suggest that the highest appellate courts typically do, and should, appeal to prevailing social standards of morality, decency and justice in giving effect to morally controversial legal provisions, and the term "anti-majoritarians" to those who reject this description of the judicial task, claiming that the Court has a duty to oppose the majority opinion when the protection of fundamental rights, and especially legitimate minority interests, are at stake. A warning is necessary, however, that this characterization may yield confusion, because some of the proponents of the theory that postulates judicial resort to current majority opinions, describe it as "counter-majoritarian".[6] This may seem ironic unless we clearly define the proper subject-matter of the appeal to the majority in our context. The proponents of the "conventional morality" theory of judicial review face a dilemma common to all those who support the right of the judiciary to (sometimes) invalidate statutes: how to defend the institution of judicial review against the charge of thwarting the majority will expressed by the legislature. One method of defence is to pinpoint the counter-majoritarian aspects of the political system as a whole: if there are some strong non-majoritarian mechanisms built into the process of democratic law-making (and, indeed, in other elements of the political system) then judicial review, counter-majoritarian though it is *ex hypothesi*, can no longer be considered a particularly suspect element of the system. If the system as a whole is not based on unrestrained majority will in the first place, then judicial review is not a deviation from the guiding principles underlying the system. In this and only this sense, the proponents of the conventional morality theory of judicial review are "counter-majoritarians": they do not believe that majoritarianism *tout court* is the backbone of the political system of existing representative democracies, and hence they do not perceive any basic inconsistency between democracy and judicial review. But, they can nevertheless properly be called "majoritarians", for they see majority moral views as an acceptable source (if not *the* source) to which the court should appeal in exercising the power to review the validity of legislation.

1. CONVENTIONAL MORALITY AND THE LEGITIMACY OF JUDICIAL REVIEW

Certainly the most fundamental argument of the anti-majoritarians is one expressed by Ely in the quotation that opens this Chapter: the argument from the division of tasks between the legislature and the highest court. It is the business of the legislature, and not of the judiciary, to translate public opinion into policies and laws; if a rationale of judicial review is to protect fundamental rights against, *inter alia*, the preference of a current majority, then this task cannot be achieved if it is interpreted in terms of the majority preference. Now this is true in theory, but relies on a number of assumptions that, in practice, do not always hold. Hence, if the argument that follows is correct, it may turn out that at least *some* appeals to "conventional morality" in the process of judicial review are consistent with the basic pattern of the division of tasks, whereby the legislature represents the majority opinion and the courts protect (among other things) minority interests. It will still not be sufficient to demonstrate that, everything considered, the majoritarian theory of judicial review is justified, for there are important problems related to the existence and discernibility of "conventional morality", as we shall see below, in Sections 2-4 of this Chapter. But it will at least show that the "division of tasks" argument, best expressed in Ely's passage which opens this Chapter, fails to demonstrate the anti-democratic character of the majoritarian judicial review.

Immediately, one can think of at least four different situations that do not fit Ely's description of the division of tasks between the legislature and the court along the "majority views/minority protection" lines:

1. The Court may feel bound *to protect the minority against itself*, on the basis of the majority's opinions. This sounds somewhat perverse, but one can well imagine that a small and very oppressive minority (oppressive, that is, towards its own members, who can be seen as a minority-within-a-minority) may violate the basic rights of its own members unless there is intervention from outside based on the accepted majority standards. There is no reason to deny the Court a role in such an intervention: appropriate legislative intervention may be politically inopportune, come too late, or be effectively blocked by a powerful lobby acting on behalf of the oppressive minority. Suppose, for example, that it is legislatively unsettled whether hospitals have a right to forcibly administer a blood transfusion, and that the faith of a small religious minority (such as the Jehovah's Witnesses) forbids blood transfusion. Suppose further that a victim of an automobile accident is in shock when admitted to the hospital, and her parents, who are Jehovah's Witnesses, are adamant in their opposition to a transfusion. A judicial decision supporting the doctor's right to administer a transfusion in such circumstances[7] will have the effect of displacing the minority will on the basis of the prevailing majority standards. This may or may not be paternalistic, depending on whether the unconscious victim would have personally chosen in accordance with his or her own group's doctrine (in our example: by refusing to accept

blood). One may speculate that in a large number of cases where the minority will is displaced by the majority standards, the aim is to protect the most vulnerable members of the minority and those whose individual interests and/or opinions do not get sufficient hearing within the minority itself. This describes, for instance, the U.S. Supreme Court decision that upheld a law prohibiting child labour against a freedom of religion challenge by Jehovah's Witnesses who claimed that it was the child's religious duty to sell the sect's newspaper.[8] Characteristically, these minority-within-the-minority cases involve the protection of the weakest members of the minority, e.g. of children, or of the sick. If such judicial intervention turns out to be genuinely "paternalistic" - that is, it is the case that a minority member is defended against his own values and contrary to his own expressed will — most of us would agree that there are some basic values that have to be enforced even against the will of the beneficiaries of the intervention, when these beneficiaries belong to the categories of persons that should be properly subject to paternalistic protection. This may be, as in our example, because we suspect that intensive indoctrination by a small, oppressive minority might have weakened the ability of some of its more vulnerable members to voice properly their own interests.

This reveals that one of the unspoken (but rebuttable) assumptions in Ely's reasoning is that the threat to the rights of minority members must necessarily come from a majority. This may or may not be the case.

2. There may be a substantial lapse of time between the enactment of legislation, expressing a past majority opinion, and judicial review, expressing the morality of today. In this situation, judicial review may be simply viewed as a method of *"updating" the content of conventional morality*. For example: a 1965 decision invalidating an eighty-years-old statute proscribing the use and sale of contraceptives[9] may be seen as repealing legislation which, although it enjoyed majority support at the time of its enactment, now stands in stark contrast with the changed morals of the community. Ely's argument that it is up to the legislature to change anachronistic statutory regulations[10] misses the point: legislative inaction does not necessarily indicate a legislative will to maintain the historical position, and any device for "updating" the substance of morals may be better, from a majoritarian point of view, than stubborn enforcement of standards that no longer enjoy community support.

This last proposition must be, of course, qualified by the proviso of all other things being equal, that is, we must assume that the new standards are no more of a threat to basic rights and to minority rights than the former ones. If they pose such a threat (or if they pose such a threat to a higher degree than the standards embodied in the legislation) then the matter falls beyond the reach of our argument here, just as it would be beyond Ely's rationale for judicial review. His argument rests upon the proposition that, while the courts are not more "democratic", they are better situated to protect the minority rights than the legislature, and so typically a bigger threat to minority rights comes from the legislature than from the judiciary.

3. The "majority" to which the court appeals in its exercise of judicial review may exist within a different constituency from the one represented by the legislature: it often happens that the court *represents a broader majority* in overruling a local majority. This is commonly the case when the superior court in a federation exercises a judicial review of state acts. When the United States Supreme Court ordered school desegregation, reversing the Southern states' segregation laws founded on the "separate but equal" doctrine,[11] and when it subsequently established that legally required racial segregation is unconstitutional in all other areas of life, the Court could be seen as acting on behalf of a national conscience as against local majoritarian standards. This is confirmed by studies that indicate a great disparity between the degree of support for racial segregation in the South and on a national level in the 1950's.[12] Perhaps a similar interpretation can be given to the Australian State/Commonwealth conflict over racial discrimination resolved in favour of the Commonwealth by the High Court of Australia in *Koowarta v. Bjelke-Petersen*.[13] Again, an answer that it is up to the national legislature, rather than to the court, to render a state act invalid misses the point: both politically (unwillingness on the part of national legislators to antagonize local communities) and legally (the legal structures of federalism which sometimes make it impossible to override the legislative will of a state), the national legislative process may be unable to vindicate the national moral consensus. As a result, judicial intervention may indeed be majoritarian, providing a roundabout way of ensuring the supremacy of the national conscience.

4. Finally, and perhaps most importantly, there may be such *deficiencies in the mechanism of translating the majority opinion into legislative decisions* that a judicial rescue operation is called for. Ely, of course, realizes this point, and one of the legitimate functions of judicial review, for him, is to "clear the channels of political change": apart from the task of reinforcing minority representation, the role of judicial review of legislation is to make sure that the government is genuinely representative.[14] But this rationale reaches far beyond the sort of actions to remove distortions of democracy that Ely suggests — ensuring that the channels of political expression and

communication are open, guaranteeing voting rights, controlling the apportionment of electoral districts, and so on. Even in a perfectly functioning representative democracy, there may be situations where majority views fail to be translated into legislative decisions.

National elections rarely reveal coherent sets of majority preferences on which all important policy choices may be based. This happens for a number of reasons, none of which is related to any malfunctioning of democracy: not all of the citizens have preferences between the alternatives proposed to them; there are situations (identified by Kenneth Arrow in his Impossibility Theorem) where individual preferences cannot be summed into social policy which would respect majority rule;[15] even if a majority exists, it may be impossible to find a voting method that satisfies the majority rule when there are more than two alternatives at issue; standard election procedures notoriously ignore differences in intensity of preferences, which may be all important when a large minority feels a strong preference for one of the alternatives and the opposing majority has only a slight preference for the other one; people often cast their votes not to express a choice of future policy but in order to punish the legislators or a government for past action, even if little can be done to change the consequences of the policy. In effect, as Robert Dahl says, "all an election reveals is the first preferences of some citizens among the candidates standing for office".[16] This in itself is no negligible indication, but it falls short of providing a coherent and comprehensive index of majority preferences on all the vital issues that the legislature may face during its term. Consequently, the elected representatives often do not know, and certainly are not uniformly bound by, the current views of their constituencies. Political democracy does not provide government by everyday consent of the current majority of the members of a society. Instead, elections give the representatives chosen a mandate only on the basis of their broad and sometimes vaguely formulated platforms. Within that scope may occur such significant departures from important social standards that intervention by the court is warranted.

Even if the opinions of the members of a legislature were completely and continuously harmonious with those of their constituents, every piece of legislation cannot receive the full attention of the representatives. Therefore, as T. Sandalow argues, the enactment of a statute does not justify the conclusion that it is an expression of majority views.[17] To attach such a significance to every enactment of the legislature would be to hypostatize the "Parliament's will" and disregard the realities of legislative decision-making. By the same token, the legislature's current silence on a matter that has been decided legislatively in the past (even if the current legislators have had an opportunity to deal with the matter) does not necessarily mean that the legislators endorse and accept the past solution. Nor does their choice of a narrower legislative solution mean that a broader approach is contrary to the will of the legislators. It may instead be that they do not know about the problem, or do not know what to do about it, or have no time to deal with it properly.

Some judges of the highest courts have long recognized this reality. In an important case before the House of Lords, *British Railways Board v. Herrington*,[18] Lord Reid considered the extent of occupiers' legal duty to take steps to safeguard trespassing children. He noted that Parliament, in enacting the Occupiers' Liability Act of 1957, omitted to alter the existing law as to trespassers, and limited itself to defining the occupiers' duties towards persons who might lawfully come on to their land. But Lord Reid refused to interpret this silence as an approval of the existing law with regard to trespassers — announced in the 1929 case, *Robert Addie & Sons (Collieries) v. Dumbreck*[19] — which imposed only a very limited duty upon owners. Lord Reid said: "It is ... possible to attribute that silence to Parliament (or those who then advised Parliament) being unable to make up their minds as to what to put in place of *Addie*".[20] Similarly, in the *Knuller* case Lord Reid warned against "the danger of drawing conclusions from Parliament refraining from legislating",[21] and denied that the Parliament's recent failure to legislate with regard to punishment of immoral acts necessarily indicated legislative approval for the common law doctrine that conspiracy to corrupt public morals is a misdemeanour. He observed realistically that "[m]uch recent legislation on this topic has all the indications of being in the nature of a compromise",[22] which implied that any search for a uniform "legislative will" would be spurious indeed. In the same decision, Lord Diplock, too, affirmed that "to infer parliamentary approval from parliamentary inaction is to take an unrealistic view of the pressure on parliamentary time under party government".[23]

In each of these four situations (protection of the minority from itself, adoption of current majority views over those of a past majority, adoption of national majority views over those of a local majority, and redress of departures from majority opinions in the representative democratic process) there is legitimate room for judicial appeal to the majority's moral standards. But the strength of the four justifications is uneven. As far as the fourth category is concerned, cases that justify the conventional-morality based judicial review must clearly be considered an exception to a general presumption that the legislature is best able to translate the majority will into decisions. For the legislator is more hard pressed than the judge to take notice of conventional morality: legislators running systematically counter to public opinion risk loss of office, while judges usually do not have to fear this immediate sanction. The legislator also has better empirical knowledge of public opinion than does a judge; politicians are usually well acquainted with the divisions of opinions in their electorate, because they often probe public opinion, using opinion polls and other devices.

So, assuming a well functioning democracy, the presumption that, by and large, legislators are responsive to the moral sentiments in the community seems well founded. To be sure, this is a rebuttable presumption, and the weaker the democratic mechanisms are, the weaker are the grounds for the presumption. This presumption is reflected, of course, in the presumption of the validity of statutes. Again, one has to stress that there can be legitimate grounds for invalidation of statutes other than incongruence with community views, such as the violation of minority rights. Concern about these grounds may result in a significant weakening of the presumption of validity. This is the doctrine expressed in the famous Footnote Four in the *Carolene Products* decision[24] — the doctrine which will be discussed in detail in Chapter 5 below. But from the point of view of our interest at this stage, restricted as it is to conventional-morality-based judicial review, the validity of such a presumption in a democracy seems well justified.

No such presumption of legislative congruence with community morality is available, however, with respect to the first three categories of situations that may prompt judicial intervention based on community standards, because in these cases (with one small exception) no overturning of the current, national legislature is at stake. There is no reason to presume that the enactments of long-dead legislators express modern community values, nor that local standards expressed by the state legislature coincide with national ones. When courts are asked to protect vulnerable members of a minority against their own group, the analysis varies depending on whether the statute at issue protects or threatens the rights of the individual. In the former case, such as when the anti-child-labour laws are relied upon to proscribe the sale of newspapers by children,[25] the presumptive validity of the statute need not be examined at all, for at issue is the interpretation of the reach of the statute, not its validity. In the latter case (consider a hypothetical statute that permits doctors to respect a refusal to have a blood transfusion administered), community standards may justify overriding the presumption of congruence between legislation and the majority will, but this does not erode the validity of the presumption generally. Unless the case can be identified with the second or the third category (i.e., the law in question is outdated, or local), such a presumption must be admitted in the reasoning.

2. JUDICIAL USES OF "CONVENTIONAL MORALITY"

"Conventional morality" has many names. The American courts appeal to "contemporary community standards", "community values", "public morality", "common views of morality", "the moral consensus", "evolving standards of decency", "the ethical standards current at the time"[26] etc. British courts make overt use of such concepts very infrequently, due partly to a tradition of parliamentary supremacy quite different from the American tradition of judicial review, and partly to different techniques of judicial reasoning, including greater reluctance to make explicit substantive value judgments. But appeals to conventional morality are built into the standards of "reasonable care", "unconscionability", "common sense", "humanity", "decency", "public morals", and the "prudent and reasonable man". Arguments about what "most people would think", or what "most people would regard as culpable", or what "to persons of normal instincts may be fairly described as perverted",[27] sometimes figure explicitly in judicial reasoning about the substance of legal duties. Appeals to the community's moral standards resonate in the Law Lords' stated aspiration to develop the common law "by adapting it to modern concepts of reason and justice and common humanity",[28] and in the imposition by them upon the jury of a duty to maintain "the corporate good sense of the community".[29] And it is, of course, conventional morality which parades under the guise of "the morality of the man in the jury box".[30] The Supreme Court of Canada has referred to "standards of acceptance prevailing in the community";[31] in Australia the courts have appealed to "[t]he general sense of a civilised community", to "a general sense [in a community] of what is decent and what is indecent", and to "conventional teaching according to ordinary standards in the community".[32] The Supreme Court of South Africa has made use of, in the interpretation of a statute, the "prevalent sentiment" among the white population;[33] examples from other common law jurisdictions could be multiplied.

There are, within this mass of references to conventional morality, two types of appeal. First, there are situations in which the court has recourse to conventional morality in order to decide about the legal status of a particular practice (that is, whether the practice can properly be restricted by law).

Examples could include a decision decriminalizing homosexuality, or abortion, or deciding about the constitutionality of capital punishment on the basis of the current moral views held by a majority. Second, there may be situations where there is no doubt about the legal status of a particular practice, but where an appeal must be made to public morality in order to give moral content to the standard by which this practice is legally assessed. Legal standards that derive their content from conventional morality include "unconscionability", "due care", and "obscenity". The Court accepts, for instance, that "obscene" publications are not protected by the freedom-of-speech guarantees, but must appeal to generally shared values to decide what qualifies as obscene.[34] In a recent case, the Supreme Court of Canada confirmed that one of the criteria of "undue exploitation of sex" (the term referred to in the statutory definition of obscenity) is whether the accepted standards of tolerance in the contemporary Canadian community have been exceeded.[35] A similar external reference is required to define the standard of "good moral character" common in naturalization law: the appeal to such a standard is not a contentious matter in itself, but the test of "good moral character" is said to be found in "the generally accepted moral conventions current at the time".[36]

It is important to distinguish between these two types of appeal to conventional morality because they do not necessarily coincide. A Court may decide, for instance, that the latter appeal to conventional morality must be made without making the former one — e.g., when the standards of what is "obscene" are moulded by community values but the legal status of obscenity is derived not from societal reprobation but from analysis of constitutional provisions.[37] Conversely, the first type of appeal to conventional morality is made without the second when, for example, the invalidity of the death penalty is decided on the basis of community values without further appeal to the scale of socially acceptable punishments for particular crimes.

The second type of appeal to community standards is clearly an easier case because it is not a matter of yes-or-no to the application of community values but rather of judgments of degree. In theory at least, it is possible to find a median or average standard of taste in "obscenity" judgments, and it may be expected that those who do not depart too far from this average in either direction will not object to its adoption. Such an approach towards ascertaining community standards on obscenity was expressed by Judge Freedman of the Court of Appeal of Manitoba: "Those [community] standards are not set by those of lowest taste or interest. Nor are they set exclusively by those of rigid, austere, conservative, or puritan taste and habit of mind. Something approaching a general average of community thinking and feeling has to be discovered".[38] But surely no "general average of community thinking and feeling" can be discovered in those hotly disputed situations where the community is divided not about the *measures* of a particular standard, but about the very *status* of the standard or of a practice. Examples include issues such as the legality of abortion, homosexuality, or the death penalty — that is, the "yes-or-no" divisions of public opinion. In disputes about *measures*, there is an underlying consensus assumed — for instance, about prohibiting obscenity — and the disagreements focus on the standards that trigger legal intervention, but truly problematic cases arise when no such underlying consensus is available. The remainder of this Chapter will focus primarily on this more difficult category of cases.

This is not to say that the distinction between these two categories (which we may call, respectively, the standard-validity, and standard-measures categories) is not problematic, or that the boundaries between them are rigid. There are situations in which judges try to cross these boundaries, and to convert the problem of the case before them from a standard-measures problem into a standard-validity problem. In an unreported obscenity decision (subsequently reversed) Judge Sweet of the U.S. District Court for the Southern District of New York held that various articles of merchandise were not obscene and dismissed the government's complaint.[39] But the way he reached this conclusion was radically different from the usual judgments of this type. Instead of demonstrating that the particular articles were within the limits of community tolerance, he declared that the community standards in New York, praised by him as "champion of free expression" and exponent of a "cosmopolitan attitude", did not allow any government restrictions of free expression. "I conclude that explicit portrayal of ultimate sexual activity ... [is] tolerated within the standards of the community, even if patently offensive or distasteful, because the community finds government restrictions and censorship of an individual's right more offensive than frequent displays of sexual materials".[40] This courageous (if futile) defense of unlimited free expression hinges on the conversion of a standard-measuring problem into a standard-validity problem: instead of inquiring into how much obscenity was acceptable by contemporary standards, Judge Sweet suggests that community standards reject the very prohibition (that is, the actual legal status) of obscenity.

Arguments developed in the course of our discussion may apply not merely to the exercise of judicial review but, more generally, to any situations in which the court is tempted to appeal to standards of conventional morality when giving effect to morally laden concepts in its judgments. With the discussion no longer confined to judiciary-legislature interactions, it does not make any difference whether the court's reference to public morality results in invalidation of a legislative act or in any other exercise of judicial authority involving the task of ascertaining the substance of public morality. When the court applies the standards of "due care", "reasonableness", or "unconscionability", the problem of the appeal to conventional morality must be addressed whether or not the application is an exercise of judicial review of legislative acts. But the political significance of such appeals is heightened in the circumstances of judicial review, so we will keep judicial review as the centre of our attention.

The question of substantive standards of judicial review has received special attention in the United States, particularly from the point of view of its uneasy relations with the principles of representative democracy, but the problem is of course much more universal. Although in most other countries courts operate within a narrower constitutional framework, the issue is also relevant to standards of judicial scrutiny of constitutionality of statutes in other countries. Examples include Canada, especially after the promulgation of the Charter of Rights and Freedoms in 1982, which provides expressly for the responsibility of the judiciary to decide whether a law is consistent with the entrenched rights, and Australia where statutes have been always open to constitutional challenge on *ultra vires* grounds, and it is hardly possible to separate *ultra vires* grounds from substantive judgments about the propriety of a law where constitutional terms contain broadly-phrased and open-ended clauses such as "absolutely free" trade among States.

If we address the problem of how conventional morality is to be apprehended by the court, a number of troublesome problems arise immediately with regard to what conventional morality actually is and how to read it. First, there are in any community a number of people who do not express any substantive opinions on a number of issues which may be the subject of the court's reasoning — for instance on the morality of abortion or homosexuality. One can perhaps say that those who are indifferent to any given issue "abstain" from the discussion and hence voluntarily withdraw from the constituency within which conventional morality on any such issue is to be ascertained. But surely this sounds more like avoiding than solving the problem: after all, "abstaining" from the vote is not identical with granting a license to a majority on the issue. Abstention may be a manifestation of dissatisfaction with all the presented options, or with the way the agenda is drawn. Further, even if people have opinions on the issue before the court, these opinions do not always cohere into complete sets of mutually compatible rules and opinions. People often hold opinions that are clearly mutually inconsistent: a student of the formation of public opinion observes that "[w]hen ordinary people are asked for political opinions, what emerges is a hodge-podge (almost) of independent and often inconsistent statements of opinion".[41] Consistency is sometimes introduced only when the attitudes and opinions are important to a person, and when he considers the community supportive of his opinions,[42] but this is not often the case with the issues tackled by the courts.

There may be (as is often the case) inconsistency between views on particular issues and more general declarations about principles. In their well-known study, Free and Cantril found that many Americans hold one set of attitudes when they consider concrete policies and another set when they are responding at a more abstract level: there is no congruence between the "operational" and "ideological" spectrum of attitudes.[43] Free and Cantril found the majority of Americans "liberal" (in the American terminology, i.e., state interventionist) on the specific or "operational" spectrum and at the same time "conservative" (i.e., pro-laissez faire) on the abstract or ideological spectrum. A court "asking" the community about its attitude to, say, homosexuality, may find a substantial inconsistency between the answers to the questions addressed in an abstract way (e.g., about freedom of sexual behaviour among consenting adults) and in a specific way (e.g., about the legal status of homosexual partners). All this applies to individual moralities; at a collective level the situation is only aggravated: not only does there not exist any substantive consensus among individuals and groups in societies about many issues which have to be addressed by the courts, but the combinations of opinions often fall into "non-congruent opinion cleavages" within the population, thus making it difficult to identify clear majorities on whole clusters of questions and so to identify overwhelming support for the underlying principles behind the competing opinions.[44]

This is a commonplace observation, and surely no proponent of the majoritarian theory of judicial review claims that there is any unanimity to be discovered in a society on such issues as homosexuality, abortion, or the moral standards of "unconscionable" contracts. We must therefore find out how they (and the courts) try to reconcile this absence of moral consensus with the postulate of an appeal to conventional morality. Judges invoke moral consensus, or community standards, in different contexts and for different purposes, and not all of these are relevant to our discussion. Some appeals to conventional morality, or to what the judges take to be conventional morality, are of *no* interest to us. First, there are statements in which the appeal to conventional morality does not play any argumentative role of its own but is merely a rhetorical or *decorative* device used in order to make a judgment more palatable. When, for instance, Justice McReynolds of the United States Supreme Court proclaimed that "[t]he American people have always regarded education and acquisition of knowledge as matters of supreme importance which should be diligently promoted",[45] he was indulging in a sort of ritualistic platitude that adds ornament to the argument but does not actually dictate or even strengthen the conclusion. Whether Americans indeed attach such an importance to education, whether on balance they consider education to be more, less, or equally as important as other activities, what practical conclusions they actually draw from this vaguely described respect for education — all this was irrelevant to Justice McReynolds' argument about the unconstitutionality of a law forbidding the teaching of foreign languages to grade-school children. After all, that law could have been supported, or at least deemed not unreasonable, on educational policy grounds (teaching requirements in a linguistically heterogeneous community composed largely of newly arrived migrants), as the dissent by Justice Holmes in a companion case indicated.[46] For McReynolds, the liberty guarantied by the Fourteenth Amendment was sufficient to invalidate the Nebraska law, without having to appeal to what the American people thought about the value of education in general.

The second type of reference to conventional morality which will remain beyond the ambit of this Chapter is concerned not with the substantive issues of the case but with the general problems of *legitimacy*. In the *Geelong Harbor* decision, the Privy Council considered whether it could interfere with the Australian High Court's decision to abstain from altering the law in Australia. Lord Diplock, arguing against such an interference, pointed out that

> the extent to which the High Court exercises its undoubted power not to adhere to a previous decision of its own must be consonant with the consensus of opinion of the public, of the elected legislature and of the judiciary as to the proper balance between the respective roles of the legislature and the judiciary as lawmakers.[47]

The appeal here is made to Australian public opinion about the legitimacy of the legislative process as such, and, although there may exist a high degree of social consensus on this legitimacy, it obviously does not provide any guidance as to the moral views on particular issues that the courts have to decide, unless the decision itself concerns the legislative process.

Third, beyond the scope of this Chapter are the *negative* appeals to consensus, i.e., those references by the judges to public opinion that serve to demonstrate that there is no current consensus on a given issue. Justice Rehnquist, in his dissent in *Roe v. Wade* argues that the very existence of public debate on abortion is evidence that the putative right to abortion is not universally accepted, and hence that, at the very least, it cannot be considered "fundamental".[48] Our focus is rather on arguments that use the positive existence of a generally accepted standard as an argument in judicial decision, though it has to be admitted that Rehnquist's point is well taken, and would have severely undercut the majority's opinion in *Roe v. Wade* if the majority had indeed relied on public support for abortion, which it did not.

3. JUDGES IN SEARCH OF CONSENSUS

The way in which judges ascertain conventional morality varies between two extremes: on the one hand, representation of one's own moral standards as the community morality and, on the other hand, total rejection of a possibility of stating what the conventional morality is. The first extreme position is approached when the judge purports to draw on his or her own experience in the community as evidence of contemporary standards:[49] it is clear in this situation that there is a high risk of giving effect to one's own opinions masquerading as the morality of the general public. When the test of community standards is perceived through the judges' eyes and experience, it seems apposite to recall Justice Frankfurter's warning against "finding in personal disapproval a reflection of more or less prevailing condemnation" and against "enforcing ... private view[s] rather than ... consensus of society's opinion".[50] The second extreme position is reached when a judge refuses, in a more or less principled way — that is, not merely because of the circumstances of the individual case in which the community standards seem to him doubtful, but because the whole enterprise of inquiring into conventional morality is seen by him as hopeless — to state what the conventional morality requires.[51]

Between these two extreme points, there are a variety of ways in which judges claim to discover conventional morality. There are, however, certain general regularities in these representations. Justice Marshall's opinion in *Furman v. Georgia*[52] provides a good example, because his reasoning hinges, to a large degree, on the conventional morality argument. As one of several independent grounds for the invalidity of capital punishment (along with its excessiveness and the invalidity of its legislative purpose) Justice Marshall asserted that "popular sentiment abhors it" and suggested that "the very notion of changing values" requires that such "abhorrent" penalties be struck down.[53] What were his methods of finding out whether capital punishment is "morally unacceptable to the people of the United States at this time in their history"?[54] To begin with, Justice Marshall refuses to attach great importance to opinion polls because

> whether or not a punishment is cruel and unusual depends, not on whether its mere mention 'shocks the conscience and sense of justice of the people,' but on whether people who were fully informed as to the purposes of the penalty and its liabilities would find the penalty shocking, unjust, and unacceptable.[55]

In effect, although Justice Marshall considered the "moral unacceptability to people" of a punishment to be one of the tests of its invalidity, the criteria of "moral unacceptability" were located in the hypothetical reactions of "fully informed" people, not in an actual reaction by people as they are. Justice Marshall followed this by citing, with approval, an opinion that "American citizens know almost nothing about capital punishment".[56] The obvious implication is that their reaction cannot be recognized as a test of "moral unacceptability" or of abhorrence by "popular sentiment". No wonder that, in this structure of argument, the actual (as opposed to hypothetical) moral views and sentiments of the public play hardly any independent role in the ascertaining of community standards on capital punishment.

Indeed, section VI of Justice Marshall's opinion (devoted to the "moral unacceptability to the people" indicium of invalidity) eschewed an empirical enquiry into public opinion, and relied entirely on a purely theoretical argument about why fully informed people *should* reject capital punishment. They should do so, he asserted, because the death penalty does not serve the social functions it is supposed to serve, because support of purposeless vengeance is immoral, because of the discriminatory effects of capital punishment, because of the potential danger of executing an innocent man, and because of the deleterious effects of the death penalty upon the entire criminal justice system.[57] All this may be plausible and wise, and might even influence public opinion if widely read, but surely it has nothing to do with identifying popular sentiments and conventional morality. On the contrary, it is a rational argument about the inefficiency and immorality of capital punishment which leaves no room for actual social reprobation as a ground for invalidating the penalty. An argument that fully informed citizens *would* share these views is unverifiable — we are told that citizens "know almost nothing" about the facts which Marshall invokes — and at any rate the assertion is irrelevant from the point of view of actual current community standards. Justice Marshall's appeal to popular sentiment must, therefore, be seen as a disguise for his own substantive morality. The pretextual nature of Marshall's reliance on popular sentiment became even more evident in his opinion in *Gregg v. Georgia* in which, in the face of the wave of the post-*Furman* capital punishment statutes, he maintained that if the American people "were better informed they would consider [the death penalty] shocking, unjust, and unacceptable".[58]

But would they indeed? Seven Justices of the Supreme Court, who probably fit the category of "fully informed Americans", announced in *Gregg*, for various reasons, that capital punishment does not necessarily have the defects that disqualify it in the eyes of Justice Marshall. This disagreement is a substantive one, and revolves around the relative merits of capital punishment from the point of view of the goals of retribution and deterrence, its alleged inherent disproportionate cruelty, its arbitrary and unequal application, and more generally, around whether it can be described as "cruel and unusual".[59] But these are precisely the matters that should be avoided in the "conventional morality" argument. In contrast, the appeal to conventional morality is redundant if the proper area of the debate is one of the relative substantive merits and demerits of the matter.

Justice Brennan attempted to invoke popular morality in a somewhat different way in his *Furman* opinion, but was no more successful. He, too, attached great weight to "unacceptability to a society" as an indicium of the invalidity of the death penalty, and yet he did not appeal to the hypothetical "fully informed" citizens. But in the absence of that manipulable construct, his assertion of *actual* moral condemnation of the death penalty by the community reveals amazing contradictions in his argument. Justice Brennan stated, in one breath, or at any rate in the space of five pages, that "this punishment has been *almost totally* rejected by contemporary [American] society", that "our society *seriously questions* the appropriateness of this punishment today", and that "contemporary society views this punishment *with substantial doubt*".[60] There is a pattern of decreasing strength of conviction about the social reprobation as Justice Brennan gradually bows to reality and injects elements of actual social practice and public opinion into his reasoning. But the use he made of this information is rather nonchalant: for instance, he claimed that the infrequency of imposition of the death penalty in the face of the support shown by the general public for the penalty through legislation, opinion polls and referendum votes "simply underscores the extent to which our society has in fact rejected this punishment".[61] At best, this is a version of the "half empty but not half full" type of argument; at worst, it is the turning of the evidence on its head.

Likewise, the fact that there has been throughout American history a gradual restriction of the range of legally permitted applications of the death penalty and a decrease in the number of crimes for which the punishment is actually inflicted does not necessarily prove, as Brennan would have it, that the very principle of the death penalty is overwhelmingly rejected;[62] it may rather mean that the general public disapproved of the death penalty for what it saw to be an excessively broad range of crimes but is now quite happy about imposing it in a narrower number of cases. In short, a comparison of Brennan's and Marshall's appeals to conventional morality to condemn the death penalty reveals the basic dilemma facing a judge who wants to use this argument in a morally pluralistic society: either the conventional morality must be concocted in such a way that it is merely a proxy for the judge's own opinions, or it will fail to support the argument, because there is an important segment of the general public that is directly opposed to the views propounded by the judge.

4. LAUNDERING DEVICES

The basic dilemma of a judge appealing to conventional morality in a morally pluralistic society has given rise to a number of "laundering" devices,[63] the aim of which is to filter the actual, divergent moral opinions of the community through the sieve of rationality. Several examples of such laundering devices, employed by judges or advocated by the proponents of the majoritarian theory of judicial review, are discussed below. Closer examination of these devices may be helpful in finding out to what extent the majoritarian theory seriously takes actual community values as plausible standards for judicial decisions.

Dean H. H. Wellington is perhaps the most radical representative of the majoritarian theory of judicial review, so it is useful to begin this short survey of "laundering" devices with a look at his theory. In two of his highly influential papers, Wellington expresses no doubts about the propriety of majoritarian standards: he openly endorses the view that "courts should seek to discover and use the moral ideals of the community as a source of legal principles"[64] and that

> [j]udicial reasoning in concrete cases must proceed from society's set of moral principles and ideals, in much the same way that the judicial interpretation of documents (contracts, statutes, constitutions — especially constitutions) must proceed from the document. And that is why we must be concerned with conventional morality, for it is there that society's set of moral principles and ideals are located.[65]

Wellington concludes that the courts (and the Supreme Court of the United States in particular) are well positioned to "translate conventional morality into legal principle".[66]

While all this sounds very unambiguous, there are some qualifiers in Wellington's texts which sit uneasily with the theory as presented. For one thing, Wellington believes that judges should "filte[r] out the prejudices and passions of the moment" and disengage themselves "from contemporary prejudices which are easily confused with moral principles".[67] Very easily indeed, especially so because Wellington himself identifies moral principles with, and locates them in, the conventional morality of the society. It is hard to see what test can be applied to distinguish moral principles and ideals from mere prejudices and passions short of applying the court's own substantive moral yardsticks, but then Wellington denies that "a court is entitled or required to assert *its* moral point of view" and maintains that it "is required to assert *ours*".[68] It is also doubtful whether Wellington's hint that, in order to discover moral principles rather than prejudices, the court should "examine the views the community expressed in calmer moments"[69] is of any use. If by "calmer moments" Wellington means periods when a particular issue does not raise a significant moral controversy, then we may suspect that in such times there is hardly any discernible majoritarian feeling about an issue. And at any rate, the very fact that the legal status of a moral principle is challenged in court indicates that it is not a "calmer moment" in the life of this principle, so the court is caught in an impossible situation if it wants to use Wellington's test. The only way out would be to consider the *past* views of the society (as expressed in "calmer moments"), but the court would then fail to give effect to the current conventional morality, which seems to be the only legitimate one in Wellington's theory.

There are other symptoms of contradiction in Wellington's theory as well. He writes, for instance, about the possibility of judicial error as to the moral ideals of the community. Just as the legislature, Wellington says, may well fail to properly express these ideals, so too the court, even though it is better suited to perform the task, "can get the community's moral ideals wrong".[70] But "empirical investigation", Wellington says, does not provide the criterion for discovering such a judicial mistake. He does not give any reason for this assertion; one would think that if moral ideals are equated with actual conventional morality, then "empirical investigation" is the only thing that really counts. But Wellington suggests that a better criterion for judicial mistake lies in "the community's reaction to a judicial decision"[71] and provides the following test: "When the Justices are right about the moral ideals of the community, their decisions become settled and accepted. The turmoil, the resistance, and the threats from other governmental entities, from private groups, institutions and individuals diminish with time".[72]

This is all rather bizarre. To begin with, Wellington seems to suggest here that the only test of a judicial error concerning moral ideals of community is a *post facto* one: everything depends on the community's reaction to the decision. But surely this is an odd meaning of an "error", for it deprives the judges themselves of any criteria of correctness to apply to their decision while they are making it. Furthermore, if the decision is followed by the "turmoil, resistance, and threats", then one can hardly maintain that there is a consonance of the decision with the moral ideals of the community, even if resistance will "diminish with time". But resistance seems, if anything, to disprove the correctness of the judicial reading of the community's ideals. Finally, Wellington suggests that both when judges "get the community's moral ideals wrong" *and* when they get them right "there may be turmoil, resistance, and threats from other governmental entities, from private groups, institutions and individuals".[73] So how is it possible to distinguish between resistance to a correct decision and resistance to a wrong one if the only test of correctness (as to the proper reading of moral ideals) is in the social reaction itself? Is it a matter of degree? If so, why does Wellington not say so? And how much resistance is enough to make a decision wrong? To make the whole matter worse, Wellington, in the context of a polemic against the anti-majoritarian theorists, recalls "the familiar fact that communities, like individuals, may well violate principles to which they adhere" and so it is not a necessary truth that "the actions of majorities are the best evidence of communities' ideals".[74] How are we then to ascertain the conventional morality if it is not a matter for empirical investigation, if the resistance to the decision is not evidence of opposition by the exponents of the conventional morality, and if what we take to be an observable pattern of moral ideals may well in fact be a "violation" by the community of the principles to which it otherwise adheres?

Wellington's problem is instructive because it displays the same pattern as Marshall's decision in *Furman v. Georgia*: it declares great deference to community standards but when it comes to construing them, both Marshall and Wellington are very selective in their approaches to the criteria of what is to count as community standards, and in fact make the actually shared moral views and ideals largely irrelevant. This resembles Dworkin's criticism of Lord Devlin's legal moralism. Dworkin has constructed a rather elaborate system of criteria of what constitutes a "moral position": in order to have one's moral views registered in the process of law-making and to qualify as a holder of a "moral position", one's reactions must pass through an analytical test which will remove prejudice, irrational emotions, rationalizations, and "parroting" and also ensure sincerity and consistency of a "moral position".[75] That certainly does not sound like giving effect to conventional morality, but then Dworkin does not claim that this is his preferred standard for judicial review.

The "laundering devices" employed in Professor Perry's theory are not much more convincing than Wellington's. Like Wellington, Perry declares himself a strong supporter of the majoritarian theory of judicial review: "conventional moral culture" (which is Perry's favourite code word for conventional morality or community standards) should guide judicial decisions, in particular in the application of the "substantive due process" principles, to which Perry devotes particular attention. Judges are both competent and obliged, Perry says, "to ascertain the contents of social conventions" and to "bring[] culturally shared ideals, sensibilities, and norms to bear on the political processes".[76] In particular, "when an individual Justice knows that his own views diverge from those of conventional moral culture, his responsibility is to defer to the public morals, not to impose his own".[77]

Again, this sounds very much like a reference to actual shared moral ideals and views, but a hidden laundering instrument operates here as well. This time it is hidden in a footnote:

> In trying to ascertain conventional morality a court should heed the basic moral principles to which social conventions subscribe and not discrete moral positions inconsistent with those principles. The latter tend to be impulsive, even irrational, venal, prejudicial; the former are a better measure of the deliberate moral character of a society.[78]

How the distinction is to be made remains unclear. But there are two elements in Perry's articles which warrant closer attention.

The first one is his notion about what constitutes "public morals". The idea here is that in ascertaining conventional morality on such issues as privacy, abortion, homosexuality, and other types of "nonobtrusive human behaviour",[79] the courts should look not at social values about what is right and what is wrong but at views about what immoral behaviour should be legally prohibited. Only those "commands to which [conventional morality] not only subscribes but believes should have the force of law and thus be legally binding on all, subscribers and nonsubscribers alike"[80] are relevant. Without such a distinction, Perry says, we cannot draw a line between "private morals" and "public morals", while it is only the latter that is relevant in the exercise of the judicial function.

The conceptual distinction between the two types of moral norms — those about what is morally right and wrong, and those about what moral wrongs should be legally prohibited — seems to be clear in theory but very difficult to apply in practice. Often the opinions belonging to the latter category are directly affected by the opinions belonging to the former one, so the distinction seems to be of little help to the courts that would have to draw such a line all the time in order to have a device of selection. Take Perry's own example, the issue of abortion. Perry's private/public morality distinction would suggest that, in ascertaining public morals, the court must distinguish between these two moral positions on abortion: 1) condemnation of abortion as wrong not accompanied by a demand for a legal prohibition; 2) condemnation of legal permissibility of abortion. The court is allowed to take account only of the latter opinions. But it seems that those who condemn abortion often do so because they equate it with the killing of unborn babies; those who hold this view will disagree with Perry's characterization of it as an "unobtrusive" behaviour in the first place. There will probably be rather few who will condemn abortion as morally wrong and yet will want to confine this strictly within the sphere of their "private" morality, without being willing to legislate this proscription. Those whose negative attitude to abortion is not combined with the demand for legal sanctions are likely to disapprove of abortion on medical, prudential, or other nonmoral grounds. So views that at first sight seem to belong to "private morality" are, typically, not views of a moral nature at all. In other words, moral condemnation of the types of behaviour referred to by Perry often operates in such a way as to convert apparent "private morality" issues into "public morals" issue, while "privatization" of these types of behaviour usually removes the matter from the realm of morality as such. This would suggest that Perry's notion of "public morals" will in practice provide little or no objective guidance by which a court can restrict the range of moral attitudes that it takes into account in the reconstruction of "conventional moral culture".

There is a second possible device in Perry's argument which may help judges to be selective in their determination of conventional morality. When

Perry asserts that judges are qualified "to determine accurately the contours of the public morals"[81] (actually he believes that judges are in a better position to perform this task than legislators, and even goes as far as to exult that the Supreme Court "is *admirably situated* to observe and to sense the evolution of contemporary moral culture"),[82] one of the main reasons he gives for this assertion is that judges themselves are not "unconventional" and hence "not unfamiliar with conventional mores and attitudes".[83] But then comes a clue:

> This is certainly not to say that against the background of the *entire* society, Supreme Court justices are conventional individuals. The entire society is hardly the appropriate point of comparison. Against the background of other political decision-makers in our society — legislators in particular — Supreme Court Justices do not appear unconventional to any significant degree.[84]

It is unclear what Perry means by this. If he means to say that judges are no less typical of society as a whole than the other political decision-makers, then his words of caution that "[t]he entire society is hardly the appropriate point of comparison" are out of place: how "conventional" (in the sense of sharing prevailing social standards) the judges are can be determined only in comparison with the rest of community. So the only other way of interpreting this statement is to read it as saying that the proper reference group for assessing judge's typicality is the group of "political decision-makers" and that, by this standard, judges appear to be representative of the accepted norms and values of this group. This is hardly a novel point, but if that is the criterion of conventional morality then the whole majoritarian theory of judicial review turns out to be tautological: the court is required to express the community standards, but at the same time it is permitted to recognize the standards of the decision-makers (including its own, since it is representative of other "decision-makers") as a proxy for community standards. The community "out there" becomes a redundant and totally dispensable factor in this interpretation, and the argument about the democratic legitimacy of judicial review loses all its relevance.

The view that conventional morality is to be ascertained through the prism of an elite (though the elite is described in different terms than by Perry) has been also expressed in a dissent by Judge Frank in a 1947 naturalization case. Discussing the "good moral character" test, Judge Frank suggested that the court should be guided not by "generally accepted moral conventions" but by "the attitude of our ethical leaders".[85] But surely in a morally pluralistic society there is no uniformity of positions taken by "ethical leaders", hence the appeal to the "ethical leadership" does not solve the problem of the indeterminacy of conventional morality. Justice Marshall referred to Judge Frank's test approvingly in *Furman*: "Judges can find assistance in determining whether they are being objective, rather than subjective, by referring to the attitudes of the persons *whom most citizens consider* our 'ethical leaders'".[86] The emphasized words indicate Justice Marshall's innovation (not explicitly acknowledged) to Judge Frank's test. They also highlight the problem: the view that conventional morality could simply be a matter of counting heads stands in irreconcilable conflict with the major theme of Justice Marshall's opinion in *Furman*, which found the test of community standards is found in the hypothetical views held by the ideal, fully informed citizens.

One of the possible laundering devices would be to allow only those moral views that are reflected in actual social practices to be registered by the court. In other words, if we perceive morality as displayed through actual behaviours and practices, we may be closer to the ideal of objectively ascertaining community standards. It is clear that there is a frequent discrepancy between beliefs and actions, between what people say and what they do, and it makes sense to claim that, in the case of such a discrepancy, patterns of behaviour reveal the "truth" about community standards better than verbal declarations. Social psychologists have long analyzed opinion/behaviour inconsistencies, demonstrating that the behaviour of a person in the presence of other people is defined by role orientations different from those that are activated by answering a questionnaire.[87] In his classic experiment conducted in the early 1930's, LaPiere found that a great majority of the same restaurant and hotel owners who accepted him and his two Chinese travelling companions in their establishments, replied in a written questionnaire, sent around by LaPiere after his travel, that they would not serve Chinese.[88] Now it may be plausibly argued that actions are a better proof of actually accepted standards than are declared opinions.

But this course will hardly resolve our problem, because there is a profound indeterminacy in reconstructing community standards through the patterns of behaviour. Further, because behaviour patterns do not cohere into one uniform scheme, the only patterns and practices that have a chance of prevailing over others are those that are supported, or at least tolerated, by the legal rules. This fact has led some to advocate detecting community standards through existing legislation, arguing that the political fact of legislation displays acceptance of a given norm by a number of people. In a strong version, this is reflected in arguments in which the very fact of existing legislation is taken to be positive evidence of the community standards.[89] In a weak version, it is reflected in opinions in which the existing legislation is taken to be evidence that the proposed standards, opposed to those expressed in the legislated ones, do not enjoy overwhelming support, hence that they are not "so rooted in the traditions and conscience of our people as to be ranked as fundamental".[90] But in both these versions, the use of legislation as evidence of moral standards defeats the purpose of the majoritarian theory of judicial review, which is to find the standard of censoring the legislation. It simply does not make any sense to inquire whether legislation is consistent with conventional morality and then to identify the legislation itself as a possible source of our knowledge about conventional morality.

The crude version of the conventional morality theory of judicial review, even with the use of the "laundering" devices discussed above, cannot withstand confrontation with the fact of moral diversity in a community. But there may be a more sophisticated and a more plausible version of the theory — one that will search for the consensus not on the "surface" of societal values, but deeper in the fabric of conventional morality. Behind the observable disagreements and lack of consensus there is, it is often claimed, a basic agreement in a democratic society about fundamental values and principles. If such a substantial agreement can be found and ascertained, then perhaps it can provide a foundation for proper standards of judicial review.

The idea of consensus on the fundamental principles is rather popular among political scientists; indeed, they often claim that such a consensus is a prerequisite of political democracy. This consensus, necessary as it is to sustain common institutions, is variously described as "the common agreement on fundamentals",[91] "a consensus on the first and last things",[92] or "unanimous ... allegiance to the structural principles of the existing society".[93] This consensus, both as postulated and as described, is identified not only with respect to the procedural principles of the operation of a political system ("the common desire to operate a democratic system")[94] but also to the general values of liberty, equality, and individualism.[95]

Whether consensus on fundamental principles indeed exists in democratic societies such as the United States is a matter of empirical investigation. It is useful to recall here the important findings by Prothro and Grigg, published in 1960 — hence in the era when moral consensus was still widely believed to exist before the moral ruptures and turmoil of late 1960's.[96] Prothro and Grigg sought to test the hypothesis that there is a large measure of consensus on the idea of democracy understood as the combination of the principles of majority rule and minority rights. They found that, although there is general consensus on the idea of democracy itself ("Democracy is the best form of government") and on abstract formulations of broad principles of majority rule ("Public officials should be chosen by majority vote; each citizen should have an equal chance to influence government policy") and minority rights ("The minority should be free to criticize majority decisions; people in the minority should be free to try to win majority support for their opinions"), this consensus disappeared when these principles were put in a more specific form. Indeed, the respondents were closer to complete discord (defined by the authors as the situation when the degree of agreement about a given proposition ranges between twenty-five and seventy-five percent) than to complete consensus: for instance, forty-nine percent of respondents believed that only people who are well informed should be allowed to vote, and only sixty-three percent believed that a person who wanted to make a speech against religion, should be allowed to speak.[97] There was also general discord about whether a Communist should be allowed to run for mayor of the city, whether a Communist legally elected mayor should be allowed to take office, and whether a person advocating government ownership of industry should be allowed to speak.

This lack of consensus on more concrete questions involving the application of democratic principles is very significant. For it is not the case that people agree about the fundamental principles while disagreing about some other, less basic values: if one declares that "Public officials should be chosen by majority vote", but at the same time believes (as more than 40% respondents in the reported findings did) that only well-informed people should be allowed to vote, or that a Negro elected mayor should be barred from office etc, then these latter statements undermine the general allegiance to the majority principle. These specific statements are the proper test of what one means by the general principle of majority rule: it is not that they may follow from the principle under a certain interpretation, but rather they are constitutive of it. So this is not, it seems, a case of conflicting views held by a given person, but rather that this person does not sincerely hold a belief in majority rule, or does not understand its meaning. Similarly, in the case of the principle of minority rights, a denial of the right to make an anti-religion speech, or of a right to make a speech favouring Communism,[98] is tantamount to a rejection of minority rights. The general endorsement of the principle of democracy turns out to be merely a verbal declaration, so vague as to be worthless. It cannot be of any use to the court if it decides to adopt the conventional morality theory of judicial review: a court, in interpreting conventional morality, cannot build upon such a declaration, because its decisions concern the applications of the principles to situations such as those described by Prothro and Grigg to their respondents, and about these situations there is more discord than consensus in the community. The basic consensus, if it exists at all, may at best refer to some fundamental recognition of the legitimacy of a system as a whole,[99] without any explicit and ordered content that could dictate the judicial decision in a controversial case.

CHAPTER 3

PHILOSOPHICAL RESPONSES TO MORAL PLURALISM

We concluded Chapter 2 on a sceptical note regarding the possibility of finding a moral consensus in a liberal society. In this, we relied (among other things) on the well known study by Prothro and Grigg about the level of agreement and disagreement on fundamental political principles in the United States. Prothro and Grigg hypothesize that persistence of the belief, among political scientists, in the existence of consensus is a result of a common fallacy — inferring empirical propositions from logical ones: it is assumed "that what people *should* (logically) believe is what they *must* believe ..., and that what they must believe is what they *do* believe".[1] The shrewdness of this suspicion can be confirmed by this recent statement about one of the tasks of political philosophy:

> The real task is to discover and formulate the deeper bases of agreement *which one hopes* are embedded in common sense, or even to originate and fashion starting points for common understanding by expressing in a new form the convictions found in the historical tradition by connecting them with a wide range of people's considered convictions: those which stand up to critical reflection.[2]

These words by John Rawls deserve closer attention, for they carry important implications for our discussion. The theory outlined in recent writings by Rawls (after his *Theory of Justice*) will be discussed in the first part of this Chapter; in the second part we will consider the implications for our discussion of Michael Walzer's conception of "shared understandings", and see whether this conception offers a way out of the dilemma posed by moral pluralism. Finally, we will consider a radical solution to that dilemma: the position of moral relativism. Admittedly, a relativistic theory is a way of reconciling the fact of moral pluralism to the moral requirements of a liberal law. As a focus of our discussion, we will use what is arguably the most influential and innovative exposition of moral relativism in recent moral theory, that by Gilbert Harman.

1. RAWLS, OR "THE DEEPER BASES OF AGREEMENT"

One aspect of the statement by John Rawls quoted above is of only indirect relevance to our discussion: it concerns the proposed aspirations of political philosophy as a device for finding the underlying basis of agreement behind apparently conflicting views. It suffices, perhaps, to say that this program for political philosophy is merely asserted without argument, and that it may be equally reasonable (or equally unreasonable) to demand that philosophy perform an opposite task: revealing basic disagreement behind apparent consensus. The task of debunking an illusory consensus seems as legitimate as the task of seeking a genuine one. But there is another aspect that is more relevant here: a quiet transition from a mere "hope" to an assertion that there may be, in a democratic society, a single body of "common understandings" which express "the convictions found in the historical tradition" and which are connected with "people's considered convictions". This point is made more clearly in one of the sentences preceding the above-quoted statement: Rawls says that the aim of political philosophy

> is to articulate and to make explicit those shared notions and principles thought to be already latent in common sense; or, as is often the case, if common sense is hesitant and uncertain, and doesn't know what to think, to propose to it certain conceptions and principles congenial to its most essential convictions and historical traditions.[3]

And in a recently published article, Rawls asserted that the aim of a conception of justice should be to shape "into one coherent view the deeper bases of agreement embedded in the public political culture of a constitutional regime".[4] So might there after all be a deeper consensus, hibernating somewhere in "common sense" or in the "most essential convictions and historical traditions", waiting for a philosopher to reveal it to its unsuspecting creators?

In order better to appreciate the significance of this theoretical proposition, it is worthwhile comparing it with a theoretical device that Rawls used initially in his *Theory of Justice*, that is with "reflective equilibrium".[5] This was a method of introducing coherence into a moral system by bringing our considered convictions and general moral principles into line with one another. Taking the most firmly held moral judgments as starting points, the aim was, first, to fashion the general principles so that they could explain initial judgments and, second, to find in these principles answers to moral questions about which we have much less assurance than about the initial considered convictions. Through a two-way process,the principles and the convictions are mutually adjusted until the ideal point is reached in which they match each other.[6]

In his post-*Theory of Justice* articles, quoted above, Rawls used language very similar to the original "reflective equilibrium": he talked about people's considered convictions and about working out a state of harmony between the convictions and principles. But there is a major difference. While in *A Theory of Justice*, "reflective equilibrium" occurred within an individual moral reasoner, in the essays quoted above equilibrium occurred (or was expected to occur) within a community. In *A Theory of Justice* Rawls made it clear that other people's considered judgments are irrelevant to the process of equilibrium:

> I shall not even ask whether the principles that characterize one person's considered judgments are the same as those that characterize another's.... [F]or the purposes of this book, the views of the reader and the author are the only ones that count. The opinions of others are used only to clear our own heads.[7]

But in a more recent version, "the opinions of others" serve a much more substantial purpose than that. In what could be termed an "interpersonal" reflective equilibrium (as distinguished from a "personal" reflective equilibrium sketched out in *A Theory of Justice*) Rawls proposed a procedure for a political philosopher to bring together the considered convictions of many people with the aim of forming a coherent body of "shared notions and principles". So this "interpersonal" reflective equilibrium is an equilibrium between people's considered convictions and the shared principles as articulated by a political philosopher.

This seems to be similar to what our "conventional morality" theorists of judicial review are looking for: constructing a deeper consensus invulnerable to the damage stemming from the plurality of moral opinions. But the problem is that this new reflective equilibrium lacks an essential feature that made the older one such an attractive device: its dynamic and flexible character. As described in *A Theory of Justice*, the considered convictions constituted only "*provisional* fixed points"[8] in the process of pursuing equilibrium: they were liable to revision in the light of freshly articulated general principles. An individual moral reasoner was expected to "go[] back and forth",[9] altering, modifying, and abandoning particular convictions and general judgments until the state of mutual fit was attained. Initial "considered judgments" could not, therefore, be viewed as unshakable foundations of a moral conception, as a set of uncontroversial fixed points: an individual could persist in developing his own sense of justice. But in the "interpersonal reflective equilibrium" such an option is no longer available, and so a good deal of the attractiveness of this device as a method of defending and reorganizing a normative system is lost.

A political philosopher, or a judge who would like to mimic the role of the former, must accept "people's considered convictions" as they are: he may play with this material as he sees appropriate (by "propos[ing]... principles congenial to ... essential convictions"[10] or by "organiz[ing] the basic ideas ... into a coherent conception of justice")[11] but he has no license as to the selection of the material itself. A political philosopher must, as it were, work from the inside of the political culture of his community, having no "authority" to revise, alter or modify the fixed points of his equilibrium: "our public political culture" constitutes "the shared fund of implicitly recognized ideas and principles" which now have to be regarded as "provisional fixed points".[12] In the "personal" reflective equilibrium there was the possibility (indeed, the necessity) of discriminating between various, mutually conflicting, moral convictions: those that were made with hesitation, or in a state of fear, or with a view to one's self-interest, could be discarded. Only those convictions that pass this test deserve the honorific title of "considered judgments" and have a role to play in the reflective equilibrium. But in an "interpersonal" reflective equilibrium we lack the authority to make such a selection. Or, rather, even after we discard the judgments made under conditions deemed by Rawls as unfavourable, and after we eliminate (as Dworkin would postulate) opinions which expressed merely emotional reactions, prejudice, rationalization of one's own interest, factual errors, and inconsistencies,[13] the result is still a set of moral judgments that do not necessarily cohere into any unitary body and within which, by virtue of the guidelines for the "interpersonal" reflective equilibrium, there is no authority to discard some opinions and favour others. If we start rearranging the received opinions too much, there is a high risk that on the way from current opinions to "considered judgments" we will eliminate some of the opinions as being tainted by prejudice or factual error simply because we morally disapprove of them, thus overstepping the limits of the authority of the searcher for the "interpersonal reflective equilibrium".

The use of the concept of "authority" in this context may seem odd, but it is not accidental, for it helps explain why there is an analogy between Rawls's vision of .the role of political philosopher and the proposed role of a judge within a conventional morality theory of judicial review. In the initial formulation of *A Theory of Justice* reflective equilibrium, connected as it was with the description of the conditions of the original position, was a device for grounding the reasonableness, not the obligatoriness, of the principles of justice. It was at best a justificatory, at worst an expository, instrument for defending certain principles as just.[14] But the interpersonal reflective equilibrium is concerned not only with reasonableness but also with legitimacy: the role of political philosophy is determined here by "the public culture of a democratic society",[15] and so a political philosopher must show proper deference to the received moral views. The principle of democracy, with its corollary of toleration, shapes the outer limits of the philosopher's (and judge's) intervention in the existing political culture, which clearly was not the case with a traditional reflective equilibrium in *A Theory of Justice*.[16] The apparent advantage is huge — merging the task of justification and legitimation; but the cost is also huge — losing a right to refashion or alter the fixed points of moral reasoning.

Such a merger of justification and legitimation cannot succeed without damaging either of these tasks. If the general principles are to be legitimate, the philosopher must remain neutral between the conflicting convictions, but if he is to be neutral, how can he find in them adequate justification for a coherent set of principles unless these principles are so vague and general as to be worthless? Rawls does not suggest any solution to this dilemma, perhaps because his treatment of the problem tends to lie at the margin of the central themes of his works quoted above. But there is another recent proposition along similar lines which is much more explicit in defending claims similar to those discussed above, and which may appear to be the best method of finding the "deep consensus" that the proponents of the conventional morality theory of judicial review are likely to find in modern moral philosophy. To test the chances of their success, we must therefore turn to this theory.

2. WALZER, OR "SHARED UNDERSTANDINGS"

Before considering Walzer's theory it will be useful to propose a simple distinction between two approaches to justification of normative moral theory: an "internal" and an "external" one. An "internal" approach would be one in which the very fact of acceptance of certain views, opinions, and principles in the community is part of the argument defending a particular moral conception, while in an "external" approach these facts do not figure at all in the argument. As a good example of an explicitly "external" approach one can mention Hare's essay "The Argument from Received Opinion", in which he rejects the view that a moral theory can be shown to be morally unacceptable by demonstrating that it is at variance with received opinion:

"Common moral opinions have in themselves no probative force whatever in moral philosophy".[17] Hare argues that it is the role of moral theory to settle moral questions, and indeed received opinions have often been displaced under the influence of a moral theory; thus received opinions running counter to moral theory cannot be taken as damaging to it.

But here we are concerned with an opposite approach. Michael Walzer has laid the general foundations for what is here called an "internal" method of finding a deep consensus in his article, "Philosophy and Democracy",[18] and showed how this method might be practically applied in his book *Spheres of Justice*.[19] His article can be interpreted as a plea for what is described above as the merger of justification and legitimation seen as the combined, and inseparable, tasks of political philosophy. He distinguishes two alternative visions of philosophy: on the one hand, the vision of a "heroic philosopher"[20] capable of detachment from his own community, "wrenching [him]self loose from the bonds of community",[21] and, on the other hand, a philosopher who "[draws] upon, [and is] radically dependent upon, the resources of a common membership".[22] It is important to see what this "radical dependence" really means, because Walzer postulates for *political* philosophy this second attitude: one which is non-heroic (in his language) or "internal" (in our terminology). The argument behind this choice is a sophisticated and complex one, but (risking a slight over-simplification) it basically boils down to the affirmation of a democratic creed. Because the conclusions of political philosophy lend themselves to (and indeed usually are intended to serve as the basis of) legal embodiment, they must not abstract from what people actually want. Walzer pleads for "philosophical restraint" understood as "the respect that outsiders [i.e. philosophers who "withdraw" from the community] owe to the decisions that citizens make among themselves and for themselves".[23]

Now Walzer does not claim, of course, that a philosopher must be bound by the views current within his community, but he does claim that when a philosopher performs a political role (presumably proposing a program for his own community to implement) he must either recognize as valid the actual desires of his people, or else be viewed with suspicion, just as "Greeks bringing gifts, of whom the people should beware, for what they have in mind is the capture of the city".[24] Generally, "[p]hilosophical founding is an authoritarian business".[25] Note the implications of this conception. First, there is an effective merger of justification and legitimacy in the "non-heroic" or "internal" philosophical enterprise. Second, this role clearly resembles that of judges who are required to ascertain conventional morality in their decisions. Judges, in this theory, are professionally required to combine the values of legitimacy (authority based on respect for people's values) *and* justification (substantive wisdom of the decision) in their activities. So Walzer's vision of political philosophy thus seems ideally suited as a model for the conventional morality theory of judicial review.[26]

To see how, and whether, this vision can work in practice, one must turn to Walzer's book, where he applies this method to the stipulation of his theory of distributive justice. He describes his argument as "radically particularist";[27] his preferred "way of doing philosophy is to interpret to one's fellow citizens the world of meanings that we share".[28] When deciding about the justice of distributive rules, we must appeal to shared understandings about the value of various social goods; "for, in matters of morality, argument is the appeal to common meanings".[29] The questions of justice should be answered, therefore, by the detection of these shared meanings, these deep understandings, these decisions about the value of distinct social goods that have already been made by people in the course of their daily life. A theory of justice need do no more than to interpret for the members of a society their shared meanings. The general thesis is that once the meanings that certain goods hold for the members of the community are properly discovered, the criteria for a just distribution will necessarily have been established.

The theory is perplexing in the face of ineradicable differences of opinion. Surely it is hard to find any answer on the morality of capital punishment in the "shared understandings" of the value of the death penalty if half of the citizenry is against and the other half is in favour of it. It is all very well to postulate the detection of common meanings and shared understandings: but what if the meanings of a given practice are not common, if understandings are not universally shared? True, Walzer envisages such a situation and postulates that in the case of disagreements about values, society must "be faithful to the disagreements, providing institutional channels for their expression, adjudicative mechanisms, and alternative distributions".[30] But this really won't do (not in the area of judicial decisions, anyway) because what we are after are substantive normative rules, not procedural rules. Walzer seems to suggest that in the case of disagreements about values the only available appeal to "shared meanings" may be to the second-degree meanings (on what to do about the disagreements) but surely these are no substitute for substantive rules. If Walzer took this point seriously, it would undermine the whole substance of his enterprise because, whenever disagreements about values are sufficiently significant, his theory of justice would turn out to be purely procedural, which it most emphatically is not. His entire book is an attempt to read substantive values from "shared understandings", notwithstanding actual disagreements, and the phrase quoted above about disagreements comes only at the very end of the book, and in parentheses, as if to indicate its marginal importance in the context of the theory! So disagreements about values do not, after all, trouble Walzer too much. Why not, if they are such a persistent and significant feature of social moralities?

One possible answer might lie in Walzer's occasional references to "deeper understandings" of social goods, presumably as opposed to the observable, current opinions which are, as it were, at the surface of the moral life of society. Walzer says that the goal of theoretical reflection upon the common life is to pick up "those *deeper* understandings of social goods which are not necessarily mirrored in the everyday practice of dominance and monopoly"[31] and, elsewhere, he suggests that a theory of justice must respect "those *deeper* opinions that are the reflections in individual minds ... of the social meanings that constitute our common life".[32] But how is one to get there, beneath the current observable views? A political philosopher (or, for our purposes, a judge) must do more than register actual moral opinions, but at the same time he must stop short of stipulating his own views from "outside". How deeply is he allowed to dive in order to ascertain these "deeper" understandings — to reconcile the competing requirements of consistency in a moral system and of respect for actual people who hold divergent views? Will they still recognize these "deeper" opinions and understandings as their own?

Answers may be sought in some of Walzer's analyses of what he takes to be those "deeper" understandings, in the societies which he discusses, of social goods that are controlled by a theory of justice. There is no room here for a more detailed discussion, so a few examples must suffice. For example, Walzer writes about the treatment of guest workers in modern democratic states and concludes that denying them those basic liberties that are attached to the status of citizenship is contrary to the principle of self-determination;[33] he postulates, with respect to the modern United States, the universal commitment of the community to the provision of medical services for everybody and, consequently, supports restricting the role of the market in medical care;[34] and he claims that the "White Australia" policy on immigration in the 1950's was an error of moral priorities, for it gave priority to the rights of white Australians to great empty spaces of the continent over the claims of necessitous strangers.[35] All these may be plausible moral stipulations, but they are not defensible in terms of "shared understandings" within the communities to which they apply. It is a generally "shared meaning" (not by all, but by a great many) among the citizens of Western European democracies that foreign workers are and should remain beyond the bounds of citizenry; it is widely accepted in America that the rights of private doctors limit their social duty to provide communal health care; and it was part of the general ethos in Australia that strangers had no initial claim to be allowed to immigrate. These claims have their roots in "deeper understandings" and "opinions" (respectively about the meaning of citizenship, of economic freedom, and of national sovereignty), however questionable they might be from Walzer's (and my own) point of view. The method of "radical particularism" does not allow for critical scrutiny of these deeper opinions, so Walzer's criticism of the practices mentioned above cannot draw support from his own methodology.

Significantly, even those critics of Walzer who share most of his substantive value judgments, such as Brian Barry, James Fishkin and Ronald Dworkin, refuse to accept these choices as the products of the reconstruction of "shared understandings" but require a demonstration in terms other than the analysis of shared understandings.[36] If questions about justice are indeed reducible to the questions: "What choices have we already made in the course of our common life? What understandings do we (really) share?",[37] then, alas, the guest workers policy in Western Europe, the free market in medical services in the United States and the White Australia policy in the 1950's reflect the choices really made, and understandings really shared, by important segments of the population in these countries.

Of course, Walzer is not blind to the rather weak support of public opinion for his stipulations and he does not pretend that he simply mirrors general opinions. The matter is, therefore, more complex, though the contrast between public opinion and the substance of his principles represented as "shared understandings" indicates that there must be something wrong deeper in the theory. The problem lies, I believe, in his theoretical views about the notion of "social goods" and what the relations are between these social goods and the substantive rules of distribution. There are two aspects of the theory of social goods, as developed in *Spheres of Justice*. One aspect, which seems sound, and which is irrelevant for the present discussion anyway, is that different kinds of "goods" generate different principles of distribution, and that these various "spheres of justice" should be kept strictly isolated from each other in order to prevent conversion of one scheme of distribution (e.g. money) into other schemes (e.g. political authority). The way Walzer defends this thesis derives its force (though there are alternative ways of arguing about it)[38] from the second aspect of the theory: the view that distributive rules follow directly from (and indeed are "internal" to) our understandings of each good. To put it briefly: social goods are constituted by common understandings of these goods, and once these are ascertained, the principles of just distribution will immediately reveal themselves to us.[39]

But the premises are defective, and the conclusions do not follow. First, what does it mean when we say that a "social good" is constituted by the meaning it has for people? This may apply literally only to those goods that themselves consist of social evaluation, such as prestige (but then the talk about "distribution of prestige" as a subject of justice does not make much sense) or symbolic honours. In the case of most other goods that are available for distribution, about which the most dramatic choices must be made, and to which most of Walzer's book is devoted, social meanings do not come in a package with the intrinsic value of the good. Money is the most obvious example of the separation of intrinsic value and social meaning, not in the sense that it has value beyond the realm of human valuation, but because its meaning does not attach to a single set of values, determining its societal distribution.[40] Walzer talks about bread as having different social meanings in different societies (e.g. it may be seen as primarily a nutritional substance, or as a religious symbol) which generate different distributional criteria.[41] But it is important to see what use Walzer makes of this example. He does not simply say that "bread" is a good which may mean different things to different people, and so they will postulate different uses and different distributions. This would be true but trivial. He says that the proposed use of bread (its social understanding) is part of its meaning, and that the distributional criteria are necessarily built into this meaning. Now this is either not true — for there is no single social meaning of bread, or money, or buildings, or whatever else, so specific as to command particular rules of distribution — or is tautological within the framework of stipulative, and rather eccentric at that, definitions.

This second interpretation of Walzer's fallacy requires explanation. Consider this:

> Distributive criteria and arrangements are intrinsic not to the good-in-itself but to the social good. If we understand what it is, what it means to those for whom it is a good, we understand how, by whom, and for what reasons it ought to be distributed. All distributions are just or unjust relative to the social meanings of the goods at stake.[42]

This short passage epitomizes the main thrust of Walzer's reasoning, and also indicates what is wrong about it. He first introduces a strong stipulative conceptual distinction: we are talking about "social goods", not goods in themselves. Now if "social goods" are defined in such a way as to incorporate their postulated uses (e.g. the nutritional use of bread as opposed to a religious one, or vice versa) then indeed the rules of distribution do not merely follow from, but are part of such a concept of "social good". Once we adopt such an eccentric notion of "social good", then it is a mere tautology to say that in order to ascertain the rules of distribution we have first to understand the social meaning of the good in question. The proper object of inquiry is then not how people understand the good, but how they want to have it distributed; the stage of reasoning attached to "social meaning" is redundant. If, however, social meaning is to play an independent role, and we refrain from incorporating the distributional criteria into the meaning itself, then any "social meaning" of the "good-in-itself" will fall short of triggering precise distributional criteria. For instance, to say that bread is seen by people in a community as a means of nutrition is to say nothing about its proper distribution. Some may postulate its equal distribution (because "we all have equal stomachs"); others, satisfaction of their basic needs first, and distribution of the remaining bread through market exchange; others, privileged distribution of bread to the fittest members of the community. All these rules adopt the same "social meaning" of bread, but the postulated distributive precepts derive from moral sources other than this meaning.

The same argument can be repeated with respect to the other examples given by Walzer — for instance to distribution of offices or of punishments (as "negative goods"). He cites these examples in order to assert that we must approach justice of these distributions historically, with the particular social meanings of these goods in mind.[43] But it is impossible to demonstrate that the social meanings attributed to these goods in any given society generate a unique distributive rule in a non-tautological way. The idea, for instance, that "offices ... should go to qualified candidates"[44] will unite both the proponents and the opponents of affirmative action, but none of them will be able to derive their views about affirmative action solely from the "meaning" of the "office". The idea that punishment is "a negative good that ought to go to people who are judged to deserve it..."[45] may be easily contested by the radical proponents of rehabilitation and/or deterrence as not being part of the "meaning" of punishment, and in any event will not help in grounding non-controversial rules for penalty-fixing. So the main thesis about the connection between "social meaning" and distributive rules invariably displays this dilemma: either it is tautological (within the eccentric construction of "social meanings") or it is a *non sequitur.*

This dilemma, actually, pervades more of Walzer's theory than the part dealing with the relations between the social meanings of goods and distributive rules. Consider the following argument about the relations between human beings and social goods:

> Men and women take on concrete identities because of the way they conceive and create, and then possess and employ social goods.... Distributions can not be understood as the acts of men and women who do not yet have particular goods in their minds or in their hands. In fact, people already stand in a relation to a set of goods; they have a history of transactions, not only with one another but also with the moral and material world in which they live. Without such a history, which begins at birth, they wouldn't be men and women in any recognizable sense, and they wouldn't have the first notion of how to go about the business of giving, allocating, and exchanging goods.[46]

Are we really "men and women in any recognizable sense" only when viewed through the history of transactions and distributions which we make, and through the transactional and distributional place into which we are born? What can be the meaning of that question? We can give it a sociological meaning, about the causal factors which shape our views on justice in a society, and say that our opinions are necessarily determined by our place in a society, and the place of our society in history. As a general position in the sociology of knowledge this would be almost trivial. And it would play no role in Walzer's structure of reasoning, the above quoted passage being located, as it is, between a thesis about "social goods" and about the separateness of spheres of justice. For ordinarily to say that our views are shaped by our experience is not to deny the validity of looking beyond our experience in order to justify our views. Clearly Walzer wants to say something more — something about what it means to be a "human being", about what the very nature of the human self actually is. He is too laconic to allow unambiguous interpretation, but he seems to imply that human beings are somehow constituted by the social goods they possess and/ or desire. But in order to connect this (controversial) notion of the self with his notion of "social goods", he would have to make some sort of claim that the validity of rules of justice is a function of a proper understanding of our selves. The argument must run somewhat like this: in order to be true to human beings, to whom social goods are to be distributed, we must construe the distributive rules in accordance with the "concrete identities" of people; since they have particular goods in their minds and in their hands, we must distribute these goods accordingly. But since what goods they have "in their minds" is just another description of how they want to have these goods distributed, the argument is tautological. All this argument effectively says is that goods have to be distributed in accordance with "concrete identities" of people, but these "identities" include their views about a just distribution. So the idea of what a concrete identity really means does not play any useful role in this argument for it is derived from, rather than constituting the basis for, the principles of a just distribution.

But perhaps there is another, non-tautological interpretation of Walzer's philosophy of the self. This interpretation would allow for selectiveness in reading what social goods people have "in their minds"; it would say that a true "concrete identity" of a person is constituted by what he actually has, and so only the actual history of a person's possessions and transactions is allowed into the reading of his identity. This interpretation of Walzer is confirmed by the fact that, in this context, he approvingly quotes William James's aphorism: "The line between what is me and mine is very hard to draw".[47] But this is not exactly what James said, nor what he had in mind. The correct quotation is: "The Empirical Self of each of us is all that he is tempted to call by the name of *me*. But it is clear that between what a man calls me and what he simply calls *mine* the line is difficult to draw."[48] James's thesis is not about the ontology of the self, not about what constitutes a human identity, but rather about the way people tend to perceive themselves, and other people, in the society. Significantly, this sentence is followed, a little further, by the following observation: "*In its widest possible sense,* however, *a man's Self is the sum total of all that he* CAN *call his*, not only his body and his psychic powers, but his clothes and his house, his wife and children, his ancestors and friends, his reputation and works, his lands and horses, and yacht and bank account."[49] Surely Walzer would not like to say that a person's horses, yacht and bank account are part of his "self" in a philosophical sense. Perhaps even more significantly, the book from which Walzer borrows James's quotation, a study by Snyder and Fromkin on the perceptions of scarcity and uniqueness, uses the quotation from James to support an empirical observation that one socially acceptable way to redefine the self as different from others is through the possession of scarce commodities.[50] This is not a proposition about the ontology of the self, but about the psychological mechanisms of a symbolic representation of a desire for uniqueness. But this is not the use that Walzer makes of the "line between what is me and mine" dictum: his proposition is about the ontological account of the human self and its constitutive parts.

In what way, other than empirical and causal, is a human identity constituted by what a person has? This is a bizarre notion of the human self, one which builds the individual history of transactions and possession into the self; it is doubtful whether it can play a useful role because, in practice, we can appreciate rules of justice which are not at the mercy of actual distributions. This is something to which Walzer's thesis, in its non-tautological interpretation, seems to boil down: if not understood outright in a normative sense as a stipulation of property rights through the people-come-to-the-world-already-with-goods type of argument (an argument that people have the right to what they already have, unless they entered into possession in an illegitimate manner, e.g., through force or fraud),[51] this can only be seen as a theoretical program for constructing rules of justice through the patterns of distribution that actually exist. The only apparent practical meaning for the proposition that the line between "what is me" and "what is mine" is very hard to draw is that, when a society attempts to remove from me part of "what is mine", it necessarily takes away part of "what is me" and thus violates my personal identity. But, apart from being eccentric, it would be an unconditionally conservative vision, one which conflicts with Walzer's substantive views about distributive justice, whenever they call for redistribution of resources.

Walzer's theory merits such lengthy discussion here because, for the purposes of the conventional morality theory of judicial review it is probably one of the best theories available these days. If, as it appears, it fails in deriving the justification *and at the same time* the legitimacy of substantive rules from shared understandings of social goods in a community, then a philosophically oriented judge has very little chance of soundly founding his standards on community norms of public morality. Walzer's problems can be seen as a philosophical equivalent of the dilemmas observed above in the arguments by judges or legal scholars who believe that a community morality, be it at the "surface" or at a "deeper" level, displayed through declared beliefs or through practical actions, can somehow dictate (and by "dictate" we mean here "justify" and "legitimize" at the same time) a coherent set of substantive rules to be applied in judicial decisions.

3. HARMAN, OR MORAL RELATIVISM

One of the important practical aspects of moral relativism concerns the legitimacy of making moral appraisals (including moral criticisms) of other societies which display different moral systems from the appraiser's own. In simple terms, this boils down to a question of whether we are justified in assessing other moral systems "from the outside" or, as Walzer's "radical particularism" would claim, the only legitimate critical moral discourse is "from the inside" - from within the perspective of shared meanings, common understandings and actual agreements made by people within the community under moral scrutiny. If moral questions are reducible to the questions about "choices already made" and "understandings really shared" among people whose arrangements are being appraised,[52] then surely these choices and these understandings themselves must remain beyond the scope of valid moral scrutiny.

Walzer's "radical particularism" might claim powerful philosophical support in some recent versions of moral relativism, notably in the writings of Gilbert Harman.[53] Indeed, the practical implications of Harman's propositions are strikingly similar to those postulated by Walzer: the only legitimate type of moral judgment[54] about other cultures is from within the system of motives and reasons of this other society; social morality is ultimately derived from actual (even if only tacit) agreement; a legitimate moral criticism of distant moral systems is restricted to pinpointing the internal incoherences of these systems, that is to say, cases where the societies are not faithful to choices already made.[55] But the theory of moral relativism is relevant to our discussion not only by virtue of its apparent support for the idea of "shared understandings", and the use that could be made of this idea in connection with the role of conventional morality in judicial decisions, but also, much more directly, it is relevant from the point of view of the discussion which will follow in the subsequent chapters of this book. For moral relativism may be thought to lend powerful support to the fundamental precepts of liberal law: if no conception of the good can be shown to be superior to another in a "non-relativistic" way, then the only path open to the liberal state would apparently be to remain neutral. To be sure, it would be a neutrality based on perplexity rather than on a firm principle, but its implications for anti-paternalism and anti-moralism of law (as discussed in the next Chapter) might be still sufficiently strong.

My discussion of Harman's brand of moral relativism will be organized around three closely interrelated themes: 1) the notion of "inner judgments", 2) the connection between these judgments and the agent's "reasons for action", and 3) the agreement-based theory of morality. The first aspect corresponds to what Lyons calls "appraiser's-group relativism": a theory which makes the validity of moral judgment relative to the appraiser's (or his group's) morality.[56] The second theme corresponds rather to the "agent's group relativism" (again, in Lyons' terminology): a theory which considers an act to be right if it accords with the norms of the agent and/or his group.

These two limbs of relativism are present in Harman's formula that "If someone *S* says that *A* (morally) ought to do *D*, *S* implies that *A* has reasons to do *D* and *S* endorses those reasons...".[57] The third theme provides extra support for both these former aspects of Harman's theory. All three should be seen jointly, as mutually connected and self-supporting pieces of a theoretical construction, and their separate treatment below is dictated only by concerns of clarity.

a. "Inner judgments"

"Inner judgments", in Harman's terminology, have the structure of judgments that someone ought or ought not to have acted in a certain way (which Harman considers to be moral "ought" judgments in a proper sense) or that it was right or wrong of him to act in this way. These have to be distinguished, Harman says, from the non-inner judgments of the type that it ought to be the case that someone acted in a certain way (which Harman labels evaluative "ought" judgments), or that it would be a good thing that he acted in such a way. This latter type of judgments, to which belong also the judgments that someone is evil or that a given institution is unjust,[58] are beyond the scope of "inner judgments" and beyond Harman's interest so far as his version of moral relativism is concerned; as to these, Harman does not claim (nor does he deny) that they are made in relation to agreement. In contrast, what is characteristic about "inner judgments" is that they make sense only in relation to a tacit convention or agreement which involves both the agent to whom the judgment applies and the speaker. They may be properly made only about those who are assumed to accept, or to have reasons to accept, the moral considerations on which the judgments are based.Inner judgments, Harman says, are used to describe a relation between an agent and an act: when we say that someone ought to have done something (or that someone was right to have done something) we presuppose that this person "is capable of being motivated by the relevant moral considerations".[59] These moral considerations constitute, as it were, common grounds between the agent and the speaker.

Now important weight is attached in Harman's argument about inner judgments to the evidence of linguistic oddity and (even stronger) to the alleged misuse of language in making an "inner judgment" about a person who is "beyond the pale",[60] that is, someone who is incapable of being motivated by our own moral considerations. Among Harman's examples are: beings from outer space which land on Earth and set about destroying people;

cannibals eating the sole survivor of a shipwreck; a professional murderer killing a bank manager; Hitler exterminating the Jews; etc. In each of these cases of what we might call "moral outsiders" it would be a misuse of language, Harman claims, to say that the agents "should not have done what they did" although we would be justified in saying (in the non-inner judgments mode) that "it ought not to be the case that the agents did what they did". For instance, we can say without oddity that what Hitler (cannibals, murderer, space invaders) did was wrong but not that Hitler *et al.* were wrong to have acted in this way.

What is puzzling is why this last formulation is alleged to be odd. Much of Harman's evidence in this regard relies on linguistic intuitions which are not sufficiently convincing to carry the burden of proof of "misuse of language". It may well be that for a number of people, who are genuinely appalled by everything that Hitler stood for (and so do not share any of his relevant moral considerations), to say that he "should not have done what he did" does not sound odd or incorrect. So Harman's thesis is perhaps less a proposition about the actual linguistic usages than a proposition about *proper* usages: even if many people use the "It was wrong of him to do" type of judgments to condemn people who are beyond their moral universe, they use this moral form incorrectly.

If that were the actual structure of Harman's argument, it would lose much of its weight and come dangerously close to circularity. For while initially "linguistic oddity" is taken to be important evidence of the connection between the "ought to do" judgments and relevant motivational moral considerations shared by the agent and the speaker, now it appears that the proper linguistic use is an inference from the construct of inner judgments. As Harman says, his "thesis [about inner judgments] is a soberly logical thesis about logical form".[61] But he cannot have it both ways: the proper structure of moral "ought" judgments is either evidence of, or a conclusion from, the convictions about shared moral considerations. It is unlikely that anyone not already holding Harman's views about the necessary relativity of inner judgments (and their connection with relevant moral reasons and motives shared by the speaker and the agent) will be convinced about the incorrectness of making the judgments of the type "He ought to have done so and so" or "It was wrong/right for him to do so and so" with regard to persons who are beyond the motivational reach of common moral considerations.

Be that as it may, let us accept *arguendo* that moral condemnations having a form of what Harman calls "inner judgments" do sound odd in Harman's examples, or in most of them. What is incumbent on him to show is that this linguistic oddity results from the "logical form", and hence that it is a *conceptual* mistake to ignore the shared moral considerations in judgments of this type, rather than for other reasons. Consequently, a way of attacking Harman's conception is to demonstrate that there may be other sources for this oddity. For instance, applying a moral "ought" to space invaders may be wrong (or odd) because we do not consider them to be human beings and so we do not think they are capable of being moral agents in the first place. This is a different reason for excluding them from the applicability of "ought to do statements", different, that is, from the lack of common motivational reasons. For we may, without inconsistency, exclude non-moral agents, such as Martians, animals and trees, from the reach of moral demands and at the same time accept that all moral agents, including those "beyond the pale", are properly judged in the "ought to do" terms. The space invaders' example does not justify Harman's conclusion because the invaders lack much more than proper motivational reasons: they lack the humanness which would make them eligible for any moral considerations, inner or non-inner. With regard to the professional murderer, Hitler and the cannibals, an important part of the "oddity" of saying that they ought not to have done this lies in the extremely low degree of likelihood of the persuasive effectiveness of such propositions. To say to a professional and ruthless murderer: "You ought not do this, it is wrong of you to do this", sounds not so much incorrect as pointless. An important aspect of our moral judgments lies in their persuasive force: as "performative utterances", they are seen as a method of convincing people to take or not to take certain courses of action. If such a persuasive effect is extremely unlikely, our efforts may indeed appear "odd". But this oddity flows from ineffectiveness, not from conceptual incorrectness related to the absence of common motivations. The plea addressed to a Hitler or to a professional gunman sounds not morally wrong but pathetically lacking in force. This sense of practical perplexity is confirmed when Harman asserts that to say "Hitler ought not to have ordered the extermination of the Jews" sounds odd because it is "too weak"; its weakness is however due, Harman continues, not to the enormity of what Hitler did but "because we suppose that in acting as he did he shows that he could not have been susceptible to the moral considerations on the basis of which we make our judgment".[62] This sounds more like a symptom of ineffectiveness (in a rhetorical sense) of persuasion than of incorrectness in the logical form of a judgment.

That the linguistic "oddity" alleged by Harman may have its source in the low degree of persuasive effectiveness rather than in the incorrectness of judging in isolation from motivations, may be additionally demonstrated by making a distinction between prospective "ought to do" judgments and *ex post facto* "ought to have done" judgments. To take Harman's own examples, the advice given to a professional gunman that he ought not to kill a bank manager, even if it is likely to "merely amuse him"[63] (as Harman suggests), does not sound as "odd" as saying that Hitler ought not to have exterminated the Jews. The reason for this distinction in oddity is, I suppose, that the former judgment is a prospective one and so we can always hope that we will succeed in convincing its addressee, while the judgment about Hitler is *ex post facto* and, from the point of view of its persuasive effect, totally pointless.

Finally, it could be said that linguistic oddity is often a matter of rhetorical inadequacy (employed sometimes deliberately in the ironic context) rather than of conceptual error: this may be why Harman claims that the "inner judgment" about Hitler is odd because it is "too weak". Churchill's saying that "democracy is the worst form of government except all those other forms that have been tried from time to time" is in this sense "too weak" and yet is correct (or not incorrect, anyway). Similarly, Darwall gives an example of a statement about someone who wins a head-to-head mile run that he came in "next to last" in the race: it is "too weak" but true nonetheless.[64] Judgments about the cannibals, the professional killer, Hitler etc. may be read as "too weak" in the same, ironic, way. If the proposition that Hitler was very, very, very wrong is correct, then the proposition that Hitler was wrong is correct. Overall, the linguistic-oddity argument does not carry sufficient weight to prove the connection between the judgments of the form, "An agent ought not to have done this", and the moral considerations shared by the agent and the speaker.

b. "Reasons for action"

Harman maintains that the "ought to do" judgments apply properly only to persons who have reasons for doing something. Harman asserts this "connection between the moral *ought* and talk of reasons"[65] by reminding us that in morality, in contrast to law, if a moral demand applies to someone, that person has a compelling reason to act in accordance with that demand. Consequently, if a person has no reason to do something (or to refrain from doing something), we lack the grounds for saying that he ought to do it. It is important to note that "having reasons for doing something" must apply to some such motivational attitudes held by the agent as "certain desires, goals, or intentions":[66] "having reasons for doing something" is not exhausted by our use of "the simple *ought* of rationality"[67] or by our "talk of obligation"[68] unless accompanied by justified assertions about the agent's motivational forces such as "desires, goals, or intentions". Hence, an inner judgment about Hitler ("he was wrong to do what he did") might be incorrect because "for Hitler, there might have been no reasons at all not to order the extermination of the Jews".[69]

This summary immediately suggests that Harman is running together two different concepts of "reasons": normative reasons and motivational reasons. Normative reasons are the characteristics of an action which justify its obligatory character; motivational reasons are the actual desires or intentions held by an agent. When Harman relates reasons for action to the obligatory nature of that action, he uses "reasons" in the normative sense (as in his sentence: "if a moral demand applies to someone, that person has a compelling reason to act in accordance with that demand")[70]. But when he links "reasons for action" with his inner-judgments thesis, he uses "reasons" in a motivational sense (as in the phrase that "there might be no reasons at all for a being from outer space to avoid harm to us").[71] So it seems that the connection between the "ought to do" judgments and the motivations of agents is achieved through the ambiguous use of "reasons", because most of us would accept the normative, but not the motivational, concept of "reasons" as a basis for the "ought to do" judgments.

But that is too easy a criticism of this theory because the problem with Harman's "reasons for action" lies, naturally, not in linguistic ambivalence or confusion. Such confusion may, at worst, result from his iconoclastic use of "moral reasons" in a motivational sense. Harman himself denies that he uses "reasons" as "motivating reasons": he says that "it is always consistent to suppose that such a reason [to adhere to a particular moral demand] is not a motivating reason because [the agent] is unaware of it, or is aware but is acting irrationally, and so on".[72] This is because, generally, reasons for action occur, in Harman's theory, not only if an agent accepts a moral demand, but also when he fails to accept this demand *only* because of ignorance or irrationality.

This is, however, a rather minor detraction from the general observation that Harman uses "reasons" in a motivational sense: the actual desires and intentions must be disallowed in the talk of reasons only if they reflect ignorance or irrationality (including "stupidity, confusion, or mental illness").[73] That this revision is rather insignificant, and does not take into account even very fundamental moral defects, is demonstrated by Harman's reluctance to include under the rubric of "ignorance" or "irrationality" Hitler's policy towards the Jews or the hardened criminals' actions towards their victims. "Certain successful criminals seem to have no reason to be at all concerned about their victims; they simply do not care, seemingly without being irrational or ignorant in not caring".[74] This is fully in the spirit of Harman's theory, for if he had allowed even very severe moral defects to count as the indications of "irrationality or ignorance" then he would have undermined the relativist nature of his ethics: he would have injected the "external" approach through the irrationality/ignorance proviso. Since he does not concede this, we must conclude that this proviso does not significantly alter the motivational nature of his concept of "reasons for action".

But, again, the root of the problem does not lie simply in linguistic confusion, for it is a deliberate and very central substantive thesis in Harman's theory that the "ought to do" statements can be triggered only by motivational facts about the agent (whether we call them "reasons" or not). The question is why we are permitted to use the moral ought only in this context. Harman does not address this question directly, and to the extent to which he avoids handling this matter, his thesis about the moral ought/motivation connection is question-begging. For, if linguistic intuition were to be a judge in this matter, we would probably have to conclude that it is a perfectly legitimate use of the moral ought to apply it to the Hitler or murderer cases quite irrespective of any inquiry into their motivations to refrain from morally improper actions.

The problem with reconstructing Harman's positive argument about the moral reasons/motivation connection is that so much of his reasoning appears circular. Consider, for instance, this rebuttal of the "external" argument which asserts that someone ought to care about other people whether or not the actual motivating circumstances influence the agent's mind:

> If S ought to care about the welfare of others in the sense that he or she has reasons to care, then these reasons are also reasons for S to act in the appropriate way towards others. But, if S ought to care only in the sense that it ought to be the case that S cared, in other words that it would be a good thing if S cared, all that follows is that S ought to act in the appropriate way in the sense: it ought to be the case that S acted in that way. It does not follow that S ought morally to act in that way.[75]

Why not? I suppose that for most people, from the fact that it ought to be the case that S acted in a particular way, it follows (at least, as a *prima facie* moral duty, subject to the consideration of competing duties) that S ought morally to act in that way. By denying this inference, Harman merely restates (rather than defends) the proposition that the moral ought is closely connected with actual motivations. The moral-ought judgment fails to follow from the "it ought to be the case" judgment only if we already accept that the moral ought cannot be asserted independent of motivational talk.

One way of establishing such a connection is perhaps through the *practical* likelihood of making an agent undertake the obligatory action. Perhaps it can be claimed that reasons for action must be capable of motivating the agent, hence of moving the agent to act in a particular way.[76] In such an argument we proceed backwards: from the effect to the cause. If an agent has not taken the proper action then we suppose that he was not motivated to do so, hence he had no reasons for doing it. But the link between the motivations and reasons is again a weak part of this chain of argument because actually we often claim that people have moral reasons for doing certain things even if they lack adequate motivational attitudes. To demonstrate that we err in saying this requires evidence which cannot be supplied by the argument just mentioned, because the hypothetical link of moral reasons and a practical capacity of motivating the agent is asserted arbitrarily. I suspect that the initial appeal of this argument (if any) may derive from the intuitive connection we make between the correctness of moral judgments and their persuasive force as prescriptions for action. Perhaps Harman's argument would gain weight within the emotivist version of noncognitivist meta-ethical theory which considers moral judgments as prescriptions and recommendations for action. Perhaps then, if the validity of moral judgments were to be fully reducible to their capacity of persuading people to behave in conformity with these judgments, the connection between moral reasons and motivations could be defended indirectly by an appeal to effectiveness. But Harman does not opt for this way of rescuing his thesis.

However, if we assume for the sake of argument that the value of a moral theory resides, among other things, in its persuasive and performative function, then Harman's theory about the reasons/motives connection displays a striking contradiction: it puts "beyond the pale" (and so, beyond the reach of moral argument in terms of the "ought to do" judgments) those who, for reasons other than irrationality and ignorance, fail to exhibit the appraiser's moral motives. In other words, in its practical operation (and from the point of view of this meta-ethical theory that is all that matters) it restricts its own preaching to the converted, while it deems pointless addressing strong moral argument towards those who do not share our moral attitudes. It thus undermines the rationale for a good deal of moral discourse, the function of which is related to moral development and reform. As one critic observed, the "inner judgments" theory is ironically at the same time too generous and not sufficiently generous: it is not sufficiently generous, because it puts "beyond the pale" all those who act on immoral (from our point of view) motives and who perhaps might be still susceptible to moral persuasion, and it is at the same time too generous, because it saves from moral blame those who act on their longstanding prejudices, for they lack a motive for doing otherwise.[77]

c. Agreement-based morality

The key evidence Harman gives for the proposition that morality rests on a tacit agreement or convention among a group of people concerns the unequal moral stringency of the duty not to harm others and the duty to help someone in need. The priority of the former is presented by Harman as a "puzzle about our moral views"[78] which can be solved only if we accept that morality is derived from an agreement among people. The argument can be reconstructed roughly as follows. (1) In our morality the prohibition against harming others is stronger than the duty of mutual aid even though from a purely utilitarian standpoint these duties should have the same strength. (2) The duty to avoid harm to others benefits equally everyone in a society since the poor (the weak) and the rich (the powerful) alike stand to be harmed by the violations of this duty; however, the duty to help those in need is much more beneficial to those weak and poor than the strong and powerful. This suggests that (3) there is a high likelihood of having mutual agreement in a society on the duty not to harm, but not on the duty to aid others. (4) In the absence of other good arguments supporting the unequal strength of these two types of duties, the agreement provides the only justification of the priority of the duty not to harm over the duty to aid. Hence (5) morality is based on mutual (even if tacit) agreement or convention.

The main thrust of the attack upon Harman's proof has been directed against stage (4) of the reasoning and has consisted in finding other, non-consensual justifications of the priority of the duty not to harm others over the duty of mutual aid.[79] But this is not the only possible line of criticism since the reasoning summarized above may be attacked right at point (1). Point (2) could also probably be questioned: one could suggest that at least *some* prohibition of harming benefits the rich more than the poor who actually might benefit from some harms (for instance, theft of luxurious items). But I will not pursue this last strategy here. Instead, I will concentrate on the status of the priority of the duties mentioned above.

Consider Harman's criticism of some of the explanations of the moral relevance of the distinction between negative duties of not harming, and positive duties of helping. Richard Trammel has argued that there are three main reasons why we are under greater obligation to avoid harming others than to help others:[80] (i) The negative duty of not harming can be discharged completely but the positive duty of helping others can never be fully discharged since there are too many people needing help; (ii) If one harms someone else, this person is necessarily harmed; but if one fails to help a needy person, that person is not necessarily left without help because there may be someone else who will help; (iii) If one harms another person, one is necessarily responsible for that other person's plight; but if one fails to help a needy person, one is not necessarily responsible for that person's needing to be helped. Harman has two types of responses against Trammel's arguments. As against argument (ii) Harman says that Trammel's distinction is merely verbal; as against arguments (i) and (iii) Harman claims that they already presuppose the unequal stringency of the duty to avoid harm and the duty of mutual aid; hence these arguments are incapable of justifying this moral distinction.

It seems to me that Harman is correct only with regard to argument (iii). Indeed, the notion of moral responsibility is parasitic upon prior moral duties and hence Trammel's point about responsibility presupposes a society in which the duty not to harm is more stringent than the duty to help others. As Harman says, "In a more egalitarian and altruistic society, which did not recognize a moral distinction between harming and not helping, you would be considered responsible for a person's plight if you failed to give the person help when it is needed".[81] Note, incidentally, that Trammel's point can easily be misinterpreted. What he is saying in argument (iii) is not that the responsibility incurred by a harming person is higher than that of a non-helping person (because then his argument about the reasons for our "moral puzzle" would be evidently circular) but rather that responsibility for causing someone's plight comes as a necessary consequence of harming but only as a contingent consequence of non-helping. So there is no moral hierarchy of responsibilities presupposed by Trammel. But Harman is right in suggesting that in a society which presupposed a general duty of help (such a duty being of equal stringency as a general duty not to harm), the failure to help would ensue in imposing a responsibility upon the non-helper. So the responsibility, but not necessarily the non-helped person's misery (because, arguably, in such an admirable society other people would give the necessary help), follows from a prior moral judgment about the moral equivalence of both types of duties in question.

Now consider Trammel's argument (ii). To the observation that someone is necessarily harmed as a result of the act of harming, whereas failure to fulfil the positive duty of helping leaves open the possibility of someone else helping the needy person, Harman replies that "this is a purely verbal point" because "if you act so that a particular person will be harmed unless someone else intervenes to save that person, that person is not necessarily harmed, since someone else may intervene; on the other hand, if you fail to help a person needing help whom no one else is going to help, that person is necessarily unhelped".[82] Trammel's argument is "verbal", Harman explains, because any case of harming can be described either as an act of harming someone, or as a case of acting in such a way that someone will be harmed unless someone else intervenes. Likewise, any case of not-helping may be represented either as a failure to help someone or as a case of failing to help someone whom no-one else is going to help.

Leaving aside the issue of whether Trammel's argument is indeed purely verbal, the substance of his proposition is that harming and non-helping are significantly asymmetrical with regard to the inevitability of the occurrence of negative consequences. By contrast, Harman demonstrates the symmetry of these two situations when consideration of a possible intervention by a third party is introduced. Since the hypothetical intervention by someone else into the relationship between the wrongdoer and the victim may avert the negative consequences in the cases of harming and non-helping alike, these two situations are relevantly equivalent with regard to the avoidability of the morally deplorable consequences.

I think that Harman is right in asserting the symmetry of these two situations, but this does not warrant his conclusions about the solution of the "moral puzzle". For if we compare the duty not to harm with the duty to help someone needing help whom no one else is going to help, it is not obvious to me that we are still justified in upholding the priority of the duty not to harm over the duty to help. This priority seems intuitive only in a simpler picture, painted by Trammel, where our attention is restricted to the wrongdoer and the victim. In such a restricted framework, it seems reasonable to believe that there will be someone else to help, and so we are predisposed to concede the lower significance of the duty to help. But in a more refined picture, introduced by Harman, where we *are aware* of the degree of likelihood of a third person's intervention, there may be situations where the unlikelihood of intervention of a third party in the non-help situation will compel us to condemn the non-help as severely as the act of harming. In such a case, stage (1) of Harman's reasoning as reconstructed above does not occur at all.

In other words: Trammel would like us to compare two situations: (a) A harms B; (b) A does not help B, while Harman says that in fact (a) may be described either as (a*) A harms B, or (a**) A harms B unless C intervenes; and that (b) may be described as either (b*) A fails to help B, or (b**) A fails to help B whom no one else is going to help. What Harman is suggesting is that (a*) and (b**) have an equal air of the inevitability of evil consequences to them, and so they seem morally equivalent. Correct, but this suggests (or at least may suggest) that the priority of the duty of non-harming over the duty of help is rebuttable rather than that it has its source in a tacit agreement. Perhaps when we endorse such a priority in abstract terms, we are reasoning in a myopic fashion, without considering the moral relevance of the likelihood of the intervention by third parties. As we refine our moral landscape, and incorporate additional considerations (such as the intervention of other parties in the wrongdoer-victim relationship), we may well be persuaded to revise our initial abstract moral convictions. And so we will remove the very foundation of Harman's reasoning about the tacit-agreement conception of morality, namely stage (1).

Such a conclusion about Harman's counter-argument to Trammel's point (ii) seems neither unlikely nor *ad hoc*. Consider the comparison of pushing into the swimming pool someone who we know cannot swim and not helping a drowning person when it would be easy for us to rescue the person. The initial judgment about the former being morally worse than the latter may be precisely the result of our common experience that, in situations such as these, there may always be some other persons who will rush in with help and so, by and large, the negative effects are more easily avoidable in the latter type of cases. In typical circumstances, then, these two courses of action do not meet the initial *ceteris paribus* condition of the whole intellectual exercise. But if we know more about the situation, and incorporate Harman's concerns about possible (non)intervention by third parties, and if we are further satisfied that the act of non-helping belongs to the (b**) category, so that there is no prospect of third-party intervention, it may be rational and wise for us to condemn the act of non-rescuing equally as strongly as an act of harming. We may further, upon reflection, qualify our initial abstract judgment about the priority of non-harming over helping by saying that, *ceteris paribus* (i.e., when the consequences for the victim are equally detrimental), harming is more reprehensible than non-helping *unless* we know that, in the case of a violation of the duty to help, no one else is going to help, in which case both these duties are of equal moral stringency. The initial judgment, taken by Harman in point (1) of his reasoning as unqualified, in fact turns out to be only a crude and inaccurate formulation of a rule about the relative importance of duties to avoid harm and to help others: the incorporation of the third-party attitude as a relevant factor helps us to refine this initial formulation.

Finally, consider Harman's rejoinder to Trammel's first point. The negative duty not to harm others can be fully discharged whereas the positive duty to help cannot, Trammel says. Harman responds that this proposition *presupposes* a moral distinction between harming and non-helping because, in the absence of such a distinction and, consequently, under the regime of a strong duty to help others (equally strong as the duty not to harm), our societies would be much more egalitarian and altruistic. In such societies the number of those who need help would be very small and so "you could help all who would benefit from your help to the same extent that you could avoid harming anyone".[83]

For one thing, it is unclear on what grounds Harman establishes such a strong connection between the altruistic/egalitarian nature of a society ruled by a strong duty of mutual aid and, on the other hand, a small number of people needing help. This connection, if anything, is contingent rather than necessary and depends, among other things, on such external factors as the overall availability of resources. One may well imagine a society in which everyone believes in a strong duty to help others and yet sufficient resources to help all the needy persons are not available. Such a society will correspond to Trammel's description about the comparative ease of non-harming as opposed to helping. Secondly, how can Harman be so sure that in an altruistic society "you could help all who would benefit from your help *to the same extent* that you could avoid harming anyone"?[84] To establish this, we would have to compare the incomparable: the number of those standing to benefit from the general observance of the duty to help with the number of the beneficiaries of observance of the duty not to harm. This is impossible because the first number can be ascertained in an empirical fashion, while the second number is discernible only after the violation of the proposed duty. We would also have to compare the costs (including the resources, energy, repression of instincts) of helping and non-harming. If the costs of helping prevail over the costs of non-harming (which seems to be obvious, even in a hypothetical altruistic society, because even the least costly act of helping requires time and effort, while abstention from harming involves none of these), then from our initial priority rule we may infer a principle that, everything else being equal, moral duties which involve more sacrifices, costs etc. imposed upon the agents are less stringent than those duties which are less demanding. Although it is a controversial principle, it may be a more reasonable candidate for a solution of Harman's "puzzle" than the tacit-agreement hypothesis: even if it fails to *justify* the "puzzling" priority rule, it helps to *explain* its popularity, which is all we need in the context of Harman's "puzzle".

Thirdly, and most importantly, Harman's rebuttal of Trammel's first argument appeals to a construction of a hypothetical altruistic society while the point made by Trammel arguably applies to societies as they are. As things stand, we know that people do not help others as frequently and efficiently as they avoid harming others. But this fact is not a *moral* presupposition of Trammel's explanation of the unequal moral weight of harming and non-helping; it is one of the *empirical* parameters within which the priority rule operates. Ironically, Harman-the-relativist interprets Trammel's explanation of the priority rule as if the only sensible interpretation were an absolutist one. Such an absolutist condition would claim that a valid moral rule must not be made to depend, in the conditions of its application, upon any empirical facts about the society in which it is to operate. But there is no reason to accept such a condition: one can be a non-relativist and at the same time claim that the choice of moral rules and of their priorities should be dependent upon the empirical facts about a given society: this choice is governed by a superior moral rule which, itself, is not relative to facts about the society. For instance, one may accept the principle that at a very low level of economic development the moral importance of the maximization of well-being should prevail (in cases of conflict) over that of maximization of individual liberty, but beyond a certain threshold of material growth the priority should be reversed. To accept this rule one does not have to be a moral relativist because the validity of this proposed rule does not depend upon the society to which it is applied: it may be claimed (without contradiction) by a non-relativist to be equally valid with regard to very rich and very poor societies. But, contingent upon the empirical facts of a society (i.e. its stage of economic growth), a different priority will follow in the observance of one and the same general priority rule. For it is the rule itself which requires us to take into account certain empirical facts about society as relevant tests for the correct application of this rule.

By the same token, the priority rule discussed by Harman and Trammel may incorporate some facts about the society, e.g., the overall level of observance of the duty of mutual aid. It may well be that one rationally takes this fact as a relevant test for weighing the prohibitions of harming and non-helping. One may say that in a society in which the overall level of mutual help is low (and, in any case, lower than the level of harming), the duty of helping is less stringent than the duty of non-harming because in such a society one cannot help all those who need help while one can easily avoid harming others. (This claim naturally assumes a moral proposition about practical ease being relevant to moral priorities, but the principle is not evidently nonsensical and in any event it need not worry us here because all we need to show is that Trammel's thesis is not tautological). However, one may accept without contradicting oneself that in a more altruistic society this priority is no longer valid because its empirical conditions do not occur. Now this argument does not involve the circularity detected by Harman in Trammel's argument, because what is *presupposed* by this particular reasoning is not the moral weight of harming compared to not-helping but an empirical characterization of a society as non-altruistic plus an unspoken assumption that the ease (or practicality) of achieving moral aims is, *ceteris paribus*, relevant to the stringency of a moral duty. Whatever one may think about the force of this argument, it is not circular in the fashion depicted by Harman. This argument would, further, commit one to saying that the general priority rule about the duties not to harm and to help, as stated by Harman and taken at face value by Trammel, is incomplete without the incorporation of a test for the overall level of altruism. So, in any event, stage (1) in Harman's reasoning must be refined by incorporating this test into a "puzzling" priority rule. But with such an addition, the hypothesis about tacit consent is no longer the only available one.

I conclude that all three of Harman's fundamental propositions, which I have identified here as the main pillars of his version of moral relativism, are deficient. He has not given us convincing reasons to accept (1) that the strong moral judgments (having the form of "ought to do" or "X was wrong to do Z" statements) may only be made about persons motivated by the same moral considerations that we endorse; or (2) that those judgments can only be meaningfully used in relation to the agents' having reasons for doing particular things; or (3) that valid moral judgments presuppose prior agreement. The discussion of the weaknesses of this recent, most influential and sophisticated, version of moral relativism, completes our survey of some philosophical responses to the dilemmas generated by the moral pluralism of liberal societies. Neither appeal to a "deeper" consensus, allegedly discernible through "deeper bases of agreement" (Rawls), nor "common understandings"

(Walzer), nor moral relativism (Harman) seems to be a successful strategy. The answer to the dilemma should therefore be found in the normative presuppositions of a liberal legal order — in the normative bases of the regime of legally protected liberties. To this aim, Part 2 of this book will be devoted.

PART TWO

LAW AND NEUTRALITY

CHAPTER 4

THE "RIGHT/GOOD" DISTINCTION, THE HARM PRINCIPLE, AND LIBERAL NEUTRALITY

We may compile a set of an individual's interests in liberty which should be protected by a good legal system: bodily integrity, freedom of expression and of the communication of ideas, freedom of thought and conscience, freedom to have or adopt a religion or belief of one's choice, privacy, protection from arbitrary interference, freedom of movement and choice of residence, freedom to adopt a life-style (including a so-called "non-orthodox" life-style) of one's choice, etc. But reciting a list of liberties that the law should protect is just the beginning of an intellectual task, not its completion. The real problem is how to define and construe them in order to provide the standards for a resolution of the conflicts among them, or conflicts between these liberties and other important social interests. The challenging problem that a legal philosopher must face concerns, therefore, the limits of protected liberties, not a list of them.

Since John Stuart Mill, the preferred method for approaching this has been by reference to the harm principle: taking it as an extreme precept, legal philosophers of a liberal persuasion have defined their attitude towards proper limits on protected liberty by proposing exceptions to, or constraints upon, the harm principle. This is nicely epitomized in Joel Feinberg's description of his own approach: "My procedure, having 'assumed' the correctness of the harm principle, will be to adopt a properly liberal skeptical stance toward all other liberty-limiting principles, and to try to go as far as possible with the harm principle alone, acknowledging additional valid principles only if driven to do so by argument".[1] In this perspective, prevention of harm to others is postulated as the only *regular*, non-problematic legal constraint upon individual liberty: all other principles (such as the prevention of moral offence, of non-harmful indecency or immorality, of self-imposed harm etc) are seen either as (sometimes) necessary and (always) lamentable evils, or are rejected outright. The non-liberal party to this dispute is not merely willing to accept *more* legal constraints and prohibitions: more important, non-liberals reject the general presumption against interference with liberty. Prohibition of private indecency, for instance, is viewed by them not as a deviation from a norm, but as an expression of a correct rule in its own right, which may be adopted by all decent people without reluctance and shame. In other words, one of the dimensions of the controversy concerns the onus of justifying legal interferences with liberty: a non-liberal party rejects the formula that all interferences require special justification while respect for individual liberty is justified by itself.

The problem for liberals is, to use the nice formula of Michael Sandel, how they can consistently "take pride in defending what they oppose":[2] for instance, how can a liberal defend the right of individuals to read pornographic books while considering pornography distasteful, or support a woman's right to abortion without condoning the moral appropriateness of abortion, or defend the right of adult individuals to use drugs while recognizing that drugs may make one's life despicable and degrading. Reliance on the attitude of moral relativism (stating that there are no objective standards of morality, hence, there are no objectively valid ways of showing that one action or lifestyle is morally superior to another) is not an attractive option, not for all liberals anyway.[3] So the most promising route available to a liberal is to draw the time-honoured distinction between "the right" and "the good", and to claim the priority of "the right" over "the good" when it comes to shaping the content of law. If we can separate our judgments about the moral criteria of the good life from judgments about moral duties, rights and obligations, then perhaps we can consistently disconnect our judgments of moral virtue/vice from judgments of the proper moral limits of legal enforcement and prohibition. If "the right" is distinguishable from "the good" (rather than being a direct inference from it, as is the case, for instance, in consequentialist ethics where "the right" is understood as that which maximizes "the good"), then there is a moral basis for demanding that law be neutral between conflicting conceptions of "the good" while enforcing "the right". This demand translates into a liberal claim that people should be free to pursue their own ends within a general framework of rules that is neutral towards these ends. Only a radical separation between the right and the good can lead us to a conclusion that not everything that is morally good ought to be legally enforced, and not everything that is morally bad ought to be legally prohibited.

A caveat is perhaps needed to stress that the "ought" in the second half of the preceding sentence is, of course, a moral "ought". For one may well introduce the argument that a distinction between moral goodness and legal regulation is based on purely prudential or practical considerations: it would still be "morally right" for the law to prohibit indecency (and there the right would be derivative from the good), but for some practical, contingent and non-moral reasons — such as administrative convenience, difficulties in evidence or high costs of investigation — it would be inappropriate for the law to punish all the vices. But this obviously is not an argument which is helpful to a liberal in the present context.

1. THE PRIORITY OF "THE RIGHT" OVER "THE GOOD", AND THE PRINCIPLE OF EQUAL MORAL AGENCY

In the version popularized by John Rawls, the conception of the "priority of the right over the good" is derived from the Kantian philosophy of individuals as persons assumed to possess a rational faculty and capable of autonomous action. The idea of treating persons as being capable of moral choice gives weight to the imperative of treating them as ends in themselves rather than as means to other people's ends. This Kantian interpretation appears in the Rawlsian "original position": particular conceptions of the good are disallowed there and the parties to the contract "do not know what final aims persons have".[4] This is so for two reasons. First, because the only relevant aspect of the self in the original position (hence, in the considerations of justice) is "moral personality" (understood, in Kantian terms, as the capacity to choose the mode of life) and not the capacity for pleasure and pain. This, naturally, presupposes that we can (and indeed, that we should) distinguish these two aspects of moral personality: the capacity for a conception of the good, and the capacity for a sense of justice.[5] Second, because to allow the knowledge of the substantive standards of the good in the original position would compromise the priority of liberty: "To acknowledge any such standard [of the good] would be, in effect, to accept a principle that might lead to a lesser religious or other liberty, if not to a loss of freedom altogether to advance many of one's spiritual needs. . . . [The persons in the original position] cannot risk their freedom by authorizing a standard of value to define what is to be maximized by a teleological principle of justice".[6]

It need not bother us now whether or not the last defense of the "priority of the right over the good" begs the question: sometimes, the priority of liberty is presented by Rawls as the *outcome* of deliberations in the original position, and sometimes (as in the last argument) it acts as a constraint upon the *conditions* of these deliberations. What does matter, in the present argument, is whether there is a strong overall fit between our intuitive feeling for liberty and the requirement for leaving the conceptions of the good behind the veil of ignorance in the imaginary moral bargaining on justice. And this fit seems to be beyond any doubt.

But the fact that Rawls has restated so persuasively the theory of the "priority of the right over the good" in modern philosophy, and that he has developed his own theory under the explicit inspiration of Kant and in direct polemic with utilitarianism, may distract attention from the fact that the conception has deeper roots in modern liberal theory which are not restricted to the Kantian tradition. Amy Gutmann draws a useful distinction between two strands in classical liberal thought: one (typified by Bentham and Mill, and traceable back to Hobbes) views human beings as sharing certain similar passions, the other (represented by Locke and Kant, and nowadays chiefly by Rawls) views people as sharing a minimal rational capacity for making moral choices and for taking responsibility for their lives.[7] The point I want to make is that, notwithstanding the tendency by Rawls to deny this, the school of "equal passions" also laid foundations for the "priority of the right over the good", not only the school of "equal rationality". The basic idea behind Hobbes' political philosophy is that, in nature, there is no basis for opinions of good and bad, and so people are certain to disagree about what is good and bad, but they can all agree on the need for peace and security. The latter need gives sense to the notions of the right, and to the sense of justice. But to bring controversies about "the good" (in our terminology) into the political sphere undermines the aim of the whole enterprise which is built upon the agreement about peace (hence, about "the right"). Including the question of the good in the political agenda amounts to the withdrawal of a person from the political community, for it means putting the grounds of sovereignty in doubt: "if any one, or more of them, pretend a breach of the Covenant made by the Soveraigne at his Institution; and others, or one of his Subjects, or himselfe alone, pretend there was no such breach, there is in this case, no Judge to decide the controversie: it returns therefore to the Sword again; and every man recovereth the right of Protecting himselfe by his own strength, contrary to the designe they had in the Institution".[8] It is clear that the sovereignty is over the matter of peace (even if Hobbes conceived it in a very expansive manner), not over the matters of what are good and bad, over which there is "no Judge to decide the controversie". Paradoxically perhaps, Hobbes turns out to be the real father of the tradition of liberal constraint which requires that matters of moral ends be suppressed in the liberal state. Characteristically, this is how a modern historian of ideas recapitulates the lessons from Hobbes: "If men could stop disputing the ends of politics and agree on the condition of all ends, they could follow privately those ends whose pursuit is consistent with the same allowance to other ends. Under Hobbes's golden rule, the universe of tolerated ends is defined by the condition of all ends, including the intolerable, and that is civil peace".[9]

We should therefore not be surprised that, with this pedigree, the "priority of the right over the good" theory resonates well with the "harm to others" principle of Mill, a writer belonging to the Hobbes/Bentham rather than the Locke/Kant tradition in Gutmann's scheme. Though Rawls does not make it clear, the way he describes the contrast between the principles of the "right" and the "good" sounds suspiciously like the Millian other-regarding/self-regarding dichotomy. He says, for instance, that the principles of the right "establish a final ordering among the conflicting claims that persons make *upon one another*" while the principles of the good are about "what is the good *of particular individuals*".[10] Hence the claim that the state has to be neutral as between the opposing conceptions of "the good" while enforcing "the right" means, for all practical purposes, that the state must not interfere with the individuals' preferences which concern themselves, their own conceptions of what constitutes a morally good life for them, while at the same time the state must enforce the 'right' actions as between individuals. But this merely paraphrases the distinction between the self-regarding and other-regarding actions so crucial to Mill's harm principle: it cannot therefore provide a justification for this principle.[11] It seems to me (and here I agree with Dworkin's argument in his essay "Liberalism")[12] that the most successful way of defending this conception is by an appeal to a certain substantive conception of equality. It may perhaps be defined as the equality of individuals as moral agents who are capable of adopting and pursuing (and, if they like, of changing) their own beliefs about what constitutes a morally good life for them. This equality implies "only" that everyone is equal in exercising the right to decide what gives value to his or her life.[13] To attribute to some members of the community the authority to decide about what is good for others (that is, to give some people power to enforce their *external*[14] preferences through legal means) would inevitably deny equal moral sovereignty for these other people over the range of decisions concerning what is good for them. In order to respect this equality, the content of law must be independent of any particular conceptions of what gives value to human life. It does not follow that the life-plans of all are equally valuable, but only that all should be equal in exercising their choice of morality for themselves (except in choosing morality which permits harming others, or imposing one's own morality upon others: such license — as we shall later see — would defeat the initial, fundamental principle of equality).

We should now attend to two objections that can be made. First, it may be objected that equality of moral agency must accord equality to those whose pursuit of the moral good requires imposition of their conception of good upon others, and second, that it must accord equality to those whose pursuit of a morally good life requires harming others. In a practical sense these two strategies of criticism are opposites: the former would suggest that our conception, in order to be consistent, would have to impose more restrictions upon individual behaviour than it openly admits, while the latter implies that our conception would have to impose virtually no restriction at all. But their common function would be to show that this conception is incoherent and self-stultifying, and that it draws the line between acceptable and unacceptable interference with individual liberty in an unprincipled, ad-hoc manner; hence, it does not qualify as a general principle governing freedom under the law.

Consider the first objection: if every substantive morality has to be equally protected against adverse interference, then presumably the same must apply to those conceptions of the good which, in order to flourish, require the imposition of paternalistic or moralistic restrictions upon the activities of individuals (because their conceptions of the good life necessarily include preferences about how other people should lead their lives). While in our conception, the "right/good" distinction would bar such a conclusion (for no interference is permitted in the realm of "the good"), the strategy of the critics must be to show that all arguments about "the good" can be easily converted into arguments about "the right", and so the distinction is untenable or meaningless (and as such cannot do its job of discriminating between permitted and prohibited interferences). "[T]here is no difficulty" John Finnis says, "in translating any 'paternalistic' political preference into the language of entitlement, by postulating an entitlement of every member of a community to a milieu that will support rather than hinder his own pursuit of good and the well-being of his children, or an entitlement of each to be rescued from his own folly".[15]

But this is too quick an argument, and merely "translating" the good into the language of entitlements won't undermine the present conception. The question is, how to interpret "postulating an entitlement of every member of a community to a milieu that will support his own pursuit of good": the key word is "a milieu". Suppose that what is at stake is the putative right to possess (read, watch, purchase, publish) pornographic materials and/or to use drugs. If, in accordance with the "entitlement" postulated by Finnis, someone claims that he cannot pursue his own conception of good in a milieu where pornography is freely available, or where he is likely to encounter drug addicts, then such an "entitlement" negates the equality of people as moral agents because, in a society where some people approve and others disapprove of pornography or drugs, equality of people as moral agents is only achievable under the general prohibition of interference with one's behaviour towards these objects. Both the pro-pornography (and pro-drugs) people *and* the anti-pornography (and anti-drugs) people can equally pursue their own conceptions regarding the place of pornography and drugs in their lives only if no-one is entitled to impose his private morality upon the others. Now imagine that an anti-drug activist (encouraged by Finnis' argument) denies this last statement: he claims that his conception of the good life encompasses the absence of drugs in his society altogether, not merely in his private life; and so the very availability of drugs to other people puts him in a situation of inequality with regard to those whose conception of the good life is either indifferent or positive towards the availability of drugs.[16] To see why this claim must be disqualified (in terms of equality) it suffices to imagine the opposite situation: no equality of moral agency is conceivable if, say, drug addicts were to make the extraordinary claim that they can pursue their lifestyle only if others are also *compelled* to use drugs (because, for instance, they cannot enjoy their addiction if they feel isolated from the lifestyle of the mainstream society). Likewise, no equality of moral agency is attainable when (conforming with the intention of the Finnis' argument, quoted above) the anti-drug and anti-pornography people claim that they can pursue their conception of a good life only in a milieu free of drugs or pornography.

But it does not follow that a liberal cannot attach any weight to the demands of those who claim that the presence of pornography or drugs destroys their social milieu, and so undermines their pursuit of good. This last claim (which is the real challenge for the right/good distinction) under some interpretations may be compatible with the harm principle: people may object to public displays of pornographic pictures because it shocks them, and hence harms their sensibility.[17] Likewise, people may object to widespread public availability of drugs in order to protect their children (who are typically and appropriately beyond the general liberal prohibition of paternalistic interventions). So some restrictions of this sort (such as rules on public sexual solicitation, on the displays of pornographic materials and on the public availability of drugs) are compatible with the equal moral agency of people to pursue their conceptions of a good life. But if a moralist claims that he cannot pursue his conception of the good in a society in which he merely knows that some people watch pornography or take drugs, because the very thought of the occurrence of these practices upsets him so much as to hinder his pursuit of the good, then such a claim must be dismissed as ludicrous, because the very fact that others watch pornography or use drugs does not hinder the pursuit of the conception which calls for elimination of pornography or drugs from one's own life. Now if this person goes a step further and claims that his conception of the good calls for elimination of drugs and pornography from his society altogether, then this comes into direct conflict with our conception of equality. So the important upshot of this very sketchy discussion is that the equality of persons as moral agents is a *fundamental* moral judgment, prior to the right/good distinction. Even if moralistic interventions can be shown (as in the passage quoted from Finnis) to be compatible with that distinction (by translating the language of the good into the language of entitlements), they cannot be reconciled with the principle of equality and, consequently, they are incompatible with the right/good distinction as interpreted *in the light* of the principle of equality of people as moral agents.

The importance of this conclusion about the fundamental nature of the principle of equal moral agency *vis-a-vis* the "right/good" distinction can hardly be over-emphasized. To realize the job this principle fulfils, consider again the distinction between the moral offensiveness of public displays of (what are thought to be) obscene pictures, acts or images (which, according to most liberals, including Mill himself, warrant restrictions)[18] and moral outrage at the very thought that some people indulge, in the privacy of their homes, or "adult cinemas", gay clubs, etc., in indecent activities (toward which, according to most liberals, the law should be indifferent). The moral intuition which allows this line to be drawn (and which holds, for me at any rate, much appeal) is notoriously difficult to justify in general terms within liberal moral parameters.[19] In his criticism of the Williams Report[20] Ronald Dworkin rejects as a *non sequitur* a proposition of Hart's (cited by the Williams Report to support its argument) that "[t]o punish people for causing this form of distress [i.e. distress at the thought of others behaving immorally] would be tantamount to punishing them simply because others object to what they do...".[21] In itself, this is indeed an extraordinary statement: moralists may easily respond that it is not their *objection* but their actual disgust, outrage or distress caused by indecency that justifies the punishment. Correspondingly, the proposition in the Williams Report that "if one accepted as a basis for coercing one person's actions, the fact that others would be upset even by the thought of his performing these actions, one would be denying any substantive liberty at all",[22] can justify a fully permissive attitude toward external manifestations of obscenity as well. If disgust caused by mere knowledge is not to be counted because it would be offensive to "substantive liberty", then the same reason would argue against counting disgust from actual sighting of the obscene images.[23] So without recourse to the principle of equal moral agency a liberal is unable to explain, or justify, in a principled way the line between offence at thought and the offence caused by external manifestations of obscenity, and his practical policy proposals turn out to be desperately ad hoc. But the principle of equality gives a proper moral weight to the distinction: when the line is drawn in such a way, all the protagonists may equally pursue their own private conceptions of the good and at the same time a possible harm to the sensibilities of some is avoided. Anything more by way of restrictions would frustrate the interests of the amateurs of pornography in the pursuit of their conceptions of the good without adding much to the anti-pornography people's interests; anything less (that is, fewer restrictions than required by the protection of individuals against unwilling exposure to offensive material) would offend the sensibility of those who are offended by pornography without significantly improving the pro-pornography people's interests. The principle of equality of moral agency, far from being an ad-hoc compromise, results in drawing a line in a Pareto-optimal way with regard to the pursuit of individual conceptions of the good life.

The same can be shown with respect to paternalistic interventions. Even if "an entitlement of each to be rescued from his own folly"[24] is not linguistic nonsense (and so can be expressed in the language of rights), it cannot be saved under the regime of equality of moral agency of all persons. For even if we maintain that paternalism gives effect to an "equal right" to rescue from self-inflicted harm, it will be undermined by an "equal right" to self-determination, i.e. the equal right of deciding about what is best for oneself. Furthermore, since typically self-determination is an important ingredient of an individual's good, the practice of defining authoritatively the conception of the good for a person regardless of her own definition of the good necessarily reduces that person's opportunity for attaining a good life. Once we adopt legal paternalism as an acceptable model for coercive legal policies, then (even if we manage to formulate it in the language of "rights") we inevitably run into conflict with the principle of equal moral agency. In turn, a consistent liberal who wants to avoid providing justification for a paternalistic program must go beyond postulating the "right/good" distinction, and must base it upon a more fundamental conception of equality.

The question now is how to combine this fundamental position with the prohibition of (and punishment for) harm to others. This is the second initial objection: do we not commit ourselves to accord the equal right of choice of morality (and of behaviour following therefrom) to non-obtrusive agents *and* to those whose "chosen form of self-realization requires that they establish their ascendancy, indeed domination, over others"?[25] In order to save the principle from self-stultification, we must find good reasons for a negative answer to this question. It is not difficult. First (and this I state with a lesser degree of conviction), the prohibition of harm does not commit us (as much as legal moralism would) to interpersonal comparisons of moral value that various acts have for various people. While there is probably an important objective ingredient in the indicia and measures of harm, observable ingredients of moral virtue and vice (short of harming others) are much less easily available to us. To be sure, this is not a radical distinction, for the very notion of harm is in itself morally laden to some extent, and — on the other hand — the moral objectivists will claim that they have objective criteria of moral value of non-harming actions. But in practice the criteria are much less controversial in the case of harm to others than in the case of immoral but harmless action: it is easier to find a common moral denominator among the competing substantive moralities regarding "the right" and defining what is to count as "harm to others" (for instance, nearly everyone will probably agree that anything which seriously impairs our health is "harmful")[26] than about criteria of the morally accomplished life. It is even a good thing that people espouse different conceptions of the "good" but that, at the same time, they share the same judgments about "the right".[27] Second (and more important), harm imposed by one agent upon the other introduces an important inequality among individuals. As will be argued more extensively in Chapter 6 below, harm disturbs the initial equality of mutual restraint upon one's own actions, equality of restraint which is correlated with equality of individual autonomy of action within limits imposed by the observance of the like autonomy of others. In this sense, a harm-producing action introduces *in*equality of individuals as moral agents: in a pre-harm situation, all equally observe the autonomy of others by restraining their actions, while harm increases the benefits (of unrestrained action) enjoyed by the offender to the detriment of the victim, whose burdens are thereby maximized over and above this minimum which is necessitated by the respect for the autonomy of others. So, if the fundamental principle behind the "good/right" distinction is about the equal moral agency of individuals, this principle cannot tolerate harmful actions which deny such equality. In this way, the principle of substantive moral equality provides a simultaneous justification for both aspects of the harm principle: the prohibition of harm to others and non-interference with the non-harmful actions.

These last remarks indicate, I hope, that the principle of equal moral agency adds an extra bite to the harm principle. The critics of Millian liberalism in general, and of the harm principle in particular, have often noted that the principle is question-begging: however we define "harm", it must make some appeal to the societal standards about what is "harmful", and these cannot avoid the specification of legitimate interests: but if the criteria of "legitimacy" of interests express the prevailing morality, then the whole purpose of the harm principle, which is to protect an individual against majoritarian societal interference is defeated. If, for instance, we define (as does Feinberg) harm as a wrongful setback to interests, then we must define independently which setback is "wrongful" and what interests (as contrasted to mere desires and wants) are legitimate. At this point, the "harm principle" turns out to be merely a derivation from more substantial principles of morality, rather than an independent principle capable of limiting the use of state coercion in the enforcement of social morality. In contrast, if we presuppose the principle of equal moral agency as fundamental, then the harm principle ceases to be merely a derivation from conventional moral standards. Harm, understood in the light of this egalitarian conception, is typically an intrusion into another person's autonomy, which hinders this other person's pursuit of her goals that are related to her own conception of the good. In this perspective, the boundaries of this sphere of legitimate autonomy need not be derived from the standards of interests that comply with any particular conceptions of moral legitimacy other than that of respect for other people's equal autonomy. For the delimitation of the legitimacy of this sphere of autonomy is, within limits,[28] neutral; it involves a comparison of the range of options (regarding her own life) available to the person before and after the putatively harmful action of another person. In this sense, the behaviour is harmful if it is Pareto-inefficient with regard to the distribution of (meaningful) options concerning the pursuit of one's own conception of the good. This explains why wicked, perverse and anti-social preferences have no claim to respect from the liberal law: it is because the criteria of "wickedness" are defined in such a way as to capture those preferences which deny (when implemented) the equal agency of other people. This principle of equal agency informs the set of initial ground-rules which help to prevent the illegitimate preferences from entering into the legal system in a liberal society.

2. THE IMPOSSIBILITY OF POLITICAL NEUTRALITY?

In *The Morality of Freedom* Joseph Raz offers two principal arguments aimed at showing that political neutrality, in the sense envisaged in this

Chapter, is impossible. However, before we consider these two arguments, it is important to note that Raz precedes them by drawing a distinction between two principles of political neutrality, which differ from each other in scope:

A: Neutrality concerning each person's chances of implementing the ideal of the good he happens to have.
B: Neutrality as in A, but also regarding the likelihood that a person will adopt one conception of the good rather than another.[29]

Clearly, the Principle B goes much further than the Principle A. It is therefore important to note that Raz announces: "[I]n the absence of any special reason to prefer A, and given that writers supporting neutrality say little that bears on the issue, I will assume that the doctrine of neutrality advocates neutrality as in B".[30]

This move, however, imposes a special burden of argument upon the liberal supporters of the ideal of neutrality, a burden which they do not wish,[31] or need, to carry. The doctrine of neutrality between the competing conceptions of a morally good life need not require that the state creates conditions in which the likelihood of adoption of particular lifestyles is roughly equal. As a matter of fact, it seems natural that the policy of strict neutrality will increase the likelihood that some conceptions of the good will become more popular (or more popular than they would have been under an alternative governmental policy) than others. This is for a number of reasons. The very adoption of a policy of liberal neutrality is, after all, based on substantive moral and political values which make a difference for the ways people perceive themselves, and themselves towards others in a community. The value of the equal moral agency of individuals, which supports the principle of neutrality, when endorsed by the law and governmental policies, will exert a gravitational pull upon the values adopted and endorsed by individuals. It is likely that people will feel reluctant to adopt the individual conceptions of the good founded on the theories of domination, fanaticism, intolerance and paternalism, especially if those people know that they stand no chance of transforming these private moralities into legally enforced policies. For one thing, people's choices are affected by available legal opportunities, and in a liberal society there will be no opportunities to coercively implement these conceptions of the good which proclaim the inequality of moral agency. For another thing, it is an inherent feature of such conceptions that they require a forceful imposition of one's values upon other people (one cannot be fanatical about religion only to oneself, without trying to impose those views upon the others, and the same applies to intolerance, domination etc). If people would realize that the ground-rules of their legal system preclude the conversion of some of the conceptions of the good into legal rules, then it will most probably constitute (in the long run) a powerful disincentive against adopting these conceptions, or an incentive to modify and ultimately abandon them.

This does not compromise the principle of political neutrality in the sense A, as defined by Raz. The individuals can still adopt any conception of the good for themselves: they can adopt a religion, or a lifestyle, or a set of beliefs, of their choice. But they cannot expect that any such conception will be equally supported by the legal system: in this aspect in which some of these conceptions will involve the imposition of certain values or behaviour upon others, they will be constrained by the legal system. Political neutrality cannot be neutral between those sets of values which are consistent with the fundamental ideals which provide the initial justification for neutrality (such as tolerance and equal moral agency) and those which are not.

As a result, people may find it increasingly useless to adopt some conceptions of the good. What is the point of persisting in a religious belief which requires the imposition of your beliefs upon "non-believers" and calls for the use of the state apparatus for this goal, if your state is totally non-responsive to this aim? Or how long can you keep calling for the state censorship of "immoral" books if the constitutional principles of your state preclude the imposition of moral censorship? Some conceptions of the good are likely to become marginalized and to fade away in a liberal state committed to political neutrality. This may result in some cultural loss but it is the price a liberal society pays for an overall gain in terms of promoting individual liberties.[32]

This is the most important reason why liberals need not go as far as to endorse Raz's "Principle B" of political neutrality. It would be defeating the reasons for which neutrality was adopted in the first place. It would drive the principle of neutrality into absurdity for other reasons as well. To proclaim, as Principle B does, that "[n]o political action may be undertaken if it makes a difference to the likelihood that a person will endorse one conception of the good or another..."[33] is to impose a condition which simply can never be met, nor even approximated, because there is a virtually unlimited number of conceivable "conceptions of the good". A liberal committed to the Principle B would face the impossible task of ensuring that any conception of the good, announced by its proponents, would have to have an equal likelihood of being adopted by the others. Would it have to include the lifestyle of a mediaeval monk? Of a Japanese samurai? Of an Aboriginal tribe member? The shape of every society imposes some constraints upon the lifestyles and the conceptions of the good which are viable and realizable. While some individuals may overcome some of these constraints by extraordinary zeal and force of will, to require an official action aimed at cancelling the differential effects of the society upon the likelihood of individual choices of lifestyles is to demand the impossible. No further argument about the impossibility of political neutrality would then be required.

Against this, it could be perhaps said that only those conceptions of the good should display an equal likelihood of being adopted (under the requirements of the Principle B) which are already favoured by a significant number of people in a given community, so that the conditions of "equal likelihood of adoption" would have to be tested against the number of conceptions restricted by what is realistic and viable. As a result, a modern liberal state would not have to be concerned about how likely it is that the lifestyles of a medieval monk and a Japanese samurai will be adopted. But such a rejoinder would always be vulnerable to the objection that limiting the spectrum of lifestyles (to which the Principle B of political neutrality applies) only to those which already have some following is arbitrary and gives special preference to the dominant, majoritarian conceptions, thus defeating the purpose of the principle of liberal neutrality which is, among other things, to protect individuals against the pressure of "moral majorities".

Finally, introducing the question of the "likelihood that the person will endorse one conception of the good or another" has the effect of raising the problem of "distorted preferences", which are discussed later in this Chapter. It is likely that a person who is aware of non-availability of a particular option will adopt a conception of the good which does not include this option: this is a strategy of reducing the cognitive dissonance in the situation of scarcity. I discuss this issue in more detail in Section 3, where I suggest some reasons why a liberal cannot embrace a doctrine of "distorted preferences", according to which such preferences, adopted for context-sensitive reasons, should be disregarded in the process of aggregating individual preferences into a collective choice. Here I just want to note that precisely the same reasons, which call for abandoning the doctrine of "distorted preferences", operate against accepting the "Principle B" of political neutrality, as expressed by Raz. For the likelihood that people will adopt some conceptions rather than others may follow the logic of "sour grapes", "endowment effects" or power relationships.[34]

Now we may turn to a discussion of the two arguments which Raz uses in order to demonstrate the impossibility of political neutrality. We should keep in mind that a liberal is committed only to "Principle A", as defined by Raz, and need not worry about the likelihood of the adoption of particular conceptions of the good. It is very important to note that Raz views his two arguments as showing not merely that *complete* political neutrality is impossible, but that even an *approximation* to complete neutrality is "chimerical"; as he correctly notes, "if political neutrality is a coherent and desirable ideal then the impossibility of complete adherence to it need not undermine its force as a political doctrine".[35] So his arguments must be stronger, and show that the very notion of political neutrality is fundamentally incoherent.

His first argument refers to the distinction between not helping and hindering. Neutrality, Raz observes, is usually attributed to actions which either help or hinder the parties to the conflict to an equal degree. And yet, one can be non-neutral by adopting a conduct consisting of non-action. The crux of Raz's argument is illustrated by the following example:

> Consider a country that has no commercial or other relations with either of two warring parties. This was true of Uruguay in relation to the war between Somalia and Ethiopia. It may nevertheless be true that such a country may have been able to establish links with either party. Would we say that Uruguay was not neutral unless the help that it could have and did not give Ethiopia was equal to the help that it could have and did not give Somalia? This will not be the case if, for example, Uruguay could have supplied the parties with a commodity that, though useful to both, was in short supply in one country but not in the other. Should we then say that Uruguay is not neutral unless it starts providing the country suffering from the shortage in that commodity? If by not helping it Uruguay is hindering it, then this conclusion is forced on us. But according to the common understanding of neutrality, Uruguay would have been breaking its neutrality if in the circumstances described it would have started supplying one of the parties with militarily useful materials after the outbreak of hostilities.[36]

A general structure of the argument is that the described situation lends itself to two opposite types of conduct, both of which may be described as neutral, or as non-neutral; hence the notion of neutrality is incoherent. Against this suggestion, I believe that "the common understanding of neutrality", referred to by the end of the quoted passage, deserves to be defended against the "conclusion forced on us", according to Raz, about the alleged non-neutrality of Uruguay exhibited by its non-aid to the country suffering from the shortage of the commodity which is plentiful in Uruguay.

The morally relevant distinction between the two alternative courses of action, suggested in the description quoted above, lies not in the fact that in one scenario we take into account only positive actions which hinder or help, while in another, we are sensitive also to non-action, if it affects the position of two warring parties. Surely there may be situations in which the failure to act is clearly non-neutral: an umpire who pretends that he does not see foul play and fails to give a free kick to one of the teams, and who persists in "non-acting" in this way throughout the match to the detriment of one and the same team, provides a paradigmatic example of non-neutrality. So even in our "common understanding of neutrality", we do not confine our attention to positive actions, but also test the neutrality (or non-neutrality) of non-actions.

Raz presents us with two scenarios. In the first one (call it scenario A), Uruguay starts supplying the militarily useful materials to one of the parties (say, for the sake of argument, Somalia), which needs it more than Ethiopia in order to achieve victory. In the scenario B, Uruguay fails to do so, though it possesses the materials. Raz is correct in saying that scenario A offends "the common understanding of neutrality", and yet at the same time he claims that the conclusion about non-neutrality of the scenario B "is forced on us". Why?

Raz's apparent answer is that in the scenario B, Uruguay is hindering Somalia by not helping it. An agent which hinders one of the parties to the conflict (or hinders the party more than the other) is clearly non-neutral with respect to this conflict. But is it really the case that by not supplying Somalia with the material necessary to achieve military victory over Ethiopia, Uruguay "hinders" Somalia, and so really there is no neutral course available to Uruguay in this conflict? I do not think so. Both Ethiopia and Somalia engage in their military conflict with a set of rational expectations about their military resources, and these expectations include, among other things, information about their foreign allies and suppliers. At the start of the conflict, they both know where they stand vis-a-vis countries such as Uruguay with respect to military supplies. If Uruguay had not been a traditional supplier of military materials, and hasn't promised to become one, then this information is part of the strategic thinking of both parties. Their comparative situation towards each other would change if, already after the outbreak of hostilities, Uruguay would begin supplying one of the parties (for the sake of argument, the one which needs these particular materials more than the other) with the militarily useful materials. This would shift the balance of military power between Somalia and Ethiopia, as compared to the starting point characterized by the initial information. It would still perhaps be a right thing for Uruguay to do, but it would not be neutral. But then neutrality is not always a right course of action. To a possible complaint by Somalia that Uruguay breaks its neutrality by adopting scenario B, Uruguay can always have a convincing reply: "But on what basis do you expect that I would start supplying you with these materials?"

The situation would of course have been different if Somalia indeed had some strong grounds for believing that Uruguay would start supplying it with military materials in its conflict with Ethiopia (even more so, if Uruguay had been a traditional supplier of such materials and broke off these supplies after the beginning of the conflict). This information, if reliable (based, say on treaties or public promises) would then form a part of Somalia's information about its resources at the point of outbreak of the conflict: a refusal to honour its obligations by Uruguay would be equivalent to diminish those resources. This would indeed be non-neutral. But this would be so because the position of Somalia would be weakened vis-a-vis Ethiopia by Uruguay's broken promise. The argument, therefore, boils down to the bases of rational expectations of both warring parties about whether or not a third party will help either of them with the necessary supplies.

This argument does not suggest that the course of neutrality is always possible: this is not crucial to our reasoning. Nor does it imply that in real-life situations it is always easy to establish what the course of neutrality requires: in our example, there may be a good deal of disagreement and uncertainty about what constitutes a reasonable basis of expectation by each of the parties to the conflict about the behaviour of the third party. But the point of this reasoning is to show that Raz's first argument does not establish that acts "which neither help nor hinder" may sometimes be non-neutral and neutral at the same time, and so that "the distinction between helping and hindering is crucial to an understanding of neutrality, *as is the distinction between hindering and not helping*".[37] This latter distinction is not crucial to our understanding of neutrality, if only we presuppose that we can establish reasonable bases of expectations about whether we will be helped by a third party or not. Again, one has to remember that these expectations do not support a judgment about the fairness or propriety of the third party's action. In international relations, just as in other areas, neutrality in not even *prima facie* right. But the only question we need to ask is whether, in the action of the third party, we may discern the bases for expectations about the future behaviour of this third party.

Now consider Raz's second argument "designed to show that neutrality is chimerical".[38] Its initial formulation is that "whether or not a person acts neutrally depends on the base line relative to which his behaviour is judged, and ... there are always different base lines leading to conflicting judgments and no rational grounds to prefer one to the others".[39] The first two parts of this statement are undoubtedly correct: it is a conceptual ingredient of the notion of neutrality that it may be asserted only with regard to a baseline, and different baselines result in different judgments of neutrality about one and the same course of conduct. But this is just the beginning of the argument; its weight depends crucially on the last proposition, that there are no rational grounds for preferring one baseline to another. In the example just considered, we suggested that the reasonable expectations about whether Uruguay committed itself to the deliveries of military materials to Somalia constitutes an intuitively strong "baseline" for assessing Uruguay's neutrality towards this conflict. There is, however, a further argument needed, because one may say that by offering (before the conflict) military supplies to Somalia, Uruguay has already compromised its neutrality anyway, so by fulfilling its promises it acts according to its obligations, but non-neutrally nevertheless. It would be bizarre to call "neutral" a party who sells military materials to one of the warring states, whether in accordance with its earlier commitments or not. On the other hand, we have just suggested that, for Uruguay to promise military supplies for Somalia and then to dishonour this promise once the war started (or to discontinue the military supplies already initiated) would also be non-neutral because it would hinder Somalia (relative to the baseline established by its reasonable expectations).

However, this suggests (at this stage) only that in some circumstances neutrality is a course of conduct impossible to pursue. Once Uruguay committed itself to sell weapons to Somalia (even though Somalia needs them more than Ethiopia), and once the war between Somalia and Ethiopia broke out, Uruguay has no non-neutral course of conduct available: it has, so to speak, lost its innocence with regard to neutrality towards this particular conflict. To honour its obligations is non-neutral, and so is to dishonour them. But to say that sometimes neutrality is not possible is not equivalent to saying that it is an incoherent notion, nor does Raz suggest such an equivalence. Rather, his second argument depends on a distinction between "comprehensive" and "narrow" neutrality. The criterion of this distinction is the substance of the help (or hindrance) as compared to the nature of the conflict. Some resources (which parties to the conflict may seek from the third parties, whose neutrality is at stake) are sought only because of the conflict. Other resources are helpful to the victory, but they present value independently of the conflict as well. Hence:

> Comprehensive neutrality consists in helping or hindering the parties in equal degree in all matters relevant to the conflict between them. Narrow neutrality consists in helping or hindering them to an equal degree in those activities and regarding those resources that they would wish neither to engage in nor to acquire but for the conflict.[40]

The example given by Raz to illustrate this distinction is again about war: to supply one of the parties with weapons compromises narrow neutrality, but to keep continuing supplies of food to one of the parties is consistent with narrow neutrality although it offends comprehensive neutrality.

The relevance of this distinction to Raz's thesis about the impossibility of political neutrality lies in the proposition that conflict in a society, towards which the liberal state is supposed to be neutral, is a comprehensive conflict; and yet all that the state can do is to adopt the stance of "narrow" neutrality. Though Raz does not explicitly make this last point (about the "narrow" neutrality as the only one available to the state), it is implied by his question: "Can one be narrowly neutral in a comprehensive conflict?"[41]

Two unclear issues are raised by this question. The first one, on which I will not base my main criticism of Raz's "second argument", is Raz's implicit presupposition that state neutrality towards conceptions of the good can only be of a "narrow" kind, or perhaps, less strongly, that the circumstances of the state's approach towards conceptions of the good lend themselves much more easily to adopting the "narrow neutrality" stance rather than the comprehensive one. In other words, in adopting a position towards the "warring parties" in a society, it is more likely that the state will provide them "neutrally" with the equivalent of arms supplies rather than with the equivalent of arms *and* food, to use the analogy of a state vis-a-vis an armed conflict of two other nations. It may well be the case, but it calls for an argument, which I fail to find in Raz's reasoning. In the absence of such an argument, the question "Can one be narrowly neutral in a comprehensive conflict?" does not lead to an obvious answer in the context of liberal neutrality because we do not know why liberal states are incapable of being "comprehensively neutral".

Another doubt is raised by the second limb of the dilemma described by Raz, namely the proposition that the conflicts towards which the liberal state would have to take a neutral attitude, are "comprehensive", that is, such that only "comprehensive" neutrality would be an adequate response. This Raz explicates in the following way:

> The conflict in which the state is supposed to be neutral is about the ability of people to

> choose and successfully pursue conceptions of the good (and these include ideals of the good society or world). It is therefore a comprehensive conflict. There is nothing outside it which can be useful for it but is not specifically necessary for it. The whole of life, so to speak, is involved in the pursuit of the good life.[42]

I am not sure how these propositions support the conclusion about the inadequacy of "narrow neutrality" to handle the conflicts between the conceptions of the good. While these conceptions are indeed "comprehensive", in the sense that they affect "the whole life", it does not follow that *all* the resources, the distribution of which is controlled by the state, affect the opportunities to choose and pursue all the conceptions of the good which have their followers in the community. Conceptions of the good can be "disaggregated" in the sense that they usually require some specific resources and protections, while other resources and protections are more or less irrelevant to the competition of this particular conception of the good with others ("more or less" suggests that the line between "narrow" and "comprehensive" conflict, just as between "narrow" and "comprehensive" neutrality is not sharp — the point acknowledged by Raz himself).[43] In Chapter 7, where we will discuss state neutrality towards competing religions, we will see that such neutrality is accomplished when the state takes some specific action (or non-action) regarding, say, the teaching of evolutionism and creationism in schools, or financing military chaplains, or allowing public prayers in state schools, etc. In the conflicts stemming from different approaches to legal prohibitions of obscene literature, state neutrality requires a specific state action in this specific domain. We may disagree about what particular action is necessitated by the principle of neutrality in these given fields, but this controversy does not result from the "comprehensiveness" of the conflict at stake; rather, the conflict can be fairly narrowly localized by all people who disagree about the specific content of a "neutral" policy. Paraphrasing one of Raz's sentences in the passage quoted above, "There is a lot outside it which can be useful for it but is not specifically necessary for it". To use his armed-conflict analogy, in such conflicts as those about religions or obscenity, the state can be neutral merely by (non-)providing "weapons" to an equal degree to the parties concerned, while the provision of "food" is not specifically necessary for the outcome of the conflict.

Conflicts between the conceptions of the good are "comprehensive" in a sense which does not negate the adequacy of "narrow" neutrality. They are comprehensive because, when people are frustrated in the pursuit of their conceptions of the good, it affects the whole of their life in a way which usually makes compensatory rewards in other spheres of their lives insufficient and inadequate. A person who cannot satisfy his desire to become a priest (due to the militantly atheistic policies of the state) will hardly be satisfied by extra opportunities created for him in the area of sport, or access to education, or opportunities for foreign travel. But this does not mean that it is impossible for the state to confine its conduct to the resources required by this person's desire in such a way as to be neutral between this person's and others' favourite lifestyles.

The major point of convergence between Raz's book and the conception endorsed in this book is the acceptance of the harm principle as a basis for restraining the coercive powers of the state. But, having rejected the idea of neutrality, Raz interprets the harm principle in a way which, as he himself admits, is quite different from a traditional liberal argument.[44] The harm principle is supported, in Raz's theory, by the principle of autonomy which he interprets in a perfectionist, rather than a neutralist, manner. And although practical consequences of his perfectionist, autonomy-based harm principle seem to be very similar to the neutralist analysis (with the single major exception: Raz allows some degree of paternalism), some attention must be given to this surprising mix of divergence (in the attitude to perfectionism) and convergence (in the endorsement of the harm principle) of these two theoretical positions.

The main *positive* reason for Raz's claim that the harm principle, in his interpretation, represents a perfectionist ideal (the negative reason being related to his rejection of the ideal of neutrality, discussed above) is that the principle of autonomy, from which he derives the harm principle,[45] is interpreted in *The Morality of Freedom* in a perfectionistic fashion. This is reflected in Raz's proposition that autonomy is not valuable *per se*, but only insofar as it is used in the pursuit of the moral good. "Autonomous life is valuable only if it is spent in the pursuit of acceptable and valuable projects and relationships".[46]

There are two essential steps leading to Raz's conclusion about perfectionism of the harm principle, each of which is questionable: (1) the rejection of an intrinsic value of autonomy; (2) the connection between the perfectionist account of autonomy and the harm principle. I will devote my attention here to the latter point, although it is clear that in the perspective endorsed in this book, autonomy is intrinsically valuable. This will be reflected later (Chapter 6.2) in the argument that, for an agent, to have more options is intrinsically more valuable than to have less, *ceteris paribus*. But even if, for the sake of argument, Raz's account of autonomy is accepted, there still remains the problem of reconciling it with the harm principle.

The problem seems to be this: the harm principle prohibits coercive interference with individual actions on any other grounds than the harm to others, hence, no interference on the grounds that an agent's behaviour is immoral or unwise is authorized. But if the harm principle is derived from a perfectionist ideal of autonomy, where autonomy is valuable only if geared to morally good actions, then it is hard to find any protection for morally bad (though harmless to others) actions in such a constellation of the harm principle and perfectionist autonomy. But then, if only morally good actions are protected against coercive interference, the harm principle would of course lose all its meaning.

Here is how Raz handles this manifest dilemma:

> [T]he harm principle is defensible in the light of the principle of autonomy for one simple reason. The means used, coercive interference, violates the autonomy of its victim. First, it violates the condition of independence and expresses a relation of domination and an attitude of disrespect for the coerced individual. Second, coercion by criminal penalties is a global and indiscriminate invasion of autonomy. Imprisoning a person prevents him from almost all autonomous pursuits. Other forms of coercion may be less severe, but they all invade autonomy, and they all, at least in this world, do it in a fairly indiscriminate way. That is, there is no practical way of ensuring that the coercion will restrict the victims' choice of repugnant options but will not interfere with their other choices.[47]

Raz offers two reasons for his surprising conclusion that autonomy, which is valuable only if used in the pursuit of the moral good, should be protected even if spent in the pursuit of the morally repugnant. The first argument is that the interference with autonomous, though morally repugnant, choices violates the independence of, and expresses disrespect for, the coerced. As for the disrespect, it is hard to find convincing grounds for the respect for an action which is morally repugnant. And disrespect for such an *action* need not imply disrespect for a *person*. To the contrary, more radical perfectionists than Raz argue that it is precisely the respect for a person which should trigger our coercive interference with morally repugnant actions.[48] As for the "condition of independence", violated by the interference with the morally repugnant action, this is true by definition. Unless Raz is willing to introduce a separate value of independence, which would be *intrinsically* valuable, and which would outweigh the value of perfectionistically interpreted autonomy,[49] it is hard to see how such a violation of "independence" could justify protection for morally repugnant though autonomous actions. And this raises the suspicion that Raz smuggles into his argument a non-perfectionist notion of autonomy (which is valuable irrespective of the moral value of autonomous actions) under the guise of "independence".

The second argument is about the indiscriminate effects of a coercive restraint which leads, as Raz claims, to restrictions not only of the victims' repugnant choices, but also of their other options, including morally commendable ones. This argument is surprisingly inadequate to the burden it is supposed to carry, namely the defence of the harm principle. For we may well cite a number of narrowly tailored, precise coercive means which focus sharply on the prohibition of the "morally repugnant" options, and where the spill-over effect will be minimal. After all, the primary concern of Mill's harm principle was not only with the *punishment* (which provides the grounds of Raz's argument) but also with *prohibition*. Moral censorship is an example which comes immediately to one's mind: the laws which prohibit "obscene" publications, but where the only sanction for the production, distribution and possession of such materials would be their confiscation, certainly do not affect the agents' capacities for all options other than to produce, distribute and possess obscene publications. Even fines (to bring the example more closely to real life) imposed upon the publisher do not affect his or her other options, or affect them only trivially. The law which prohibits the sale of contraceptives, similar to the one invalidated by the United States Supreme Court in *Griswold v. Connecticut*,[50] assuming that the only sanction supporting it would be confiscation (or even a fine, but not as severe as to seriously affect the options available to the punished person) is hardly defensible on the grounds of the harm principle, and yet it does not affect the persons' liberty to act in areas other than their sexual life. Raz's argument is, at best, an autonomy-based argument against the penalty of imprisonment for morally repugnant actions, but is not sufficient to reject all coercive prohibitions of immoral (though harmless) behaviour. In conclusion: the perfectionist account of autonomy is inadequate to support the harm principle; the one cannot be reconciled with the other.

3. LIBERAL NEUTRALITY AND "DISTORTED PREFERENCES"

The hardest problem area for liberals, as far as the application of the principle of equal moral agency is concerned, is with respect to addictions and other serious distortions of preference-formation. Intuitively, even for a liberal there is little to be said for a strong laissez-faire attitude toward individual preferences resulting from drug dependency, permanent drunkenness etc., and yet coercive interference may be seen as overturning the substantive conception of the good of the agent, which should be anathema to a liberal. This, I suppose, is more of a practical than a theoretical problem. In theory at least, the line can be drawn between those preferences which are admittedly silly, irrational or debilitating but which do not result from any grave corruption of the decision-making capacities of the agent and, on the other hand, those which result from a defect in individual decision-making. A person devoting all his leisure time to impassively watching silly TV soap operas does nothing to develop his own rational capacities and self-fulfilment, but these are not the goals that the state may properly foster through the use of coercion: decisions about a person's conception of the good are his own in a meaningful sense. But decisions resulting from drug dependency or made under alcoholic compulsion are not decisions freely made, in the sense that the agent has not exercised his choice in a meaningful sense of the word (this applies, of course, to the stages subsequent to the initial decisions about embarking upon an addictive course: the initial choice leading eventually to the surrender of one's full freedom of action need not be, eo ipso, unfree). People act under the influence of various constraints in their capacity for choice: a compulsive TV viewer or a member of a fanatic religious sect may, from this point of view, appear to belong to the same category as the drug addict. But there is a difference: as Leslie Farber argues, while in the case of "an addiction to shopworn ideologies ... [people] forfeit, in wilful dedication, the very capacities of spirit and intellect that might set them free", there nevertheless remains "the possibility of a response, however minimal at first, to some human claim". In contrast, "[c]hemical deadening, if pursued, will, by its very nature, render such capacities eventually heedless to any call".[51] This difference, however difficult to apply in practice, is crucial as far as the liberal principle of neutrality goes. The principle implies respect for individual choice, harmless to others: the question to be asked therefore is: whether there was a choice? If the function of drugs (and, by analogy, alcohol) depends largely on "the chemical deadening of important imaginative and critical capacities",[52] then the preferences resulting from the process do not express any actual choice between the options available to an individual. A person who is dependent on drugs or alcohol, and who is no longer able to exercise any judgment or choice, is for this reason beyond the protection provided by the harm principle and should be properly treated paternalistically, along with children and the mentally ill.

The distinction between seriously corrupted preference formation (such as in the case of addictions) and imperfect life-choices which have to be respected is, of course, less determinate and clear in practice than it is in principle. But the position of liberal neutrality calls for scepticism towards any arguments which advocate disregard for individual preferences on the basis of imperfections in the process of preference formation. Such arguments have recently been put forward forcefully by Jon Elster[53] and scholars inspired by his writings, in particular Cass Sunstein.[54] The basic insight of Elster's theory, relevant to our discussion, is that expressed preferences are a very fragile basis for collective decisions insofar as they are shaped by the external constraints which corrupt the process of preference-formation. This happens for instance in the case of the phenomenon of "sour grapes" where preferences are adapted to the (externally determined) range of possibilities: options that are seen by an agent as realistically unattainable are perceived as unattractive in order to reduce the dissonance between what is wanted and what is possible to attain. Cass Sunstein applies Elster's theory to the operation of the legal system and argues generally that whenever existing preferences are traceable to legal rules, then it would be wrong to justify legal rules by reference to expressed preferences. This is illustrated by the "adaptive preferences" (including the case of "sour grapes": preferences are distorted by the agent's awareness of the non-availability of certain options), "endowment effects" (where preferences are attributable to the legally shaped phenomena of ownership or non-ownership) and preferences distorted by the relations of power.

The preference-distortions theory, being a modern and sophisticated restatement of the traditional conception of "false consciousness", carries, unfortunately, the inherent dangers of unlimited paternalism built into the latter conception. Once we agree that the existence of external determinants of preferences warrants a dismissal of these preferences as non-authentic, there is virtually no limit to a total disregard for actual individual wants in shaping the legal system: all wants and desires can be traced to some external determinants (which include the legally shaped ones). Surely the very fact that preferences are context-dependent cannot, in itself, disqualify them, because then we will be committed not only to disregard those preferences which express adjustment to the context but also those which resist and challenge the context. As David Shapiro has put it, under the theory which disqualifies context-dependent preferences as unworthy of official respect, "even the individual's best efforts to cope with a hostile environment may be brushed aside".[55]

The problems inherent in the theory which proclaims that preferences are non-autonomous (hence disqualifiable) if "the source of preference change is not in the person, but outside him — detracting from his autonomy"[56] are evident if we consider a list (arguably, non-exhaustive) of non-authentic preference changes under this theory: "adaptive and counter-adaptive preferences, conformity and anti-conformity, the obsession with novelty and the equally unreasonable resistance to novelty".[57] That a person decides to adapt his or her substantive preferences (i.e. first-order preferences, as explained below in this Chapter) to what is perceived as possible, or to what other people are doing, or to what the agent had been doing in the past etc., may after all be a matter of that person's "authentic" second-order preference, in the sense that its source is not "outside" the person but stems from that very person's aversion to (or passion for) novelty, conformity with generally accepted behaviour etc. To disqualify these preferences as non-authentic is question-begging because, while their informational source is indeed external to a person (e.g., information about a set of available opportunities), the tendency to use the information as a factor inclining one's choices in a specific direction lies "inside" the person. An infinite regress looms large in such reasoning, of course, because one can always sensibly ask whether there exist any "external" determinants of such a second-order tendency to change one's first-order preferences in one way rather than another (e.g. by adjustment to the environment rather than by challenging it, or *vice versa*). But this danger of an infinite regress only highlights how unhelpful the argument is about disqualification of exogeneous preferences.

This can also be shown by reconstructing the moral insight behind the disregard of context-dependent preferences: it seems that only those preferences should count which were formed in a fully autonomous fashion, that is through the process over which a person had control. But surely this is an impossible requirement: an individual's preferences are only partly subject to his or her will, and the language of "forming", "choosing" and "changing" one's preferences falsely implies the voluntariness of the process. We may "identify with" our preferences, to use Scanlon's formulation, but this is just another way of saying that they are our own, and often it would be inappropriate to introduce the notion of "responsibility for" or "control over" our own preferences.[58] Whether the determinants are "external" or "internal" is irrelevant from the point of view of the issue of "responsibility" for preferences: consider, at the extreme, the preferences formed as a result of, or in response to, one's (undeserved, of course) disability or disease. An involuntary pedigree of preferences does not make them less authentic or unworthy of respect. Or, to take another example, does it really make any difference to our decision about the legal treatment of sexual preferences whether one's sexual orientation is a matter of free personal choice (which, more often than not, is not the case) or is beyond the realm of deliberate control (hence, the responsibility) of an agent? The origins and the mutability of sexual preference, especially in the context of homosexuality, are the subject of vigourous debate, and generally at least this seems settled: that the acquisition of homosexual orientation is not subject to one's control.[59] But this, of course, does not make homosexual preferences any less worthy of respect than if they were deliberately chosen. If anything, this provides an additional argument *against* the disregard of these preferences (because such disregard would amount, in practice, to official penalization for immutable characteristics). Indeed, the fact that certain tastes and desires are "voluntary" often serves to support the argument against counting them in the collective aggregation of preferences.[60] But we need not get embroiled in this dispute here: the point merely amplifies the contention about the lack of any necessary moral connection between the voluntariness of preferences and their positive weight in the process of collective (and legal) aggregation. But if there is no such connection, then it is hard to see how the distaste toward context-dependent preferences can be sustained.

To be sure, it does not follow that the principle of neutrality must accommodate all expressed individual preferences (assuming, of course, that they are not harmful to others). There are some uncontroversial cases, for instance of clearly mistaken preferences: where a preference, for its validity in the eyes of the preference-making agent, crucially depends upon the truth of the statement of facts, and this statement is clearly false (consider Mill's example of a person who is ignorant of the fact that the bridge, upon which this person is about to step, is unsafe). There are also certain categories of preferences which, although expressed, are in fact subordinate to some other, more important, preferences which allow us to overturn the former ones. Donald Regan distinguishes between "ultimate" and "instrumental" preferences: his example is of Jones willing to go to Chicago (an instrumental preference) in order to see his friend Brown (the ultimate preference).[61] If Brown is in fact in Los Angeles, then (assuming that Jones was candid in declaring the reason for his intended trip to Chicago) there is no problem in overriding his instrumental preference for going to Chicago. But it is an easy case for a liberal: once we conceptualize the full actual meaning of Jones' preference as "I want to go to Chicago in order to see Brown", then to prevent Jones from going to Chicago when we know that Brown is in Los Angeles does not amount to a disregard of this preference (though, naturally, it may be wrong for some other reasons, for instance in connection with

Jones' privacy).

To the same category belong the second-order preferences, i.e. preferences about preferences. John Harsanyi illustrates these with the case of an "alcoholic [who] presumably has a strong first-order preference for drinking but may have a clear second-order preference for breaking his drinking habit".[62] In this case what happens is not so much that, as Harsanyi suggests, the first-order preference is "irrational" but rather that it is effectively displaced by the other, prevalent preference of breaking the habit. To enforce the latter against the former is therefore consistent with the agent's own ranking of his preferences and does not pose special problems for the principle of liberal neutrality (though problems of a practical nature may arise when we agree that, as Goodin suggests, first-order preferences should be overridden by *implicit* second-order preferences, that is by second-order preferences implied in a person's actions: how determinate is guidance provided by a person's conduct to formulate her "true" preferences?).[63]

The strategy of pre-commitment belongs to the same, non-controversial, in principle, category: people may *ex ante* exclude certain options by which, as they know, they may be tempted in future. Ulysses ordering his crew not to follow his future orders to untie him from the mast provides a paradigm for a set of an antecedent second-order preference not to have one's future first-order preferences respected.[64] Again, this situation can be expressed in the language of a simple ranking of conflicting preferences. Finally, to this broad category belong what Robert Goodin calls "reciprocal forbearances" which occur when "each agrees to forgo his opportunities for gain at the other's expense, on condition that the other likewise forgo opportunities for gaining at his expense".[65] What is not clear is why Goodin believes that the observance (by the collective-choice makers) of such reciprocal forbearances belongs to a category of "laundering preferences". The rule of mutual forbearance strictly follows the agent's cost-benefits calculus which suggests that mutual tolerance is more beneficial to him than gains at another's expense in a non-tolerance environment. Hence the top preference of this person may be fully formulated as to have one's freedom of action respected on the condition of this agent's respect for the freedom of others. No preferences are being "laundered" but rather an expressed ranking of preferences is properly enforced.

These are non-problematic cases. These cases (clearly mistaken preferences and subordinate preferences) *and* the general rule excluding the harmful preference (on the basis of a violation of the principle of equal moral agency) exhaust between them the types of preferences which have to be disregarded under the ground-rules for a liberal legal system. However, to disallow preferences on the basis of the imperfections of the preference-formation process, and in particular on the basis of external constraints affecting the process of preference formation, is a step which cannot be reconciled with the principle of equal moral agency. To take an example of the "sour grapes" phenomenon: a housewife in a male-dominated society deciding not to pursue her education but rather to spend her days unfulfilled at home, does so in anticipation that in that society her future options of a successful professional career are seriously limited: why bother to study? While her preferences are adapted in a "sour grapes" fashion to external social constraints (which are, among other things, legally affected) and shaped by the existing system of domination and power, these are still meaningfully *her* choices. We may deplore the predicament of a victim who reduces her sense of frustration by downgrading in her eyes the value of unavailable choices, but it does not follow that we may disregard the actual choices.

This does not mean that the liberal is committed to a myopia about the injustice and domination in the social background against which individual choices are made. The conclusion, however, is to improve the background and not to disregard the choices. The principle of equal moral agency provides a yardstick for censoring a legal system which establishes unequal life opportunities for different groups: the principle of equal moral agency requires that the opportunities to pursue one's own conception of the good life be equally accessible to people. The social and legal systems which generate the concern by Elster and Sunstein about sub-optimal choices, obviously do not measure up to this principle: the "sour grapes", "endowments effects" and the power-shaped preferences reflect socially constructed constraints, as opposed to the inevitable, natural ones, such as the impossibility of human beings to fly, which also affect the range of expressed preferences but do not come under the category of "sour grapes". Such social constraints, when enforced by the legal and social systems, do not support equal moral agency for all members of the society.

Note, incidentally, that when I describe the substantive conception of equality which underlies the liberal approach to civil liberties, I am avoiding the most popular formula, used both by the proponents and by the critics of liberal equality, namely that of "equal concern and respect". I suppose that the idea of equal moral agency suffices to ground the principle of non-interference with personal non-harmful (to others) choices; in turn, "equal concern and respect" is vulnerable to a number of criticisms which suggest that it is either too ambiguous, or incapable of restricting the state interference in conformity with the liberals' intentions. The modern *locus classicus* of the "equal concern and respect" is in this passage from Dworkin: "Government must treat those whom it governs with concern, that is, as human beings who are capable of suffering and frustration, and with respect, that is, as human beings who are capable of forming and acting on intelligent conceptions of how their lives should be lived".[66] "Equal concern" and "equal respect" raise some problems, though of slightly different character.

The idea of "equal concern" lends itself to paternalistic interpretations, inconsistent with its Kantian presuppositions and with the intentions of the proponents of the idea. John Finnis, for one, suggests that "there is no difficulty in supposing that a 'paternalist' political programme may be based on a conception of what is required for equal concern and respect for all; for paternalists may well consider that, for example, to leave a person to succumb to drug addiction on the plea that it is 'his business' is to deny him the active concern one would show for one's friend in like situation...".[67] While the emotive potential of Finnis' example seems to advance his argument, we need to realize that, so understood, "concern" (where state coercion is analogized to a sympathetic friend) contains the seeds of virtually unlimited interference with liberty regarding personal lifestyle. Significantly, Finnis draws this inference himself: "'I wish someone had stopped me from...': if this can rationally be said (as it can), it follows necessarily that even the most extensive and excessive programme of paternalism might be instituted without denial of equal concern and respect to anybody".[68]

The point is that "equal concern" has to be combined with "equal respect" and these two concepts do *not* play the same role. While the requirement of "equal concern" calls for the active role of the state towards, for instance, alleviating individuals' undeserved misery or educational handicaps (in order to minimize their "suffering and frustration" to the extent they are unable to do so themselves), "equal respect" requires recognizing their autonomous choices as valid. A good deal of criticism of the idea of "equal respect" exploits the ambiguity of the word. "Respect" can be understood as an attitude akin to praise, as a positive evaluation of the person respected. The critics of the "equal respect" idea point out (correctly) that the very fact of humanness is a much too thin ground for equal respect for everybody.[69] But "respect" has another, value-free, meaning, as in "I respect your decision, though I do not approve of it". It has nothing to do with esteem, praise or honour, but merely denotes refraining from interference with a person or his choices. As Stanley Benn observed, "to respect someone requires at most forbearance, a stand-off relationship...".[70] Those who claim (as Finnis does) that "equal respect" has a paternalistic potential fail to see its distinctiveness from "equal concern"; those who claim (as R. M. Smith does) that "equal respect" lacks a moral basis understand it in a value-laden way; but "equal respect" in its liberal-equality use is *both* distinct from "equal concern" and taken in a value-neutral sense. Respect displayed by a government which treats people as "human beings who are capable of forming and acting on intelligent conceptions of how their lives should be lived"[71] is value-neutral in the sense that it does not engage in the substantive assessment of these conceptions, and so the argument about the lack of moral basis for that respect misses the point.

4. THE "PRIORITY OF THE RIGHT OVER THE GOOD" VERSUS THE BALANCING PROCEDURE

The basic aim of the principle of liberal neutrality based upon the right/good distinction is to provide a device for accommodating conflicting moralities in one legal system, while respecting the equality of all the participants, without creating a constant threat to the stability of the system from any of the moralities. The "right/good" distinction provides, therefore, an answer to the fundamental dilemma addressed in this book, and can be seen as a basis for a principled framework for a compromise among conflicting values. To describe its significance it may be useful to contrast it with an alternative approach to such compromises, namely the approach of weighing and balancing all the competing values and ideals. Such an approach has been enunciated recently by Guido Calabresi, and since it is a very influential approach (and certainly holds much appeal, especially for judges in morally controversial cases), it may be useful to show why it is unacceptable for a liberal who opts for a principle of neutrality.

Calabresi demonstrates his position with respect to a particularly troubling case of the clash of fundamental ideals, namely to the issue of abortion. In a landmark decision *Roe v. Wade*[72] the Supreme Court of the United States overturned a Texas anti-abortion statute on the basis of the right to privacy. The main criticism by Calabresi is that, by resting its verdict on the premise that a fetus was not a person, the Court has committed the unforgivable sin of "emarginating" a large segment of the American public by effectively telling them that their beliefs and ideals are rejected as invalid and outside the boundaries of American law. It was, according to Professor Calabresi, a signal to the "pro-life" groups that their deeply held beliefs are unworthy; in consequence, the decision "made it impossible for the opposing views to live with each other".[73]

What was the alternative approach which would have helped avoid such a consequence? According to Calabresi, the Court should have professed its respect for the beliefs of all those in conflict and "recognize the values on the losing side as real and significant".[74] Even if more weight, in the present case, has to be given to one of the opposed beliefs, *both* sets of beliefs (i.e. "pro-life" and "pro-choice") could be accommodated within the constitutional framework by respecting the losing beliefs as worthy, and by "look[ing] to a time where it may be possible to accommodate both sets of beliefs".[75] With regard to the issue of abortion this could have been done, according to Calabresi, by conceptualizing the real issue in *Roe v. Wade* not as the matter of the right to privacy but as the conflict between two values: equality of the right to engage in sex *versus* preservation of fetal life. The real trouble with the prohibition of abortion is that it discriminates against women with respect to access to sex: if the Court's decision were presented as a balancing act between two important (though not absolute) values, its outcome would be seen as respecting the beliefs of both sides. It would, according to Calabresi, "tell[] the losers that, though they lost, they and their values do carry weight and are recognized in our society, even when they don't win".[76]

It is beside the point in this chapter whether indeed the issues of abortion are better handled in terms of discrimination against women rather than (as the Court decided) in terms of the right to privacy: actually I do not wish to enter into the merits of the abortion debate at all. My concern here is more general, about the proposed procedure of legal compromise between competing moral beliefs and ideals in a pluralistic society. For it is precisely this diversity of beliefs that triggers the liberal "right/good" distinction, and the significance of the "balancing" procedure is that it tries to replace it by a method better suited, according to Calabresi, to the aim of including and preserving moral diversity within a society.

It may seem at first blush ironic that the very decision which is considered by many as an example of an *ad hoc*, opportunistic compromise,[77] is criticised by Calabresi as excluding compromise and reconciliation of diverse beliefs. But this irony is instructive: the Court would have escaped Calabresi's criticism if, instead of affirming categorically the principle of privacy as embracing a woman's right to terminate her pregnancy, it engaged in the weighing and balancing of competing values of equality and preservation of fetal life. But on what basis could such a balancing act be said to result in a pro-abortion or an anti-abortion verdict? To say that after a careful balancing of two conflicting values one ultimately outweighed the other may be an effective rhetorical device for reducing the dissatisfaction of the "losers", but it says nothing about the actual moral grounds of the outcome of the balancing. Surely in order to decide about the relative importance of these two conflicting values one has to appeal to a higher principle. But this is exactly what Calabresi refuses to do because it would immediately "put beyond the pale" those who reject this higher coordinating principle. So what Calabresi's balancing proposal boils down to is a rhetorical device: as long as the Court does not tell us how it is balancing the two values (that is, it does not disclose its higher coordinating principle), it may nominally adhere both to the principle of equality of women with respect to sex *and* to the principle of a fetus' right to live.

But this sounds like a prescription for hypocrisy: it tells the Court how to cover up its actual moral choice rather than how to make it. Calabresi reaches this strange result because he wishes to achieve a compromise between the conflicting beliefs in a pluralistic society without being willing at the same time to concede what we stressed earlier in this chapter: that there must be some basic ground rules that all substantive preferences must satisfy in order to be registered in the legal process. If no such ground rules are required, then all the postulated principles are of the same weight and are freely entered into the weighing and balancing procedure. The liberal solution outlined earlier in this chapter differs fundamentally from that procedure by insisting on the initial ground rules for moral bargaining: all the principles registered in the law-making process must respect the equal moral agency of all individuals. This principle, which implies that all individuals have equal rights over their private lives, does not have to compete on an equal basis with a putative principle which would deny this right to some, since the latter one does not respect the basic principle of equality of individuals as moral agents who are capable of choosing and pursuing their own moral conceptions.

The comparison of these two approaches indicates, I hope, the main reasons supporting the superiority of the principle of liberal neutrality based on the principle of "equal moral agency" over the "weighing and balancing" approach. For one thing, the latter approach does not provide any principled explanation of the moral intuition that some preferences about other people's conduct must be disqualified at the outset. Calabresi makes it clear, for instance, that he would disqualify racist preferences,[78] but it is hard to see what general principle, consistent with the "weighing and balancing" approach, would ever allow us to draw the distinction between racism on the one hand and, say, anti-homosexual or anti-contraception beliefs on the other.

Second, and consequent upon the former observation, the proposed "balancing" formula falsely indicates to the "losers" of the present moral calculus that their beliefs are basically as legitimate as the winning ones, except that in this particular case they happen to succumb to others. But they are not: racist preferences are not even initially as legitimate and valid as non-racist ones.[79] A principled liberal must make it clear that the law has no business saying to everyone: all your preferences, however illiberal and harmful to others they happen to be, have a place in our legal system. There are, for a liberal, some beliefs which are beyond the pale and which must be disallowed from even entering into the forum of societal moral bargaining: they are those which offend the liberal ground rules for dealing with differences in moral beliefs.

Further, the "balancing" procedure for reaching compromise promotes, on the part of those whose preferences require the imposition of their conceptions of the good upon others, false expectations that despite the present setback they may well achieve their goals the next time around. Significantly, this is how Calabresi describes the implicit message of the Court (engaged in the "balancing" process) to the "losers": "Your views matter, and are worthy. They are part of our law and on many occasions they will be upheld. On *this* occasion, however, they do not prevail".[80] But this procedure is educationally counter-productive: instead of educating people that some illiberal attitudes have no place in a liberal community, the "balancing" procedure is complacent toward these attitudes. In consequence, the balancing procedure is inherently destabilizing since the procedure of weighing and balancing is ultimately intuitionist. We are precluded from affirming a categorical higher principle: if we could affirm it, then presumably it would have to be balanced against a corresponding counter-principle of the same order, and we would find ourselves in a regress until we affirmed one principle as fundamental, thus offending the requirement of a compromise. Hence, the standards of the compromise are uncertain and non-transparent. The decision reached can be easily overturned without the injection of any new moral ingredients for consideration, but merely by attaching a slightly different weight to the principles at stake.

Finally, the weighing and balancing formula of compromise fails to take any notice of the familiar "liberal dilemma" of both condemning private immorality and defending the individual right to be (what we may consider) immoral. In the balancing calculus, there is no room for such a combination of attitudes: a private condemnation of an immoral action simply enters into the balancing by reducing the weight of a liberal's predisposition to protect it.

In contrast, in the liberal reasoning, based as it is on the equal moral agency of all, a principle of the protection of non-harmful (even though immoral) actions prevails over one's distaste for the immorality *before* it enters the arena of moral bargaining about the content of laws.

The fact that Calabresi developed his procedure for dealing with the clashes of moral beliefs on the basis of the discussion of abortion, rather than of other morally controversial legal issues, makes a contrast between his approach and the liberal-neutrality approach less clear than in the cases of other clashes of moralities. There are two reasons for this. First, in the case of abortion, but not in the case of homosexuality or pornography, one can theoretically imagine a situation of a future reconciliation of these opposing views. Calabresi supports his idea of compromise with the following prediction: "One can imagine a time and a technology in which a woman who wished an abortion could have the fetus removed without pain or risk to her ... [and that] women who wished to adopt babies, could have that same fetus implanted in them and brought to term".[81] One *can* imagine such a future reconciliation of the conflicting values in the abortion debate, and this makes a plea for an *ad-hoc*, tentative compromise slightly more convincing. But no such reconciliation is conceivable with regard to the conflicting beliefs about homosexuality (one cannot have, in one and the same society, freely practicing homosexuals and people living in a homosexuals-free milieu), contraception or pornography.

Second, a clash of moralities is most "pure" when some people demand prohibitions of behaviour which offends them without causing any observable harm (except the "harm" inseparable from the moral outrage). But one of the crucial characteristics about the abortion debate is that one party claims that there is a clear "harm to others" situation (i.e. to fetuses equated in this argument with living persons), while the other party denies this. If a fetus *is* a person, then abortion is murder and therefore is properly within the ambit of the harm principle. I will not go into this debate here because, as indicated earlier, my purpose is not to pronounce upon the merits and demerits of legalized abortions but rather to consider the different approaches to reconciling conflicting moralities in a pluralistic society. But clearly a metaphysical question about the definition of human life precedes the moral arguments about the legitimacy of the right to abortion. This, however, is not the case with issues such as homosexuality and pornography, for with respect to these problems we encounter strong and persistent demands for prohibition, even regardless of detectable harm to others.

5. THE HARM PRINCIPLE AND THE REDISTRIBUTIVE STATE

One may ask whether the conception underlying a liberal approach to liberty-rights would prohibit the redistributive and regulatory functions of the state, to which modern liberals are often committed. Their endorsement of some degree of wealth redistribution is a matter not only of contingent political, but also of fundamental philosophical commitment. For if the ideal of positive freedom defines the evil to be attacked as the fact that important human opportunities are determined by factors beyond the agents' control, then we know that a great many social inequalities result from such morally arbitrary factors. A legal system committed to positive freedom in its protection of equality-rights commits itself, by implication, to a wide-ranging egalitarian and redistributive programme, aimed at equalizing those opportunities and resources which are directly attributable to factors beyond the control of the agents whom they concern. But, on the other hand, the conception of equal moral agency which underlies the protection of liberty-rights would appear to narrow down the coercive role of the state to the prevention of harm to others. Isn't there a contradiction here?

No. The "harm principle" (interpreted through the priority of the right over the good and through the conception of equal moral agency) says that prevention of harm to others is the only legitimate, regular justification of legal coercive interference with individual autonomy. But there is nothing in the redistributive, egalitarian theory of the state which calls for a wider use of coercion against individual autonomy than this. For to say that redistributive transfers amount to *coercive interference with autonomy* begs the question: it presupposes that people have strong initial rights to pre-redistribution shares of resources. Such a theory has to be supplied independently of the claim that absolute private property is a prerequisite of individual liberty because this is precisely what is at stake in the argument about redistribution allegedly amounting to coercion. Without an independent theory justifying rights to private property in the pre-redistributive state, to say that imposition of redistributive transfers upon the better-off involves a coercive intrusion into the individual's autonomy is a *non sequitur*. It may be claimed (and this is a theory which I, for one, accept)[82] that we do not have any strong moral claims to the shares of wealth we hold before redistributive transfers modify this pattern of distribution, since we cannot properly derive these claims from our personal "desert" only, and to a large degree this pre-redistributive pattern is shaped by factors which are arbitrary from a moral point of view. One way of defending such a theory would be by recourse to the Rawlsian idea of the "common pool" of benefits derived from the assets which are morally arbitrary (such as natural abilities or the accidents of birth in a particular social position).[83] But I do not need to defend this theory here: it requires a moral defense just as any other moral theory of property does (e.g., about "mixing one's labour with things" or about proper entitlements derived from legitimate acquisitions and transfers). They all belong to the realm of theories of distributive justice. But unless one shows by an independent argument (that is, independent from the property-freedom connection) that the putative "givers" (that is those who lose out on the redistributive actions of the state) have strong rights over the resources which they control before the redistribution, there is no substance in claiming that to forcibly deprive them of the surplus necessary to compensate others for morally arbitrary disadvantages is "coercive interference with autonomy".

It is important, in this context, to avoid the semantic error consisting in presupposing a "moralized" concept of coercion, whereby to describe an act as coercive is to condemn it. For one is tempted to say that a putatively coercive redistributive transfer is not really "coercion" unless those from whom a surplus is extracted and transferred to the worse-off have prior legitimate rights over their holdings (which, as I have suggested, begs the question and calls for a criterion of legitimacy which must be provided independently). But to say this would be to replicate a libertarian error of implicitly using a "moralized" concept of coercion. If libertarians believe that the legal protection of private property maximizes individual freedom, they must disregard the coercion against the non-owners inherent in the legal protection of property, and the only explanation that can be given to such a myopic approach is that they find an assault by a non-owner upon the existing distribution of wealth unjustifiable, and therefore the coercion against the assaulters — justified. If *that* use of coercion is deemed not to be restrictive of liberty, it may be only on the basis that the use of the word "coercion" is implicitly restricted to the unjustified uses of force. As G.A. Cohen argued in his polemic with Antony Flew, such a "moralized" concept of freedom and coercion presupposed tacit approval for a status quo, which is seen as a natural state of affairs, hence the forceful protection of this status quo is not viewed as coercive.[84] The use of coercion to prevent deviations from that status quo is not viewed as coercion; the institution of property is therefore viewed as fundamentally non-coercive.

But this "moralized" account of coercion is not only questionable by virtue of its in-built conservatism; it is also conceptually muddled, as one immediately realizes on contemplating an uncontroversially justifiable use of coercion by the state against the convicted murderer (assuming, for the sake of argument, that the penal law under which he has been convicted and punished is fair). In this case we do not object to the use of word "coercion" to describe the actions of law enforcement agencies, regardless of their legitimacy. Why therefore deny the use of this word to describe force used against those who attempt to change the established patterns of wealth in ways that the valid law deems improper? Because *their* action is illegal in the first place? But so is that of the murderer, and yet the official reaction does not lose its attribute of coerciveness. The reason might lie elsewhere: just as we do not complain that natural restraints of our actions are "coercive" (to say that I am "coerced" to stay at home by the stormy weather would be, at best, a *façon de parler*), so if we happen to view the current distribution of property as equally natural, we tend to ignore the coerciveness of legal mechanisms aimed at protecting it.

And yet surely there is no reason to deem any current distribution of property, whatever it might be, as a "natural" fact, equally as "natural" as weather conditions. It is a complex outcome of the combination of legal rules regulating contracts, employment, inheritance, familial division of property, taxation, torts, expropriation or confiscation with or without compensation etc., and of human actions undertaken in the context of this pre-existing legal regime.[85] There is nothing "natural" about these rules in that they represent the value judgments and policy decisions of law-makers; they enforce public choices which are inherently controversial (for any particular regime of the tax law one can propose an alternative one, which will result in a different distribution of wealth, etc). These rules are just as coercive as the rules which govern the use of force against violators of the status quo: no more and no less.[86] Hence the appeal to "coercion" is not effective in the argument about the possible applicability of the harm principle to the question of redistribution of wealth: both a redistribution and a failure to redistribute are equally "coercive". The use of a "moralized" concept of coercion, whereby to establish the fact of coercion is to condemn it, only conceals the truth that any distribution of wealth in a society at any given time is the result of legally sanctioned coercion.

However inconclusive as to the question of whether the harm principle may accommodate the redistributive functions of the state, the above analysis is instructive because it brings into our discussion the issue of the baseline of "naturalness".[87] Consider the paradigmatic use of the harm principle": A attempts to hit B; the law prevents him from doing this (or, if too late in preventing it, punishes him). Legal action fits the account which triggers the harm principle because it is a coercive interference with A's autonomy: A would like to be autonomous in the use of his arm, and the law prevents him from doing so, on the basis that this particular use of his autonomy is illegitimate. Now consider a simplified case of a redistributive transfer: C is forced to pay (against her will, of course) 20% tax on her income, and the state uses the funds thus obtained to confer welfare benefits on D, who is unemployed. In what way is A's situation relevantly different from that of C?

The answer is this: to say that C's autonomy is violated (in an analogous way to the violation of A's autonomy by state officials) would be to presuppose that the pre-redistributive state of affairs is a natural baseline by reference to which the violations of autonomy are measured. This is a general though tacit presupposition of the talk about violations of autonomy: it presupposes a pre-existent situation in which that which is taken away through the violation of autonomy had belonged to the coerced person (or was under the person's control in a "natural" sense, i.e. not as a matter of legal entitlements). A's use of some parts of his body is "natural" in that it can be described in natural terms, without appeal to legal rules. The point at which law enters into the picture marks the moment at which the violations of autonomy occur: that happens if the range of options available to A has been restricted (regardless of whether or not these restrictions are legitimate — otherwise we will repeat the error of using a "moralized" concept). In contrast, there is nothing "natural" about the situation "before the redistribution" in C's case; her alleged rights to the pre-tax income are a matter of legal rules which define her entitlements in the light of currently valid law. When, say, the law removes some of C's rights to her deceased grandfather's estate in the form of death duty, there is no point at which she "has had" the inheritance in a natural sense, independent of the operations of legal rules. Her claim to (the part of) the inheritance is a matter of the law of succession (which could have well been quite different, e.g. by excluding the grandchildren from intestate succession altogether), and also the prior property entitlements of her grandfather which have been the result of the operation of specific and contingent legal rules. To locate a "baseline", by reference to which we will measure all the deviations as restricting the autonomy of the agent, would be to claim that at this particular point a given distribution is "natural", pre-legal. That is precisely why we could measure the interference with A's autonomy from the point at which his capacity to use his body was "natural". But in the case of C, to locate this baseline between her pre-tax and post-tax status would be purely arbitrary.

The harm principle governs the use of legal interference with a person's autonomy. It therefore imagines a point at which a person is in a "natural" state, that is in a state which can be described without resort to legal rules (just as it was a philosophers' fantasy that there was a "state of nature" in which law did not operate, so too it is a lawyers' fantasy that no human action can be described without resort to legal rules). This applies to A but not to C. That is why the harm principle does not apply to the redistribution of property: it can neither delegitimize nor validate it. Consider again a general concept of the restriction of liberty: it is such a manipulation of one's environment as a result of which the coerced person must make a choice (consistent with the coercer's wishes) which is worse for the coerced person than the situation before the coercion occurred, in the sense that the number of options available and attractive to the agent is more limited than before the coercion (this concept paraphrases Hayek's definition of coercion as "such control of the environment or circumstances of a person by another that, in order to avoid greater evil, he is forced to act not accordingly to a coherent plan of his own but to serve the ends of another").[88] It is an unabashedly non-perfectionist definition (in that it does not relate the coercion to the ideal-regarding standards but to the coerced person's perspectives, however we happen to judge them), and rightly so, considering the anti-perfectionist nature of the harm principle. This description applies to A, but not to C: we cannot measure her after-tax situation by reference to the pre-tax status because *she had never been there*! She never was in a situation analogous to that of A before the law's action; there wasn't such a moment in which she "had" more while now she "has" less. Her autonomy has not been restricted because there is no reason to locate the baseline from which to measure the autonomy-restrictions at the pre-redistribution stage. To be sure, redistribution may be deemed "just" or "unjust", but to rest such judgments on the claim of the violation of autonomy is question-begging: redistribution is neither more nor less coercive than non-redistribution, and its merits and demerits must be argued independently. As to these arguments, the harm principle is agnostic.

The final question worth a brief mention here is how to square the harm principle with the state funding of, and support for, the arts, education, and related areas of spiritual pursuit. This, together with the problem of redistribution discussed above, underlies an answer to the question: Must a state based on the harm-principle be libertarian? The argument about redistribution suggested a negative response to this question; the discussion of support for education and art expands the proposition that liberals committed to neutrality need not be libertarian in the sense of the advocacy of a minimal state.

While the issue of state support for education and the arts found prominence in recent discussions about the meaning of liberal neutrality,[89] it is perhaps worth mentioning at the outset that the problem is less crucial from the point of view of the doctrine which identifies the harm principle as the centerpiece of its moral theory, because the harm principle is fundamentally concerned with the coercive state action which leads to direct prohibitions on certain uses of the individual's liberty. While in the state's spending of the taxpayers' money there is undoubtedly an element of coercion, and such spending must be based on a properly defended general theory, it nevertheless does not raise problems of equal moral weight from the point of view of the harm principle as the direct prohibitions flowing from the criminal law.

Nevertheless, *some* justification is necessary, and there has been a good deal of suspicion expressed that the state's support for education and arts, however justified, cannot be neutral between conceptions of the good because the spending priorities necessarily reflect a prior endorsement of specific moral and aesthetic values. This, however, is not the only plausible explanation of state action in this area. Such action may well be defended on the basis of the inevitable market failure to sustain different types of artistic and educational activities; without collective support they risk disappearing or being accessible only to privileged groups in a society. Interestingly, the actual arguments in political discussions about the proper level of state subsidies for the arts in West European societies indicate that the concerns about preserving diversity and guaranteeing accessibility, rather than an official preference for "good" aesthetic values, are the main operative arguments behind the policies for subsidizing the arts.[90] State support aims therefore at preserving the diversity of artistic and educational activities, and at making the choice available to those who would be excluded from benefiting from or participating in them in a situation of the costs of art and education being regulated by the market alone. It also provides a partial answer to the complaints about liberal insensitivity to the issue of preference-formation. As mentioned earlier in this Chapter, various defects in the process of generation of preferences substantially weaken the political norm demanding the state's respect for individual preferences as they are, rather than as they could have been under more favourable circumstances. State support for education and arts aims at enabling people to take a reflective, critical attitude toward their own tastes, desires and preferences, by providing them with opportunities to test and experience a variety of conceptions of the good. Diversity of existing spiritual, cultural and intellectual opportunities (hardly possible under a system which gives no support to the arts and education) provides a framework within which the preference-formation process is more authentic, and the outcome of the process — more credible as an expression of "genuine" individual preferences.

While some cultural activities (e.g. sport) can be fully supported by the market, others (e.g. opera) cannot survive without extra subsidies (and if they can survive, then they do so in an impoverished form and/or only accessible to the privileged few). State support for opera rather than for soccer is justified not on the basis of the official preference for the aesthetic worth of opera as opposed to soccer, but on the basis of (1) making the choice between opera and soccer meaningful (preserving the vitality of opera), and (2) making it meaningful to all on a roughly equal basis (maintaining low prices for opera tickets). This is a precondition for the opportunity of the worse-off to follow their chosen conception of the good life, which may well include going to the opera. Without a diversity of options and without the accessibility of diverse aesthetic and educational pursuits to a general public, the equal moral agency of people to pursue their conceptions of the good becomes meaningless. State subsidies for arts belong, therefore, to the category of measures which merely "enlarge the portfolio of opportunities for citizens to realize their chosen conceptions of the good".[91]

Can the above argument apply as well to the transmission of specific moral values through the state (or state-funded) educational system? Not really, because the value of the instruction (specifically at the primary and secondary level) does not necessarily and fundamentally lie in the diversity of options accessible to schoolchildren. Rather, it is believed that a good elementary education must convey certain basic moral values in an unambiguous and unconditional way. But the recipients of this transmission of values are properly beyond the sphere of anti-paternalistic and anti-moralistic protection: the liberal state is prevented from using the coercive means to enforce specific moral conceptions upon mature, adult individuals. On this basis it is understandable why we accept that the higher level of education, the broader should be the range of choice available to a student.

The point remains, nevertheless, that if an elementary education in a liberal state is allowed to transmit specific and substantive moral values, then there must be room for such values in the process of policy formation. This is true, but there is no reason to expect that the policy- and law-makers will be free of substantive moral conceptions guiding the principles of the good life. The harm principle prevents them from enforcing these values against adult individuals through coercive and authoritative decisions — but this principle does not apply to the education of children.

CHAPTER 5

LIBERAL NEUTRALITY AND THE SPECIAL PROTECTION OF MINORITIES

In Chapter 4 we argued that the specificity of liberal presuppositions on the neutrality of law lies not so much in the insistence on the primacy of liberty (after all, the liberals cannot make any special claim to the appreciation of the value of freedom, though they certainly may be able to make a special use of it) but rather in a particular interrelation between the libertarian and egalitarian considerations. More specifically, we argued that the libertarian substance of the harm principle does not preclude the redistributive functions of the state: such a preclusion would be justified only if we had accepted a prior "baseline" of a particular distribution of wealth produced by the legal regime of actual societies as something "natural" and pre-legal.

This argument indicates the strong egalitarian potential of the related conceptions of neutrality, harm principle and equality of individuals as moral agents. In this Chapter, some of the egalitarian implications stemming from the last Chapter will be addressed more directly. We will approach this issue by taking up what is probably one of the most controversial legal questions, namely the justification of special protection of disadvantaged minorities. But rather than discussing various arguments against and in favour of affirmative action (an arguably interesting topic but rather well covered in the modern jurisprudential literature), we will approach the issue from a different angle. By following up some of the arguments in Chapter 2 about the institutional divisions of tasks between the legislatures and the judiciary, we will consider the question of whether there is real justification, *in the liberal conception of neutrality*, for special judicial protection of disadvantaged and powerless minorities.

At first glance, such a supposition may appear surprising: whatever other arguments for a special minority protection can be supplied, they are hardly compatible with the principle of neutrality. After all, neutrality (as defined here) requires disregard for (or impartiality between) substantive conceptions of the good shared by different individuals or groups in a society. Special protection of minorities would have to identify, as an evil to be eliminated, the fact that some groups are victims of unreasonable prejudice by the rest of the society, but in order to determine what prejudice is "unreasonable" (or, indeed, what belief amounts to a "prejudice") the law-maker would have to make precisely the sort of judgment that the principle of neutrality seems to forbid.

This is the fundamental dilemma which will serve as a focus for our considerations of the principle of special judicial protection of minorities and its relationship to the principle of liberal neutrality. Our argument will focus on one particular doctrine of the American constitutional law which, I believe, contains the most promise for solving the dilemma identified above. I will argue that the doctrine of special protection of "discrete and insular minorities", derived from a celebrated argument by Justice Stone in the decision *Carolene Products v. United States*, if re-interpreted in a manner proposed in this Chapter, is well suited to provide support for the special protection of disadvantaged minorities in a way which does not offend against the principle of liberal neutrality.

1. DEMOCRACY AND MINORITIES: THE MEANING OF FOOTNOTE FOUR

Judges in the Anglo-American legal tradition, with which this Chapter is mainly concerned, are fond of declaring their deference to the legislative will and their unwillingness to conduct a critical scrutiny of the validity of properly enacted statutes. Representative democracy, it is tacitly presupposed and sometimes openly asserted, has a quasi-miraculous faculty of self-correction: the best remedy for the defects of democracy lies in the democracy itself. As one prominent Australian judge recently announced, "The chief protection [of our citizens from an oppressive majority in Parliament] lies in the democratic nature of our Parliamentary institutions".[1] This of course leaves open the problem of the possible oppression of a powerless minority by the Parliamentary majority: appeal to the good sense and wisdom of the majority itself does not sound very reassuring for those who fear that their claims will not receive proper attention or a proper hearing from the legislators. It is in this context that the *Carolene Products* doctrine may be usefully considered.

Carolene Products was one of the many cases typical of the period in which the Supreme Court abandoned the practice of casual invalidation of New Deal laws and was prepared, instead, to support a growing number of government regulations by adopting a very deferential, rationality-based review of economic legislation. In order to uphold challenged legislation all that was required was that the Court be satisfied that the legislation rested upon "some rational basis within the knowledge or experience of the legislator".[2] By that standard, federal legislation that prohibited the shipment in interstate commerce of filled milk seemed eminently reasonable to Justice Stone. But there was a problem: if such a loose scrutiny was applied across the board it would make the Court powerless vis-a-vis the legislature in the areas of civil rights and liberties. So, in order to avoid this, Stone hinted in his footnote that the decision did not preempt the question of whether other regulations might be subjected to a less deferential kind of review.

There was nothing particularly ingenious in postulating a two-tier system of judicial review: lenient scrutiny of economic regulations and stricter scrutiny when dealing with civil liberties. But what *was* ingenious was the *rationale* offered for the latter. For to leave the matter there, and to simply assert that civil liberties are so fundamental from the point of view of constitutional values that the legislature could not be trusted by the courts, and so a tougher scrutiny must be applied compared with economic matters which are somehow constitutionally less important, would inevitably raise the two notorious difficulties which had led the Court into a crisis which ended only in the late 1930's: a "natural law" difficulty and a counter-majoritarian difficulty. The former is raised by the question of how one is to construe and interpret Constitutional values inherent in open-ended clauses in an objective way: the controversies surrounding *Lochner*[3] indicate how vulnerable the Court was to the criticism that it imposed its own values under the guise of an interpretation of "substantive due process". To apply such standards in invalidating laws affecting civil liberties would be to repeat the same sin that the Court was accused of committing with regard to restrictions on labour relations in *Lochner*: it would merely substitute the natural-law of the liberal Left for the traditional natural law of the Right. In turn, the counter-majoritarian difficulty, mentioned earlier in Chapter 2 of this book, stems from the problem of legitimacy: even if open-ended clauses of the Constitution require substantive value judgments, why should the nine unelected, unrepresentative and life-tenured lawyers be entrusted with the right to replace the value judgments of the duly elected representatives of the people?

The main attraction of *Carolene* lies in its permitting a strict scrutiny of laws affecting civil rights (and keeping a proper deference to legislation in other areas) while avoiding the natural-law and the counter-majoritarian difficulties. To the natural-law objection, Footnote Four offers the response that it is not the substantive judgments of the representatives which are being overridden, but it is merely the defects in the process of reaching these judgments which are being corrected. To the counter-majoritarian objection, the Footnote's answer lies within the realm of the value of majoritarian legitimacy itself: the only statutes which can be truly legitimate are those which are the product of a genuine majority will and where no group is ignored merely because it lacks adequate access to democratic decision-making.

The main potential of the Footnote as an inspiration for anti-discrimination law lies at the very end of the third paragraph in the "prejudice against discrete and insular minorities" proviso. It suggests that "prejudice against discrete and insular minorities may be a special condition, which tends seriously to curtail the operation of those political processes ordinarily to be relied upon to protect minorities" and therefore that it "may call for a correspondingly more searching judicial inquiry..." . The "prejudice against discrete and insular minorities" is seen as triggering strict scrutiny because the groups adversely affected by laws reflecting such prejudice cannot effectively resort to the normal, political corrective process. It is interesting that the only two cases which illustrate this point in Justice Stone's footnote initially appear to have nothing to do with any disadvantaged minority. *McCulloch v. Maryland*[4] was one of the grand decisions of the Marshall court that shaped the federal-state division of powers, one in which the incorporation of a bank by the Federal Government was upheld as constitutional, and the state's right to tax a federal bank was rejected. In *South Carolina v. Barwell*[5] a particular state regulation affecting interstate commerce was invalidated. The relevance of these citations becomes clear only at closer inspection of the specific passages to which Stone refers. In *McCulloch v. Maryland* he refers to those pages where the Court asserts that "the only security" against the abuse of taxation power lies in the fact that these are the government's own constituents who are being taxed. The implication is that one cannot harm oneself; however, this protection against abuse disappears when the state wants to tax outsiders, in this case, by taxing a Federal bank, "since not all of the electors of the Union are represented".[6] In *Barwell*, a footnote referred to by Stone asserts that when the main burden of a regulation falls upon non-state residents, the normal political restrictions typically expected when state interests are affected, are not likely to occur.[7] Hence, while neither of the two cases match the language of the "prejudice against discrete and insular minorities" clause (non-state residents are neither discrete, nor insular, nor a minority, nor even typically a target of prejudice), the spirit of the principle is clearly indicated: those who cannot affect legislation politically, should get judicial support when trying to repeal the act they find offensive to their interests.

The true meaning of the *Carolene* Footnote became evident during its judicial life: the "prejudice against discrete and insular minorities" test has been invoked since 1970 (if we do not count a reference by Stone himself)[8] to invalidate, or to try to invalidate, laws burdening Blacks, aliens, the young, minor political parties and independent candidates, prisoners, the poor, and the mentally retarded. Not all these efforts have been successful,[9] and some judges seemed to contradict themselves in claiming or rejecting the status of a "discrete and insular minority" for one and the same group.[10] But the history of the judicial uses of *Carolene* has been rich and instructive, and Justice Powell was certainly right to call it "the most celebrated footnote in constitutional law".[11]

2. "PREJUDICE", "PRINCIPLE" AND NEUTRALITY

"One person's 'prejudice' is, notoriously, another's 'principle'".[12] This may well be true, and in the light of our argument in Chapter 4 it would appear that the courts should, as far as possible, avoid drawing the prejudice/principle line when allocating and enforcing rights: in a liberal-egalitarian vision of a just legal order, the law must not take sides in ideological disputes, and should keep an attitude of neutrality towards competing ideologies and world-views. The construction and interpretation of rights, on this theory, must not enforce any substantive conceptions of the good life about which people in a morally pluralistic society disagree, but should merely guard the enforcement of basic ground rules of social cooperation (such as the protection of the equal autonomy of every individual) which are neutral as between competing conceptions of "good".

Now there is an ironic twist in the "One person's prejudice is another's principle" dictum: those who endorse it usually urge the courts to draw a line between prejudice and principle. Rather than debunk the illusory nature of the distinction (thus demonstrating its uselessness in judicial decisions), on the contrary, they magnify it by adding extra weight to "prejudice". Ackerman's argument is a good case in point: three pages after restating the "One person's prejudice..." maxim, he concludes: "The difference between the things we call 'prejudice' and the things we call 'principle' is in the end a substantive moral difference".[13] His argument is that *Carolene* and its most vigourous proponent John Hart Ely[14] are wrong in suggesting that *prejudice* against minorities may be a meaningful factor in a test for justifying a strict judicial review: what is "prejudice" (Ackerman says) is ultimately a matter of our substantive normative judgments. Those "things" called principles impose "ultimate limits on pluralist bargaining" in a democracy;[15] everything beyond these limits is, presumably, "prejudice". Ackerman's argument is that the notion of prejudice in *Carolene* and that put forward by Ely erroneously focus on the process alone, and that it is an illusion that we can tell "prejudice" from "principle" without inquiring into the value of the substance of particular preferences. Once we engage in such a critical scrutiny, however, the pedigree of a given preference turns out to be irrelevant.

This is a broadly accepted view: Ely's defence of the *Carolene* standards generated wide protest against his disregard for substantive tests of illegitimate "prejudice".[16] But if this "normative judgments" view propounded by Professors Ackerman, Brest and Tribe is to be accepted, it comes at considerable expense to the principle of neutrality in ideological controversies. For if "prejudice" is indeed a matter of who is right and who is wrong, then we might as well abandon the liberal neutrality project altogether. We might then simply say that the courts will disregard those views which are wrong, and which we may (although no argument would hang on this characterization) call "prejudice". But then, in an ideologically pluralist society, we abandon the hope of finding common ground rules that will allow us, in a neutral fashion, to relegate some preferences beyond the framework of a liberal bargaining bazaar for reasons other than merely because "we" ("we" the legislators, "we" the popular majority of the day, or "we" the majority of an appellate court who happens to hear the case) do not like them. In other words, the task before us is to outline a theory of invidious discrimination against minorities that would not depend on which side, in an underlying controversy, is right; a theory that could command agreement about which groups should obtain special protection even in the face of substantive disagreement about which negative external preferences towards minorities are wrong ("prejudice") and which are right ("principle").

I believe such a theory is available which would avoid the Scylla of Ackerman's "normative judgments" approach and the Charybdis of Ely's processualism, and the way is indicated by *Carolene* itself. Consider *Watson v. City of Memphis*:[17] the Supreme Court of the United States refused to allow the city of Memphis to delay the desegregation of its parks and recreational facilities; the city feared that quick integration would lead to interracial disturbances, riots and turmoil. To be sure, the dangers anticipated by the city were real, so a true Millian liberal could perhaps invoke the "harm principle" in defending the city's action (or rather, in this case, inaction). But the Court refused to attach any weight to racist prejudice and bias.

What is the best interpretation of this refusal? Is it Ackerman's view about substantive principles which put racism beyond the consideration, as too odious a doctrine to be allowed into pluralist bargaining? Compare *Watson* with *Village of Skokie v. National Socialist Party of America.*[18] The plaintiff village, inhabited mainly by Jews, and largely by survivors of German concentration camps, sought to enjoin the Nazi Party from conducting demonstrations within the village or, at the very least, to enjoin the Nazis from wearing the swastika. The village lost: the Nazi Party's right to demonstrate and to wear the swastika in a predominantly Jewish settlement was affirmed. Superficially, *Watson* and *Skokie* are equivalent from the point of view of disallowing private bias and distaste to enter into the enforcement of rights, and confirm the "One person's prejudice is another's principle" dictum. But such a conclusion strikes us as outrageous: it would equate racial prejudice with anti-Nazi feelings. Our task is to find moral grounds for this intuitive outrage, and the basis for the distinction.

Now one possible reason for this non-equivalence of *Watson* and *Skokie* is suggested by Ackerman: if we exercise moral judgments about the substance of "prejudice', then the external negative preferences of white racists in *Watson* (who do not want Blacks to interact with Whites) are not equivalent but opposite to the external negative preferences of Skokie villagers (who do not want the Nazis to demonstrate in their neighbourhood).[19] While under the doctrine of near-absolute free expression the Skokie people must still be made to tolerate Nazi marches and demonstrations, we can certainly find a great deal to sympathize with in their predicament, and can only accept the Court's decision about the Nazi's right to demonstrate with reluctance and as a "lesser evil" to a prior restraint. This is a different (indeed, an opposite) response to the one raised by the white racists who would like to have their preferences registered in law when decisions about desegregation in parks, or custodial rights of interracial marriages, are concerned.

But if we draw the distinction along this line, it all boils down ultimately to the difference between the "good guys" (anti-Nazis) and the "bad guys" (white racists), and hence, to the distinction between a good and a bad ideology. An alternative way, suggested by *Carolene*, is to inquire into the nature of the *group* which is the target of the negative preference in question. In *Watson* the target group was the Black minority, in *Skokie* it was the American Nazis. The difference in our moral response to these two groups lies (according to this alternative interpretation, which I wish to offer) not in the fact that their "ideologies" differ (what is the ideology of Blacks as a group?) but rather in that the former answers the description of a socially disadvantaged group, which needs extra protection from possible legislative indifference or hostility, while the latter does not. So the logic, if not the letter,[20] of *Carolene* explains the moral distinction between the Blacks and the Nazis as target groups of laws which have to be tested with a different degree of scrutiny by the court. At this stage, it of course still begs a number of questions, which I will take up later; the only point I wish to make now is that if such a distinction can be defended, we may well find a solution to the dilemma raised by the conflict between ideology-neutrality and the selective disqualification of only *some* biases and preferences. Hence, we may ascertain illegitimate prejudice without falling back on normative judgments about "good" and "bad" preferences.

It follows that in the test of "prejudice against disadvantaged minorities", it is the "disadvantaged minorities", and not the "prejudice", which is truly operative. Now does it make sense in the *Watson/Skokie* context? After all, Nazis may be depicted to be a "disadvantaged" minority, just as the Blacks are, if we consistently screen out from consideration all the substantive judgments about the worth of their preferences. For one may claim that the American Nazi Party, by virtue of being at the fringes of the political system, has very little access to the legislative process, and its members are generally disliked by the community at large. So, unless substantive judgments about their ideology enter the picture, we cannot deny the equivalence of Nazis in *Skokie* and Blacks in *Watson*.

But this is a myopic view. The notion of a protection-deserving minority in the *Carolene* sense does not apply to every loser in the political or legislative decision-making process. If this were to be the proper understanding, it would carry very little weight: any vote produces a majority and a minority, and it is appropriate in a democracy that those who are in the minority must submit to a majority view. To add that democracy calls for majority rule *and a respect for minority rights* does not really solve the problem, because what the minority rights should be is precisely the question at stake here. It is not even good enough to say that a minority in the *Carolene* sense is one which is systematically and perpetually on the losing side in the political and legislative process.[21] Such a description would, perhaps, fit the American Nazi Party, but it would still not entitle it to any extra protection from the judicial system, for there is no reason to believe that such a perpetual minority's predicament is a result of "a special condition, which tends seriously to curtail the operation of those political processes ordinarily to be relied upon to protect minorities".[22]

The difference between the Nazis in *Skokie* and the Blacks in *Watson* is indicated by the very spirit and rationale of the third paragraph of *Carolene*.

Why would Stone choose to advocate a special protection for "discrete and insular" minorities, rather than for "disadvantaged" minorities, regardless of their discreteness and insularity? Professor Ackerman shows convincingly that neither discreteness nor insularity is really relevant in identifying the groups which require special protection from the legislative process: some groups which are anonymous (e.g. homosexuals), or dispersed (women), or both dispersed and anonymous (the poor), may well deserve more protection than the "discrete" and/or "insular" groups.[23] Ackerman is right; he is also right in pointing out that often the characteristics of discreteness and (in particular) insularity may be a strong political asset, rather than a liability. And yet there is a rational core in Justice Stone's description: both "discreteness" and "insularity" are *social* characteristics, that is to say, they are the attributes of the group regardless of its position in the formal structure of power. They apply to the group before it begins playing the pluralist wheeling and dealing game, and independently of the outcome of the game. While Stone's choice of these two particular adjectives may and should be disputed, the lesson to be drawn from the spirit of his description is that the conditions of special vulnerability of minorities cannot be simply reduced to their minority status in the legislative process, but have to do with their position in civil society. Legal disadvantages which have to be severely scrutinized by the court, petrify, strengthen and freeze, but do not create, existing structures of social disadvantage and discrimination. The group's reduced access to law-making is not simply a tautological matter of being outvoted, not even a matter of always being outvoted, but more generally, of coming to the process from a disabled social position. Legal and political defeat is but a complement to the social deprivation, the stigma of inferiority, and the general powerlessness of a group which, together, form a coherent pattern of overall disability.[24]

Whether Stone had precisely this theory in mind or not, it is clearly consistent with the rationale of the third paragraph. It is only when we see the minoritarian status of a group in the general social context of the overall pattern of disabilities that we may begin to appreciate the conditions which "tend[] seriously to curtail the operation of those political processes ordinarily to be relied upon to protect minorities".[25] A group which is locked into a pattern of economic disadvantage and deprivation of educational opportunities, or a group which is the object of widespread social stereotypes which induce others to perceive members of that group as incapable of performing particular jobs or public functions, cannot expect proper protection from the legislative process. This is the factor which justifies a "more searching judicial inquiry" into laws which disadvantage such groups.[26] This is the line which divides Blacks as a socially disadvantaged group which still suffers the effects of past formal and societal discrimination from Nazis who simply happen to be in a minority by virtue of their unpopular views. But their "minoritarian" status is trivial from the point of view of the considerations which guide paragraph three of the *Carolene* footnote: it is not a part of an overall pattern of disability and societal discrimination.

The question may still linger whether the above strategy helps avoid the trap indicated by the "One person's prejudice is another's principle" dictum. The danger it exposed was the inherent subjectivity, hence controversiality, of depicting illegitimate views as "prejudice", but the cure its proponents advocated — a direct appeal to substantive, normative principles, which put some attitudes and preferences "beyond the pale" - was destructive to the liberal conception of neutrality vis-a-vis substantive conceptions of the good. The strategy advocated here, relying as it does upon the identification of socially disadvantaged minorities, is attractive only if consistent with the promise of neutrality, that is, if the identification of such minorities is reasonably noncontroversial and does not hinge upon substantive judgments regarding negative preferences targeted at these minorities. In order to play its role, it must — as far as possible — rely on "objective" characteristics, and avoid moral judgments about "unfair" or "undeserved" deprivations.

Since the preceding sentences may sound somewhat extravagant, it is necessary to clarify the function played by the identification of a group as disadvantaged. Such identification is not *conclusive* in the decision about the rights conferred upon, or the burdens borne, by the group. This identification is important, however, in the decision as to how far the democratic legislative process can be trusted to treat such a group properly: it is inspired by the *Carolene* insight that the law must protect more stringently those groups which cannot protect themselves politically in a democratic state. So it may well be that, at the end of the day, the law which burdens a socially disadvantaged group will yet be found by the court to be valid, but the presumption of validity must be much weaker, for the group does not enjoy the routine protection afforded by the democratic process.

The crucial question is whether the indicia of those groups which cannot protect themselves politically, and therefore deserve extra protection through a legal system, can be ascertained with a certain degree of "objectivity" and can be agreed upon by people who otherwise disagree about substantive political ideologies. A good way of testing the *Carolene* approach (in the interpretation suggested here) is to subject it to a "parade of horribles", often used by the proponents of the normative-judgments approach. If we disregard normative judgments about whether particular groups deserve the substantive rights they claim, and concentrate instead on the "discreteness and insularity" (or any such other "objective" indicia) of the groups in question, the argument goes, are we not then forced to support special protection for burglars, extortionists and exhibitionists?[27] All these groups can be depicted, after all, as suffering traditional disadvantage and vilification: if the *Carolene*-inspired approach prevents us from enquiring whether the disadvantages and vilification are *justified* or not (in which case we would be pushed into a substantive mode of inquiry), then we will probably end up with an obviously counter-intuitive demand for holding suspicious a good many criminal laws, addressed, as they are, against "discrete and insular" minorities of burglars, extortionists etc.

Now we have seen in what ways "Nazis" are different from "Blacks" as a target group of a disadvantaging law: the former are not a minority in a social sense.[28] Neither are extortionists, burglars and exhibitionists: they do not constitute "groups" which define the identity of its members in such a way as to dramatically reduce their say in a democratic political process. Perhaps a good point at which to begin the analysis is by saying that no-one is born into a group of burglars, while one is necessarily born into a racial minority group. Hence, the burdens imposed by the law disadvantaging burglars are easily avoidable, but the burdens imposed by racial or gender classifications are not.

To be sure, it has sometimes been noted that the immutability of a classifying trait is neither a sufficient nor a necessary indicium of "suspectness": perfectly legitimate classifications based on intelligence or strength (immutable properties) suggest that it is not a sufficient indicium, and laws disadvantaging aliens or the poor (mutable criteria) are used to show that it is not a necessary one.[29] But one must not protest too much. The poor or aliens are not in the same category as burglars from the point of view of the immutability of a criterion identifying their group membership. While the poor and aliens can hope to have their group classification altered in the future, at present they cannot help but suffer legally defined burdens. However, the prospective burglar can change his mind and easily desist from his unlawful course of conduct. So for some groups at least, the immutability criterion works quite well as a test for disqualifying classifications that disadvantage, and the intuitive principle that there is something presumptively wrong in burdening people along lines which they cannot cross, and on the basis of characteristics which are beyond their control,[30] seems confirmed by specific examples given above. The significance of immutability (or "immutability-like" criteria, such as alienage and poverty) is further compounded by a reflection that in the case of alterable characteristics it does make sense to say that the law may wish to discourage people from joining a particular group (e.g., from becoming a burglar), but it would definitely be eccentric to say that the law might burden people in order to discourage them from becoming black, or poor.[31]

But then what about homosexuals[32] or Catholics?[33] If we abandon criteria requiring the substantive assessment of a group's proposed right, laws disadvantaging these groups will easily escape the charge of using "immutable" classifications. At this stage, it is important to reflect upon the rationale for disliking immutable classifications. It is not merely the fact that a person cannot physically escape his characteristics which should worry us. It is also worrying when, in order to escape legal burdens, a person must pay an extremely high price in terms of what constitutes someone's spiritual, moral or intellectual identity. Hence in the case of legal burdens against homosexuals, the situation matches the rationale of our distrust of immutable classifications: a person is either unable to change his group membership,[34] or can do it only by abandoning a very important part of himself.[35] The only way of escaping anti-homosexual law is by repressing or rejecting one's sexual preferences: even when this is not impossible, it carries enormous personal cost. This is not the case with extortionists or burglars.[36] I suggest that we can make such a distinction without falling back on judgments to the effect that stealing is "bad" while homosexuality is morally neutral.

This is also the case with regulations directed at religious groups: it is possible to change one's group-membership, but the costs are usually very high. But an important qualification is needed here: it is not the fact that a classification burdens a religious *group*, but rather that it burdens a religious *minority*, which makes a regulation immediately suspect. For we must always keep in mind the underlying rationale of the *Carolene* test which aims at extra protection for those groups which cannot protect themselves through normal, political channels. Hence when Tribe mentions "laws burdening Catholics" with the implication that they are evidently more suspect than "laws burdening pickpockets",[37] my response is that it all depends: not because there is any moral equivalence between Catholics and pickpockets (though admittedly these two categories may partly overlap) but rather because pickpockets are not a social group in the *Carolene* sense at all, and Catholics are not necessarily a powerless *minority* properly covered by the *Carolene* protection. One would be hard pressed to find a *Carolene*-based suspicion concerning a statute imposing extra burdens on Catholics passed by the Italian Parliament; it would be preposterous to believe that such a law reflects the legislature's indifference or hostility towards the dominant religious group. In turn, the laws disadvantaging minoritarian religions, or religions disfavoured by the dominant power elite, fall easily within the *Carolene*-inspired suspicion. Constitutional protection of freedom of religion has therefore (to the extent to which it is reviewable by the courts) special significance with regard to marginal, or generally unfavoured, religions.

As a number of critics have noted, a group deserving extra judicial protection need not necessarily be "discrete" (in the sense of being non-anonymous) and "insular" (in the sense of territorial concentration and/or isolation). What does matter is the *rationale* behind the "discrete and insular" characteristics: it is that the status of group members, in order to justify extra judicial protection in terms of the *Carolene* rationale, must be determined by the fact of group membership more strongly than by other social indicators. To take a different example, a Black in Australia is first of all a Black — and this means for him much more, in terms of determining social and political clout, than the fact of being an urban dweller, a boomerang thrower, or a single parent. But being a Pole means relatively little in Australia: it is just one of a number of indicators, generally not a decisive one. The social significance of group membership is relevant to our considerations because it determines when the *Carolene* rationale should become operative. An Australian of Polish origin cannot complain about her disproportionately low impact on legislation due to her Polishness: she can still affect public life in a number of roles. But a Black can complain about political powerlessness, and he has few roles in which he can participate in public affairs which would override the social status determined by his colour. The point of this comparison, in our context, is not to distinguish between a fair and unfair situation of ethnic or racial determination of status, but merely to acknowledge the objective (hence "neutral") fact of the varying degrees to which group identity determines one's status. These differences are crucial from the point of view of the neutral *Carolene* rationale of protecting politically powerless groups.

These differences will generate a continuum: at the one extreme will be groups more like the Aborigines in Australia (or, to take a religious-groups continuum, more like Jehovah's Witnesses), at the other, groups more like Polish Australians (or Catholics in America). But that the distinction admits degree does not imply that the differences are insignificant or the distinction impossible to make. This is the mystification behind the popular "We are all minorities" argument of the critics of special judicial protection for disadvantaged minorities. The argument, voiced both in the judicial decisions[38] and in the academic writings,[39] disregards the fact that not all minorities are alike from the point of view of the *Carolene* rationale. The enthusiasts of a pluralistic model of politics claim that the political power of minorities is actualized through their entering alliances and coalitions with each other: by forming mutually beneficial pacts various minoritarian groups can amplify their political influence on these issues where their particular interests are affected.[40] But the whole point of *Carolene* is that to some groups this path is not available: for instance because they are too weak economically to effectively play political games, or so unpopular among the electorate that supporting their cause is a liability for politicians rather than an asset, or because widespread social stereotyping makes other groups unwilling to enter into coalitions with them. These are all *objective* indicia of disability related to the past history of legal and social discrimination, to a lower social status of a group, and to objective victimisation by popular ideologies. This "objectivity" of indicia of disabilities needs to be reasserted in the face of the argument that if "neutral" segregation of various groups generates the feeling of inferiority on the part of a weaker one, this is merely because this group "chooses" to put such a construction upon segregation.[41] Reducing publicly caused suffering to individual paranoia is a striking example of what Robert Merton called a "sociological euphemism" - the kind of conceptual apparatus that helps us ignore "social structures which are so organized as to systematically inflict pain, humiliation, suffering, and deep frustration upon particular groups and strata".[42]

Contrary to Justice Rehnquist's belief, discrete and insular minorities (in the *Carolene* sense) are not to be easily found "at every turn of the road",[43] and contrary to Justice Powell's view, in order to trigger the *Carolene* rationale it is not sufficient to note "that one group is disadvantaged by a particular piece of legislation, or action of government".[44] Rather, the group must be disadvantaged by the fact that its access to law-making is particularly limited due to social disadvantages the group suffers *as a group*. To deny the ability of the courts to make such distinctions between groups[45] is tantamount to attributing to the judges a strangely selective myopia: they may be aware of the socially constructed judgments about what contracts are "unconscionable", what degree of care is "due" and what punishments are "cruel and unusual", but they are prohibited from knowing what social groups in their own societies are isolated from mainstream political life by virtue of their social disadvantages.

A general strategy, advocated in this Chapter, is to de-emphasize the subjective (and hence, eminently controversial) factors in the legal treatment of discrimination against minorities, and to focus instead on the objective criteria, related to social characteristics of a group which is the target of disadvantaging laws. More specifically, with reference to the terms used in Footnote Four, it suggests that it is not so much "prejudice" (which is indistinguishable from "principle", unless we make a substantive assessment of the particular external negative preferences in question) but rather the underlying rationale behind the "discrete and insular minorities" characterization which should play a major operative role in judging the discriminatory nature of the law.[46] This rationale derives from the general philosophy behind Footnote Four: that minorities which cannot protect themselves through political corrective mechanisms should be given extra judicial protection, and although neither "discreteness" nor "insularity" need to be taken literally as the indicia of such groups, the reason for focusing on some such objective characteristics (which indicate political powerlessness grounded in more general social disadvantage) is valid and convincing.

But, of course, this is not the whole story about discrimination; politically dominant groups may also be affected by unfair and unequal legal treatment. There may be a disproportionate, unjustified allocation of burdens among various groups which does not answer the criteria of the *Carolene* description. But these are trivial cases, and while they should be corrected, no special distrust of the capacity of the political process to do so is justified which would call for judicial intervention. Twenty years ago, a judge of the US Supreme Court, writing about a referendum system which indirectly adversely affected a black minority, said: "The majority needs no protection against discrimination and if it did, a referendum might be bothersome but no more than that".[47] Interestingly enough, twenty-six years earlier the Chief Justice of the Australian High Court used the same argument, if not the language, when referring to the application of the constitutionally guaranteed freedom of religion to restrictions on the activities of Jehovah's Witnesses: "The religion of the majority of the people can look after itself. Section 116 [of the Constitution of Australia] is required to protect the religion (or absence of religion) of minorities, and, in particular, of unpopular minorities".[48] Though *Carolene* was not mentioned in either of these cases, the insight was precisely the same: the majority may be able to protect itself through political mechanisms, and so may *some* minorities by entering into mutually beneficial coalitions with others, but to other minorities this option may not be available because of their particular social position. The lesson to be drawn from this insight is that special, extra-parliamentarian protection of such minorities is needed. This is perfectly compatible with a liberal conception of neutrality vis-a-vis competing substantive moral judgments about the relative value of external preferences expressed by various groups towards each other in a society.

CHAPTER 6

LIBERAL NEUTRALITY AND THEORY OF PUNISHMENT

Earlier in this book, in Chapter 4, it was suggested that the liberal neutrality position need not (indeed, must not) be neutral between the non-harmful (to others) conceptions of the good and the conceptions which call for an action leading to inflicting harm on others. It was suggested that exclusion of respect for some preferences (harmful for others) is based on the very principle of equal moral agency on which liberal neutrality, and the priority of the right over the good, are founded. Now is the time to explore this idea in more detail.

It is all the more important since, in recent years, there have been a number of interesting and influential theoretical proposals put forward which have as their common denominator an implicit or explicit rejection of anti-perfectionism in thinking about crime and punishment. Whether one believes that the criminal harms himself rather than profits from committing a crime, or whether one believes that the real purpose of punishment is to benefit the convicted criminal, by facilitating his moral regeneration, by helping him to repent and to regain the position of a trusted member of society, the common feature of these suggestions is a rejection of neutral, anti-perfectionist morality which denies that there may be such standards of true interests of a person which are opposed to the observable preferences and options of an individual. In particular, the "perfectionists" reject the "non-perfectionist" idea that the criminal may really benefit from the crime, and that punishment may fail to further one's self-interest.

The distinction between these two positions is well displayed in the discussion of the concept of "moral harm" by Joel Feinberg (though that particular discussion is not conducted by Feinberg in direct connection with the issues of punishment).[1] A Socratic and Platonic tradition in thinking about immorality and wickedness, Feinberg reminds us, consists in equating immorality with moral sickness, and in believing that immorality is really unprofitable to the immoral person. In contrast, Feinberg himself rejects the idea of "moral harm" and suggests: "When a remorselessly wicked person *appears* to be flourishing, and there *appear* to be no reasons to suppose he is not, then I 'assume' that he is indeed profiting from his wickedness, and try to fashion my theory of harm and benefit to save the appearances".[2] The proponents of the moral harm theory reach their (paradoxical to common sense) conclusion about the wicked person really being harmed by his wickedness because they find it intolerable that he should not suffer; in consequence, they fashion their theory "not to 'save' but to explain away the appearances".[3] But Feinberg's view is that it is by no means an obvious truth (indeed, it is contrary to the observable facts) that the wicked must necessarily be in a harmed position.

This is also a general point of departure from which our argument will proceed. And since the recent growth in the popularity of perfectionism in thinking about criminal justice undoubtedly has its roots in the rise of communitarian, anti-liberal theories of justice in general,[4] so our discussion of criminal punishment will be conducted by referring to the concepts moulded by thinking about distributive justice. In short, this Chapter will propose and defend a particular, substantive principle of retributive justice viewed as an application, and an extension, of a broader principle regulating the distribution of benefits and burdens in a society. The origins of this broader principle are mainly in the domain of economic justice, or more generally, in a normative theory of the distribution of material goods as well as economic and educational opportunities.

1. FROM COMPENSATORY JUSTICE TO A THEORY OF PUNISHMENT

Consider this proposition:

> The principle that unpleasant, onerous, and hazardous jobs deserve economic compensation, unlike the claim that superior ability deserves economic reward, is an equalitarian one, for it says only that deprivations for which there is no good reason should be compensated to the point where the deprived one is *again brought back* to a position of equality with his fellows. It is not that compensation gives him more than others (considering everything), but only that it allows him to catch up.[5]

There is probably nothing particularly startling or revealing, much less eccentric, about this statement. It affirms a familiar moral truth about the role of compensatory rewards in situations of higher-than-average burdens. This truth appears often in the literature on economic justice,[6] and no doubt it functions as a broadly shared intuition in conventional moral thinking in a variety of situations — not merely, as in Feinberg's proposition, with regard to material compensation for effort. A similar intuition (that it is the role of compensatory action to restore initial "equality" or "equivalence"), but with regard to making good special injury or handicap, is well captured by Bruce Ackerman who says: "A blind citizen has a right to insist that others make a *greater* sacrifice of their rights in non-genetic domains if overall equivalence is to be achieved".[7]

I hope that at least some readers will recognize these propositions about compensatory justice as being consistent with their own moral views, and that the opinion that the aim of compensation is to create a certain sort of "equality" (or "equivalence") is quite deeply entrenched in our moral thinking. But Feinberg's metaphor about "bringing someone back to a position of equality with his fellows" through compensatory rewards, read literally, is puzzling. For it seems plausible to believe that a beneficiary of the compensation postulated by Feinberg was not in a position of equality with his fellows *before* undertaking a more onerous or hazardous job: the hard social reality of economic inequalities suggests that the very fact that some people do more unpleasant work than others is one of the results of their disadvantaged position with regard to educational and employment opportunities. Hence, they cannot be brought *back* to a position which they did not occupy in the first place.

And yet, the idea implicit in Feinberg's proposition strikes such a familiar and powerful moral chord that it is definitely worth rescuing from the above-mentioned objection. The rescue, I suggest, can only be this: the view that compensatory practices "bring people back to a position of equality with their fellows" is intelligible only if we presuppose a particular, initial pattern of balance of benefits and burdens in society, and look upon deviations as contrary to social justice. This picture removes the grounds of both doubts just mentioned: against the background of this idea the difficulties inherent in the metaphor of "bringing back to a position of equality" can be overcome. In conclusion, if we think that it is *just* to compensate people for some deprivations or burdens (such as those described by Feinberg), and at the same time we feel that this compensation brings about a balance of benefits and burdens, then this balance must be taken as an overarching, coordinating principle of social justice.

Now if we apply this general principle to the practice of punishment, the result will be the vindication of a well known theory of punishment as the restoration of balance by the imposition of extra burdens upon those who have usurped more than their fair share of benefits. But this theory, whose *locus classicus* is an influential article by Herbert Morris,[8] and which has been — with lesser or greater variations — advocated by Jeffrie Murphy, John Finnis, George Sher and others,[9] has not usually been expounded as a *product* of a fully-fledged theory of distributive justice, which may be worked out initially with reference to the distribution of socio-economic goods (as I would propose doing) and only then extrapolated onto the sphere of punishments.

This theory, which justifies the institution of punishment in terms of the ideal of "balance of benefits and burdens", may be succinctly stated as follows.[10] Criminal law is concerned with maintaining the equal distribution of a specific set of benefits among the members of the community: in particular, the benefits of autonomy of action within a sphere which should be beyond interference by others. In a well-ordered society, where criminal law is by and large just (i.e., does not provide for unequal protection of autonomy-rights for some members of the community to the detriment of others), this equality may well coexist with inequality in a number of other dimensions, in particular in the distribution of economic wealth (though, as we will note later, a drastic inequality of economic benefits may produce inequality of the autonomy protected by criminal law). The enjoyment of these benefits by a person is correlated with another person's duty not to interfere with the exercise of recognized rights to autonomy. This is a prerequisite for the effective use of an autonomy-right; it may be enjoyed only if others restrict their activities (or, in very exceptional circumstances, such as in the case of legally imposed duties of rescue, if others do specific things prescribed by the law). Those restraints that are prerequisites for the effective use of the benefits of autonomy can be represented as burdens upon a person's life since they cut off a number of options which would otherwise be available to this person.

Harm inflicted on a victim by an offender constitutes the limitation of the victim's use of his rights. By infringing those rights, the offender intrudes upon the enjoyment of his victim's autonomy and thereby oversteps the bounds of his own range of autonomy in such a way as to limit his victim's autonomy. As a result, the distribution of benefits secured by the criminal law has undergone a change: the legally recognized frontiers between any two persons' spheres of autonomy are moved to the victim's detriment. The *status quo ante* with respect to the initial balance of benefits and burdens is upset since the offender has arrogated to himself part of his victim's sphere of autonomy and he has renounced some of his own burdens: namely, the burdens of self-restraint (which, as we have said, are a prerequisite for other people's enjoyment of equal benefits).

This initial balance can only be restored by a reallocation of burdens. If an offender has renounced some of his fair package of burdens, the balance will be restored when he suffers more burdens than would be normally required to safeguard the enjoyment of rights by other people. Just as with the allocation of benefits under distributive justice, where additional rewards correspond to desert (or to unmet basic needs), so in the case of punishments the burdens inflicted by a society correspond to the degree of illegitimate benefits gained by the offender. It is a *re*distribution after the wrongful distribution (of benefits of autonomy and correlated burdens of self-restraint) has taken place.

2. THE "BALANCE OF BENEFITS AND BURDENS" MODEL REVISITED

Most of the criticisms of the theory outlined above have been aimed at showing that neither law-abiding behaviour, nor criminal action, fit the description in terms of "benefits" and "burdens", i.e., that law abiding conduct is not necessarily burdensome, nor is criminal invasion of other people's rights necessarily beneficial to the offender. I will consider these two types of arguments in turn.

As to the burdensome nature of self-restraint, the usual objection is that it is psychologically untrue with regard to many people, and in any event it cannot be held to be a necessary but is at best a contingent truth, that restraining one's action towards others is a burden in a person's life. As one student of criminal law observed, usually we do not "suffer a burden in abstaining from the core crimes of murder, rape, arson, robbery, and burglary".[11] But to validate the model of "balance of benefits and burdens" no such empirical truth about our alleged dissatisfaction about restraint is necessary. It is sufficient to state that self-restraint (or an externally imposed restraint) is burdensome *as compared to* unlimited freedom of action, by virtue of a purely conceptual calculus that it is always better to have more options from which to choose than less, even though we do not seriously contemplate trying some of these extra options. Even if in principle I do not like bananas, I am better off if I may chose from among bananas, apples and pears, rather than only from among apples and pears. The range of choice in itself is a value: if unrestricted liberty gives me all the options that I have in the situation of self-restraining behaviour *plus* some extra options, then in my private common-sense calculus an agent who can chose from a wider range of options is better off than in a situation of restricted choice.

But is she really? In a well-known essay "Is More Choice Better than Less?" Gerald Dworkin suggests that an affirmative answer to the title question is far from obvious, and that often having fewer choices is preferable to more. If Dworkin is right, one limb of the "balance of benefits and burdens" theory of punishment is badly defective.

I will indicate by way of examples what I believe to be the common defect in all seven cases which, according to Dworkin, display choice-situations in which "more choice is not necessarily to be desired". One preliminary proviso of his discussion of these seven cases is the *ceteris paribus* requirement:

> Suppose, for example, A says to B that if B is offered more options with respect to some matter, A will kill B. Here what makes B shun additional choices has nothing to do with the nature of the choices or the nature of choosing, but rather an arbitrary cost attached to the increase in choices. The presence of this cost is too contingent to count against the choices.[12]

I believe that none of Dworkin's examples which appear to contradict the proposition that "more choice is better than less" satisfies the "other things being equal" clause, or else the costs are too contingent to count against more choices. The first two cases in Dworkin's essay concern various decision costs: costs of information, time, effort and responsibility related to selecting from among a broader range of options. While these costs are real, common sense suggests that, as a rule, they can hardly outweigh the benefits of being able to choose from a broader range of options as compared to a narrower one. For if the extra options are clearly undesirable, the costs of renouncing them are very low (I do not spend much time agonizing whether to buy bananas or apples, if I detest bananas really strongly), while if these extra options offer benefits which I am likely to enjoy, the costs of deciding are likely to be outweighed by the benefits of having this choice. To use Dworkin's own words, the presence of these costs "is too contingent to count against the choices".

A third case, discussed by Dworkin under the heading "Pressure to Conform", is of a different nature. Dworkin suggests that legal denial of certain options may in fact benefit the decision-maker, who in the circumstances of a broader choice is subject to pressure by others to behave in a way which may happen to be contrary to the agent's deep wishes. Discussing the inheritance of wealth, Dworkin says:

> ...the wealth holder herself may be worse off by having the option. She might prefer to spend all her wealth on herself and leave none to her heirs. A law that denies her the option of leaving her money to others frees her from the expectations and pressures of others.[13]

But then, this very law denies the same option to persons who genuinely wish to leave their wealth to others. While superficially it may seem that the person in Dworkin's example is worse off by having an option the by-product of which is to generate pressures upon her by potential inheritors, this effect is produced by the fact that what Dworkin sees as the extra option (i.e. being able to leave one's wealth to others) affects the initial situation in a way which makes the overall position deteriorate. It is not that a person has an option A (not leaving wealth to others) *and* an option B (leaving wealth), but rather, by virtue of a new fact description (a person really does not want to leave wealth; her relatives would exert pressure upon her, etc.) introduced by Dworkin, option A has now additional costs attached to it. So the full description of option A is: not leaving wealth to others while others exert psychological pressure upon you, and you being so sensitive that you are likely to suffer in consequence. But then, the *ceteris paribus* clause is violated: "more choice" means in this situation not *extra* options but *different* options.

This, I suggest, is the case with all of Dworkin's other examples. For instance, the availability of divorce (hence, an extra option as compared to a no-divorce regime) has the effects, Dworkin says, of changing "the expectations brought to the marriage, the ability to tolerate imperfections of the marriage partner, the sense of commitment to the marriage",[14] and as a result, the overall situation of the couple may be worse off as compared to their position in the absence of the possibility of divorces. While the psychological effects of the availability of divorce noted by Dworkin may or may not occur, it is clear that when they do occur (and there is nothing endemic to the availability of divorce that they must occur), the initial situation is not the same as in a no-divorce regime and so the *ceteris paribus* condition is not respected.

Finally, Gerald Dworkin considers cases in which the extra options should be ruled out on moral grounds: for instance, the possibility of purchasing release from a system of conscription is wrongful.[15] Correct, but this is still advantageous to an agent: the notion of "advantage" or "benefit" is independent of the moral worth of the basis of the advantage. This is consistent with the anti-perfectionist position adopted in Chapter 4. Advantages may be immoral and based on egoistic motives — this is the whole point of punishing for arrogation of unfair advantages. But we gain nothing by redescribing them as non-advantageous to the agent.

An attack on the second aspect of the "benefits and burdens" model is aimed at showing that not all crimes bring benefits to the criminals (or that even if they do, this is merely a contingent and not a necessary element of a crime, and so cannot be part of the justifying principle for *all* punishments), and that the gravity of the crime is not a function of the value of the benefits acquired by the criminal. It seems at first that only some crimes bring about tangible benefits to the criminal, the most typical being crimes against property. But then the wrongful redistribution brought about by the thief may be redressed by restitution, which is independent of the punishment proper. Thus it would appear that even in the case of such typically "advantageous" crimes as theft, punishment cannot be depicted as a restoration of the balance of benefits and burdens because the punishment is meted out irrespective of whether or not the fruits of illegal activity are removed from the thief and restored to the victim.[16] This argument seems to be all the more forceful with regard to non-economic offences: while we may identify a range of non-tangible "benefits" derived by the criminal from the act of careless driving, assault, or rape, the punishment is meted out whether or not these benefits actually occurred (i.e., whether or not the offender derived particular satisfaction from his careless driving, from assaulting other people, etc). Moreover, the punishment is not necessarily proportionate to the amount of satisfaction gained by the criminal: an assailant who actually felt a sadistic satisfaction while mugging his victim need not be punished more severely than one who did not. Further, the "benefits" seem to be even less obvious in the case of punishable attempts, criminal conspiracy and other forms of non-complete crimes.

This line of argument rests on a fundamental misunderstanding about the nature of the benefits acquired by the criminal, and about the nature of the values protected by criminal law. The major value protected by the criminal law is the autonomy of citizens within the limits determined by a requirement of a similar autonomy of others. Each person's immunity from interference can be enjoyed only on the condition that other people observe self-restraint. The fundamental benefit which a criminal acquires from violating the rules of criminal law is a benefit of non-self-restraint, that is, a benefit of renouncing the burdens imposed by the criminal law. All other benefits are contingent and incidental: they may or may not occur.[17] The very fact that we can intelligibly distinguish between restitution and punishment provides confirmation that — in our moral intuitions — the act of non-self-restraint is in itself an unfair benefit, over and above other, more tangible benefits.

Once we appreciate the real nature of the benefit produced by a crime, the central core of the argument about the "non-advantageous" crimes collapses. But how about the proportionality argument? It has been argued against the present theory that, for instance, "crimes against property often bring more benefits to their perpetrators than do more serious crimes against persons (crimes including violation of more precious rights)".[18] If this is correct, our theory would have to require more severe punishment for the former crimes, which is seriously counter-intuitive. But this argument again misunderstands the nature of the benefits involved: crimes against property may bring more *economic* benefits to the perpetrator, but these benefits are only contingent to the occurrence of crime. The value of the benefits protected by criminal law, i.e. of immunity from interference by others, is measured by the value a particular sphere of human autonomy has for an agent. Hence, if in the generally accepted hierarchy of values freedom from assault on our life is more precious than freedom from invasions of our property, then the benefit of non-constraint with regard to the former is higher than with regard to the latter. To refer back to the last quotation, the "violation of more precious rights" is, by its very nature, more beneficial to the criminal because the benefits he removes from his victim are more precious to the victim. The relative importance of the sphere of autonomy violated by the offender constitutes a measure of the advantages he derives from his act.

Richard W. Burgh has recently criticized this point by saying that the value of "profit in wrongdoing" should be measured by the strength of the inclination to commit a crime (because "[t]he stronger the inclination, the greater the burden one undertakes in obeying the law"),[19] but since the strength of the inclination to commit a crime is usually not proportionate to the gravity of the crime, the "balance of benefits and burdens" theory results in a counter-intuitive conclusion about the lack of proportionality between the gravity of crime and severity of punishment. A proportionality can be maintained, says Burgh, only if we presuppose that "the strength of the inclination to commit a crime is directly proportional to the gravity of that crime"[20] which, according to Burgh, is more often than not untrue: compare your inclination to avoid taxes with the inclination to commit a murder.

The error in Burgh's argument seems to lie in the identification of the value of non-self-restraint with the actual, psychological tendency to commit some illegal acts rather than others. This tendency is, however, affected not merely by the value of the result, but also by the likelihood of bringing it about, by the degree of risk-aversion, by the troublesomeness of the action leading to the desired result, etc. I am more inclined to apply for a position of Lecturer than for that of Vice-Chancellor at a university, but this does not mean that the former represents a higher value for me. Hence the actual inclination to choose one option rather than the other is not the sole measure of the value of the optimal result of pursuing this option. So, after all, there is no inverse proportionality between the value of the benefit of non-self-restraint (which, in our theory, is a ground and a measure of justified punishment) and the seriousness of the crime.

By the same token, criminal attempts and criminal conspiracy are properly punishable, because the liberty to set about the course of criminal activity amounts to renouncing the burdens necessary to observe other people's autonomy. The benefit of individual autonomy is meaningful only when we know that others will not even *try* to invade it; otherwise, the insecurity inherent in a general licence to attempt invasions upon others would render our autonomy valueless. And, in any event, the offender's benefit in renouncing his self-restraint is already actualized at the stage of undertaking illegal activity, not only when the intended end-result is achieved.

This would leave unanswered the question of why attempts deserve less penalty than completed crimes. Michael Davis, who derives the standards of severity of punishment from an imaginary auction where licences to commit crimes are sold, suggests that a licence to attempt would be worth less than a license to do a complete crime.[21] My own view is that the general principle that attempts necessarily deserve less punishment than the corresponding completed crimes cannot be sustained in justice. That the courts normally award lighter sentences for attempts can be seen (from the standpoint of the theory proposed here) either as a morally defective practice, or as one based on considerations other than those of justice. Interestingly enough, considerations of deterrence do not seem to unambiguously support this tendency, either. The usual explanation, that less harm results from attempts than from complete crimes,[22] is not available in our theory which substitutes the notion of benefits and burdens for the concept of "harm". Significantly, the writers who identify "dangerousness" and the related "culpability", rather than "harmfulness", as the basis of a justified punishment, are reluctant to accept a general principle of lesser punishments for attempts.[23] So perhaps the principle of lesser penalties for attempts represents one of the irrational (or morally indefensible) features of actual criminal justice systems: an expression of a sense of relief by a society that the harm has not been completed, rather than a strict application of justice?

Can our theory be squared with the usual defences and excuses, such as insanity? After all, a case could be made that even an insane person may obtain benefits from the illegal action, and so punishment would then be justified, contrary to our accepted practices. Consider an instance of an insane woman who, by killing her tyrannical husband in an uncontrolled attack, does obtain the benefit of freeing herself (though not deliberately) from her life-long oppression. But if we appreciate again the true nature of legally protected benefits, we see why there is no ground for the restoration of the balance of benefits and burdens through criminal punishment in this case. An insane person does not *act* in a sense which might be regarded as enjoyment of her freedom (to a lesser degree this may apply to provocation — hence a reason for seeing provocation as a mitigating rather than an exculpating factor). The benefits which are normally acquired by an offender are the benefits of unrestrained liberty of action, but this is not a proper description of an act committed by an insane person. There is no broadening of her freedom; in no way are the constraints on her behaviour reduced. For that reason, punishment in such cases is unjustified. Far from being incompatible with the common defences of insanity, the "balance of benefits and burdens" model provides justification for accepting these defences as proper grounds of exculpation.

Similarly, this model of punishment helps explain some standard court practices with respect to other defences and excuses which are generally accepted as just (e.g. self defence, where a potential victim resists an attempt to remove the benefits of his autonomy by a criminal who renounces her share of burdens), and those which are usually not accepted by the courts or criminal codes as exculpating criminal behaviour (e.g. intoxication, where knowingly putting oneself into an uncontrollable state is an exercise of liberty beyond the bounds of tolerance dictated by respect for other persons' liberty). But this is not to say that any single judicial doctrine about excuses and defences can be neatly squared with the balance of benefits and burdens model. For one thing, there is no uniformity among the legal systems of the modern world about many particular exculpating circumstances. More importantly, however, if a theory of justice is to have some controlling and critical function, we must be prepared to use it in order to scrutinize and review actual legal practices: it would be preposterous to suggest that a good normative theory must yield to discordant facts. On the one hand (in accordance with our "reflective equilibrium" strategy), a theory must be embedded in *some* actual social practices; on the other, it must provide a standard for criticizing other ones. The balance between an explanatory and a critical function of a theory is not easy to strike, but we must not be upset whenever a judicial habit or a doctrine fails to "confirm" a normative theory of just punishment.

One such area of inconsistency may be the defence of mistake of law, which is generally not accepted by the modern criminal justice systems. But the principle *ignorantia iuris non excusat* cannot be accepted unconditionally by a proponent of the "balance of benefits and burdens" model. For the benefits acquired by the criminal are real only when she knowingly (or at least negligently) oversteps the bounds of her legally determined freedom. If she is unaware of these bounds, we can only justify punishment by pointing out that she took unfair benefit in not inquiring (while others did) as to the legality of a particular act. Quite apart from the danger of infinite regress immanent in such reasoning (she should have known that she ought to have known... etc), it often dramatically clashes with social realities: some people may genuinely, and through no fault of their own, be unaware of criminal-law-imposed duties. This may be the case concerning persons raised in a foreign culture who had not been exposed to those socializing institutions of their new country which serve to instruct people about the norms underlying the criminal law. Similarly, this may apply to members of close-knit, segregated communities, isolated from the rest of the society, who are unable to absorb the majoritarian values reflected in the criminal law of the land.[24] In these cases, punishment may perhaps be justified on the grounds of deterrence (as an extra incentive for people to make a special effort to acquaint themselves with valid law), but not on the grounds of justice. This conclusion is consistent with H.L.A. Hart's general principle which asserts that criminal liability should be imposed only if the defendant had a fair opportunity to conform his conduct to the law.[25]

3. CRIMINAL JUSTICE AND SOCIAL INEQUALITIES

Perhaps the most serious argument against the theory of punishment proposed here is that it ignores (or, even worse, rationalizes) socio-economic inequalities and the role of law in maintaining and perpetuating these inequalities. If punishment indeed aims at restoring the balance of benefits and burdens, it is argued, it should take into account not only the redistribution of benefits and burdens resulting from the crime, but also the disequilibrium *before* the crime. A criminal is often, *before* committing a crime, in a disadvantaged social position. The crime, in such a situation, may be considered as a restoration of a balance of benefits and burdens. To represent punishment as restoring the equilibrium of benefits and burdens is to seriously believe that in real life such a balance exists; in this way, this theory could be seen as a device of ideological distortion or of the justification of social inequalities. As one critic observed, "punishments are often imposed upon those already unfairly low on the scale of benefits and burdens. To represent them as having unfair advantages over others is ironic at best".[26]

Initially one might say that this argument is based on precisely the same sort of misunderstanding as some of the objections canvassed above: that it identifies the "benefits" with the material privileges rather than with autonomy of unrestrained action, and "burdens" - with material deprivation, rather than with self-restraint. If we see the main aim of criminal law as being to safeguard a particular distribution of *these* particular benefits and burdens, leaving the distribution of socio-economic goods to other instruments of social control, then the point about socio-economic deprivation as undermining the "balance of benefits and burdens" model collapses.

But the matter is more complicated than this and the objection cannot be disposed of so easily. For one thing, a particular criminal justice system may enforce and protect an unequal distribution of the particular benefits which *are* properly at the centre of attention of criminal law, i.e. it may grant more benefits of autonomy to some, and impose more restrictions on the liberty of others. With regard to such a system, an argument that our model fails to justify punishment will be correct, but I do not think this discredits the present model in any way. In accordance with what was said before about the critical role of the substantive moral theory, we must not assume that our model of punishment will explain and justify each and every act of punishment, even under the most unfair legal systems. The point is that the only unfairness which will result in the refusal to justify punishment under this theory, is unfairness in the allocation of the benefits of autonomy and burdens of self-restraint among various groups and individuals in a society. When such unfairness occurs, punishment cannot be seen as restoration of a previous balance, for such a balance did not exist in the first place. An illegal act (condemned as "criminal" by a particular legal system) may well be seen, from the standpoint of our theory, as an act of "doing justice" - of restoring the balance of benefits and burdens. A critical potential of this theory is that, with respect to unjust legal systems (in the particular sense of injustice concerning the allocation of autonomy and self-restraint), justification of punishment is transformed into justification of a violation of law. However, unless we accept the thoughtless maxim *dura lex sed lex*, it is not embarrassing to this theory.

However, real-life legal systems do not neatly fit into one of two categories so that either they observe equal distribution of benefits of autonomy, and then we do not have to worry about socio-economic inequalities, or they do not, and then disobedience is justified. Drastic socio-economic inequalities may pervert formal equality of law because important deprivations may substantially reduce individual autonomy, even when on the face of it criminal-law prohibitions apply equally to all. When, to take an example rich in its symbolic connotations, the United States Supreme Court upheld, in *Clark v. Community for Creative Non-Violence*[27] the Interior Department's ban on sleeping in Lafayette Park in Washington D.C., it echoed the majestic equality of French law that Anatole France described so well so long ago. And a powerful dissent by Justice Marshall in the same decision, pointing out that the Court has been remarkably insensitive to the plight of the poor,[28] strikes a familiar chord in those of us who can discern the idiocy of the idea of "equality" in a law which forbids rich and poor alike to sleep in the park.

This insight may find its way into the current theory of punishment through a re-interpretation of "autonomy". Even if we grant (as this theory assumes) that criminal law is properly concerned with the allocation of the benefits of autonomy only, there is no reason to be blind to the fact that the volume of individual autonomy may be determined not merely by the criminal-law rules, but also by the socio-economic stratification within which a particular criminal law operates. If we have a theory that the socio-economic conditions which are necessary to make use of our freedom affect the degree of freedom we have, and not merely "the value" it has for us (as John Rawls or Neil MacCormick would have it),[29] in other words, if we refuse to draw the distinction between factors which determine the worth of freedom and factors constitutive of freedom itself, then important socio-economic inequalities produce inequalities in the autonomy we enjoy. There is no room here to defend such a theory of freedom,[30] nor to test its applicability to real-life situations of economic inequalities. But it seems plausible that at least some such inequalities may affect — in our moral convictions — the degree of blameworthiness of the criminals who belong to economically deprived social classes. A proposal to consider economic deprivation as one of the mitigating factors can be seen as matching the idea that autonomy is unequal when social goods and inequalities are very unequally distributed.[31]

4. LIBERAL NEUTRALITY AND CRIMINAL PUNISHMENT

The point I made earlier in this Chapter about possible inconsistencies between the practice of actual criminal-law systems and our model of punishment indicates that the critical status of the theory must permit us to postulate a proper range of punishable crimes. This implies that the "benefits" and "burdens" themselves must be defined in a manner independent (to some degree, at least) of the actual catalogues of crimes in particular legal systems. If "benefit" is defined purely in terms of taking the liberty not to obey the positive law, then the normative principle that the role of punishment is to restore the balance of benefits and burdens does not add anything new to the formula that violation of a legal rule calls for punishment. If any violation of a rule becomes immediately a "benefit", then the "balance of benefits and burdens" formula is redundant; we may as well simply state that punishment is justified whenever a rule is broken. But if this formal legalistic principle is unsatisfactory as a substantive principle of punishment, then "benefits" (of non-self-restraint) and "burdens" (of self-restraint) must have a meaning independent of the existing positive law. In other words, they must correspond to the reality of social cooperation in which abstention from interfering with other people's autonomy is an actual prerequisite for enjoying equal autonomy in particular spheres of action.

When seen in this way, the "balance of benefits and burdens" formula acquires its status as a substantive moral principle, related as it is to one from among a number of competing political philosophies. This is a central point of my argument: while the theory of "balance of benefits and burdens" may be inferred from a substantive theory of distributive justice which incorporates a particular principle of compensation, it may be maintained with sense in the realm of punishment only if we at the same time presuppose a particular political philosophy with regard to the value of the equal individual autonomy of persons in society. For violation of the criminal law can be understood as a transgression upon another's autonomy, and punishment as the restoration of a prior balance, only if law aspires to enforce equal autonomy of individuals in the first place.

In this, my conception of punishment differs from Michael Davis' "unfair advantage" principle which "is consistent with any theory of what the criminal law should forbid or allow (provided the criminal law is conceived as part of a relatively just legal system)".[32] Davis explains his position by saying: "This is so because (ordinarily) any law within a relatively just legal system creates a cooperative scheme most departures from which would take unfair advantage".[33] To my mind, however, even within "a relatively just legal system" (which, I presume, is meant to denote law which does not impose unequal punishments as a function of group membership, and where penalties are not disproportionately harsh and cruel), violations of *some* legal rules do not constitute any unfair benefit. For instance, violation of paternalistic laws (such as safety helmet requirements) or moralistic laws (e.g. the prohibition of the sale and use of contraceptives) does not benefit the offender *to the detriment* of someone else. This, generally, applies to all so-called "victimless crimes". To argue that they give an "unfair advantage" to the offenders one has to identify the "advantage" with any violation of a valid rule, so that by definition any offender takes advantage of law-abiding people. But then the whole talk about benefits and burdens is rendered redundant.

So, at this final stage of our analysis, it is inevitable that we introduce a broader picture of the role of the state with regard to individual autonomy if we want to keep our model of punishment coherent. This broader political philosophy must incorporate a certain view of the limits of the exercise of state coercive power: it must view the maintenance of equal, most extensive autonomies of individuals as defining the general principle justifying coercive interference with individuals. In a broad sketch, this liberal-egalitarian theory is consistent with the view about the proper limits of legal coercion as outlined in Chapter 4. It excludes punitive interventions based on paternalistic or moralistic grounds because the metaphor of restoration of balance of benefits and burdens is clearly irrelevant there. The liberal egalitarian theory, based on neutrality toward the competing conceptions of the good, justifies the punitive action of the state only by the need to protect the equal autonomy of all. The sphere of "self-regarding" action (in the language of the "harm principle"), or pursuit of one's conception of the morally good life (in the language of the "priority of the right over the good"), must be beyond the limits of intervention by the criminal law.

Perhaps extra evidence of this connection between the "balance of benefits and burdens" theory of punishment and the liberal theory of state action can be provided — somewhat perversely — by some of the recent criticisms of this particular conception of punishment. In her interesting essay, M. Margaret Falls criticizes what she calls the "reciprocity theory" of punishment (which is identical with the one expounded in this Chapter) by pointing out its incompatibility with a moral tradition which postulates that "in doing evil one harms oneself rather than profits".[34] This tradition, which M. M. Falls endorses, and which she derives from Kantian moral teaching, must undermine the view that it is punishment's aim to re-establish the equilibrium of benefits and burdens, since if "doing evil harms the evildoer" then "the burden of obedience [to law], if accepted, is actually a benefit", hence "there is no profit for punishment to remove".[35]

In turn, John Deigh (in an article published before Falls's paper) shows convincingly the clash between the "balance of benefits and burdens" theory of punishment and the view that punishment benefits the criminal. According to this view, punishment renders a benefit to the criminal by providing him with "the means necessary for his moral regeneration" and "expiation", by "facilitat[ing] reconciliation, a renewal of good relations" and by "reliev[ing] the weight of one's guilt and quiet[ing] one's conscience".[36]

These arguments point at two sides of the same coin: that their theories of punishment are ultimately based on a perfectionist moral theory of law. Falls applies perfectionism to crime, Deigh — to punishment; both end up with conclusions that are at odds with our theory of punishment. It is true that if we rest our political theory on a theory of the good (a conception of the morally good life, a prescription for a good moral character, etc) which a state should enforce over other, competing theories of the good, then the criminal offender, in acting contrary to this conception, harms himself by failing to pursue what is morally good. Short of preventing this self-harm, the only means available to render him moral help is through punishment. If indeed "willing the morally good . . . is the highest human good"[37] then the criminals are simply myopic in not seeing what is really good for them and they should be protected from themselves.

But the liberal theory of the state rejects perfectionism as a theory about the range of state coercive powers; it rejects the idea of an enforceable good independent of the actual preferences expressed by actual people. This does not mean, naturally, that the state has to be neutral as between non-harmful and harmful (in the sense of postulating harm to others) moralities. The usefulness of the "balance of benefits and burdens" theory of punishment is that it explains *at the same time* why it is not permissible to interfere within the individual non-harmful sphere of action (even if there are strong moralistic or paternalistic reasons to do so) *and* also why it is legitimate (indeed, obligatory) to punish transgressions of other people's autonomy. A harm imposed by one agent upon another introduces an important inequality among individuals: it disturbs the initial equality of mutual restraint upon one's own actions which is correlated with equality of individual autonomy of action within limits imposed by the observance of the like autonomy of others.

Once we adopt this normative philosophy of the state with regard to the conceptions of the good, the criticisms by Falls and Deigh collapse. A crime is "a good" to the criminal, for we are prevented in our theory from defining the enforceable conception of the good which would conflict with the agent's expressed preferences, and a punishment is "the bad" as long as the individuals concerned would rather avoid it than submit. Falls' and Deigh's objections are valid only within the perfectionist moral theory — but this is a theory which liberals reject (at least as a prescriptive theory to be enforced by law).

CHAPTER 7

NEUTRALITY OF LAW TOWARDS RELIGION

While the concept of neutrality does not lend itself in an obvious manner to the discussion of judicial protection of minorities and of the theories of criminal punishment — the two areas discussed in Chapters 5 and 6 — it is no doubt very much at home in the area of the relationship between law and religion. One may say that the law-religion relationship is a natural locus of the liberal neutrality. The idea of a secular liberal state, i.e. the state which neither gets involved with matters religious nor inhibits in any way religious expression and activities, has been long understood as best encapsulated by the idea of the state's neutrality toward religion. Indeed, the Supreme Court of the United States has repeatedly declared that the Constitution requires the government to pursue a policy of neutrality regarding religion, and that, in accordance with that constitutional mandate, the Court must "enforce[] a scrupulous neutrality by the State, as among religions, and also between religious and other activities"[1].

"Neutrality is what is required",[2] proclaims Justice Blackmun in the same decision. But what is required by neutrality, is by no means clear and unambiguous. It is an illusion that the answer to this question may be found in a semantic dissection of the word "neutrality", or in seeking help from other areas where the concept of "neutrality" has often been applied, notably in international law. It is not the case that the semantic lack of clarity of the word is the source of disagreement, but rather that this disagreement hinges upon the controversy about the normative weight of various purposes and ideals contained in a cluster of values captured by the liberal ideal. Hence, in order to clarify the concept of "neutrality", and decide about a preferred interpretation with regard to the law-religion relationship, we must first elucidate our vision of the ideals served by the liberal and secular state regarding individual beliefs and organised cults.

1. TWO PRINCIPLES

The relationship between the state and religion in modern secular nations is regulated by two principles: the separation of the state and religion, and the freedom of religion. While, in general, these two principles seem to be coextensive, and the separation of state and religion is often seen as the best guarantee for religious freedom, one can also imagine the fulfilment of one of these two principles being accompanied by denial of the other one. One can imagine, for instance, a perfectly secular state in which religion is purged from public life altogether to the detriment of religious freedom (say, the state refuses to grant permission to build new churches, or to provide fire protection to religious buildings), as well as, on the other hand, a state which secures religious freedom while at the same time officially endorsing and encouraging one particular religion (but without coercive prohibitions against the other religions, or against non-religious beliefs), thus satisfying the principle of religious freedom, but not of the separation of state and religion.

As reflected in legal norms, these two principles correspond to two legal principles: the principle of non-establishment of any religion through law (henceforth referred to as the Non-Establishment Principle or Clause) and the principle of free exercise of any religion (henceforth: the Free Exercise Principle or Clause). These two principles have been entrenched in a number of constitutions and bills of rights, including the Constitution of the United States[3] and the federal Constitution of Australia.[4] Just as with the political principles of separation of the state from religion and of religious freedom, so in the case of legal principles their coextensiveness is largely illusory. It occurs, no doubt, in easy cases, where both the Non-Establishment and the Free Exercise Principle are threatened; say, in the case of coercive imposition of specific religious observance by the state upon its citizens. But as far as modern liberal societies are concerned, these easy cases are highly unlikely to occur and they need not bother us here. With regard to hard cases, the two principles display some tension in their mutual relationship.

At its most general level, this tension is due to the fact that while the Free Exercise Principle calls for some degree of governmental accommodation of religion, the Non-Establishment Principle in contrast calls for suspicion towards any such accommodation, and it detects in them impermissible governmental assistance to religion. This suggests that the conflict between the two principles stems from the fact that the Free Exercise Principle has an expanding dynamic built into it (calling for a positive and active legal attitude towards claims to have one's religious requirements respected through legal accommodation, exemptions and privileges), and this very dynamic threatens to undermine the disengagement of the state from religious matters demanded by the Non-Establishment Principle.

At a more specific level, the tension between the two principles may be illustrated by the current judicial interpretations of both Religion Clauses of the First Amendment in the United States. The valid construction of the Establishment Clause derives from *Everson v. Board of Education*[5] of which the practical outcome was, ironically, to validate a specific form of indirect state aid to religious schools, namely the state-financed transportation scheme available to students of both public and non-public schools. The Court announced in *Everson* a set of separationist prohibitions:

The "establishment of religion" clause of the First Amendment means at least this: Neither a state nor the Federal Government can set up a church. Neither can pass laws which aid one religion, aid all religions, or prefer one religion over another.... No tax in any amount, large or small, can be levied to support any religious activities or institutions, whatever they may be called, or whatever form they may adopt to teach or practice religion.[6]

These famous dicta have an unmistakeably rigourous and absolutist ring to them ("No tax in any amount, large or small..."). On this basis, twenty-four years later, the Supreme Court set a general standard of the Establishment Clause, which seems to forbid any governmental assistance to religion whatsoever. In *Lemon v. Kurtzman*[7] the Court announced that in order to conform with the Clause, government action must: (1) have a secular purpose, (2) have as its primary effect neither the advancement nor the inhibition of religion, and (3) avoid excessive governmental entanglement with religion.[8] While the third tier of the test clearly admits judgments of degree ("excessiveness" of entanglement), and so arguably does the second tier (what effect of a legislation is "primary"?), the first tier is formulated in categorical, yes-or-no terms.

In contrast, the Supreme Court's interpretation of the Free Exercise Clause involves balancing the state's interest in achieving valid governmental aims and the individuals' interests in exercising their religious objectives without state interference. The modern fountainheads of judicial construction of the Free Exercise are *Sherbert v. Verner*[9], a decision in which the Court found unconstitutional the denial of unemployment benefits to a Seventh-Day Adventist after she had been fired for refusing to work on Saturday, and *Wisconsin v. Yoder*[10] where the Court invalidated the imposition of criminal penalties upon Amish parents who refused to send their children to a public high school. In both cases the decision came as the outcome of a weighing and balancing process. But no such weighing is involved in the anti-establishment standard. In consequence, an exemption upheld in applying the Free Exercise balancing test may, even on the face of it, contravene the Non-Establishment Principle if it lacks a "secular purpose" or if it has as its primary effect the "advancement of a religion". The conflict between the two principles can be illustrated by the situation in which an implementation of the Free Exercise claim will offend the Non-Establishment Principle (when for instance, religion-based exemptions may be seen as privileges not available for non-adherents to a particular religion, or for non-believers), and *vice versa*, by the situations in which the Non-Establishment claims may be viewed as denials of the Free Exercise requirements (when, typically, a state refusal to provide aid to religion is seen as inhibiting the exercise of religious freedom).

There are two conceivable strategies for solving the tension between the two principles. One is to postulate the priority of one over the other. Not surprisingly, those who choose to adopt this strategy stipulate the priority of the Free Exercise Principle over the Non-Establishment Principle[11] ("not surprisingly": because on the rhetorical level, the Free Exercise Principle sounds like a more fundamental principle describing an important *aim*, while the Non-Establishment Principle has the air of being "merely" an institutional device about the proper *means*). How unsatisfactory this solution is, is sufficiently indicated by its consequences. If the Free Exercise Principle is to be unconstrained by the Non-Establishment Principle then there is virtually no conceivable limit to official endorsements of religious beliefs and ceremonies. This would create, first of all, an intolerable situation for non-believers. Secondly, this would pose real threats to minoritarian religions and cults. If the Free Exercise claims were to be unconstrained by the Non-Establishment Principle, then the state would have to get embroiled in inquiries into the reasonableness of religious claims for assistance or exemption. Otherwise, any sincere religious claim, however outlandish, would have to be respected and that would quickly lead us to quite absurd consequences which would be unacceptable even to the most ardent proponents of the supremacy of the Free Exercise Principle. But such inquiries into the reasonableness of religious claims would inevitably reflect a majoritarian bias. It is the constraint exerted by the Non-Establishment Principle vis-a-vis the Free Exercise Principle which frees the courts from inquiry into the substantive worth of religious beliefs. Hence, the implausibility of the strategy of priority of the Free Exercise Principle over the Non-Establishment Principle lies in the fact that such a priority would lead to undermining these very values which are to be served by the principle of religious freedom: the values of free choice and pursuit of any religious beliefs (or of rejection of religion) without any governmental inhibition.

A second strategy for reconciling the two principles is by appeal to a higher coordinating value which is supposed to be served by the two principles. By showing that the two principles respond to different types of problems within a unified pattern of values, the second strategy may show that each of these two principles has a proper place in the jurisprudence of religious freedom, and that the conflict may be solved by reflecting upon the best way to promote a more fundamental value.

This Chapter advocates an approach to reconciliation of these two principles along the lines of that second strategy. Our appeal is, consistently with the earlier chapters of Part II of this book, to the ideal of legal neutrality toward competing conceptions of the good, and more particularly, toward religious conceptions of the good (which includes also neutrality as between religious and non-religious conceptions). Anticipating possible objections, it is important to observe that it is *not* a restatement of the political principle of separation of state and religion, nor of its legal equivalence, namely the Non-Establishment Principle. After all, there is nothing in the principle of "neutrality" that necessarily commits one to the strategies of no-aid, or disengagement, or non-entanglement (rather than, respectively, to the strategies of equal aid, equal involvement and impartiality). But, while it is not a reformulation, it may well support a no-aid interpretation of the Non-Establishment Principle as the best means to solve the conflict between the Non-Establishment Principle and the Free Exercise Principle in particular cases. So the anticipated objection of an initial bias toward one of the two principles may at this stage be rejected: the principle of neutrality toward moral (and religious) conceptions of the good seems to resonate equally well with the Non-Establishment Principle (because non-establishment or disengagement is presumptively neutral, though the converse is not necessarily true: there may be also other forms of neutrality than non-involvement), and with the Free Exercise Principle (because equal freedom to pursue one's harmless conception of the good underlies the strategy of neutrality).

2. LEGAL DEFINITION OF RELIGION

The tension between the two principles outlined above is reflected in the controversy about the legal definition of "religion": the Free Exercise Principle favours a definition of religion which is ultimately unacceptable under the Non-Establishment Principle. The natural tendency to apply the principle of neutrality to the free exercise of religion leans toward an expansive concept of "religion", for any limits upon the concept threaten to leave some genuine "religions" (which happen not to match the definer's expectations about what the "religion" is about) outside the category of beliefs deserving protection under the Free Exercise Principle. Any definitional limitation therefore involves the danger of discrimination based on a definitional bias against unknown, or unpopular, religions (precisely those which are in the greatest need of legal protection). But, as we will see, any extension of the concept of "religion" inevitably comes under fire from the Non-Establishment Principle because it undermines the legitimacy of the routine state regulations in the areas previously (i.e. before the definitional extension) held "secular". In an era of expanding social and economic functions of the welfare state, the Non-Establishment Principle must therefore call for the narrowing down of the scope of "the religious".

But even apart from the problems raised by the definition of "religion" under the Non-Establishment Principle (a problem to which we will return later), is there any substantive definition of "religion" which could avoid the dangers of discriminatory bias (under the Free Exercise Principle) and at the same time distinguish meaningfully the religious and non-religious beliefs, codes of conduct, and bodies? The history of the religion clauses jurisprudence of the Supreme Court of the United States and the High Court of Australia warrants a good deal of scepticism about the possibility of an affirmative answer. In their attempts to forge a non-discriminatory concept of "religion", both these courts bravely rejected a number of conventional notions about what constitutes "religion". First, and least controversially perhaps, both these courts rejected the legitimacy of judicial inquiry into the "truth" or "falsity" of beliefs claimed to be religious; in a memorable sentence by Justice Douglas of the United States Supreme Court (cited also by the Australian High Court): "Heresy trials are foreign to our Constitution".[12] Second, both courts rejected confining the concept of "religion" to theistic beliefs only.[13]

But from this point on, the lines of argument about the definition of "religion" in the two court's decisions part company. The United States Supreme Court adopted a consistently subjective-functional approach, in which virtually the only restraint upon the "religiousness" of a given belief is the sincerity with which it is held, and the function it plays, but not its tenets. This test was set forth in two conscientious-objection cases. In *United States v. Seeger*,[14] in interpreting the scope of exemption from military service based on "religious training and belief", the Court extended the exemption upon those who rejected dependence on a Creator for a guide to morality, and concluded that "[a] sincere and meaningful belief which occupies in the life of its possessor a place parallel to that filled by the God of those admittedly qualifying for the exemption comes within the statutory definition."[15] The process was completed by *Welsh v. United States*,[16] a case of a conscientious objector who expressly struck the word "religious" from his application and who claimed to ground his anti-war beliefs on readings in history and sociology. A plurality of the Court nevertheless found him to be religious, and explained the *Seeger*'s test (the person's "own scheme of things") as intended "to indicate that the central consideration in determining whether the registrant's beliefs are religious is whether these beliefs play the role of a religion and function as a religion in the registrant's life".[17] While under *Seeger* "essentially" non-religious views (for example "political, sociological or economic" beliefs) were still denied exemption, under *Welsh* such a possibility became foreclosed and the exclusion of exemption had been confined to considerations of "policy, pragmatism, or expediency", as contrasted with a "moral, ethical or religious principle".[18]

The Australian High Court refused to go as far as that, and explicitly rejected the subjectivist-functional approach: it found that the subjectivist-functional definition (not labelled in this particular way) had an effect of "expand[ing] the concept of religion beyond its true domain".[19] In its place, the Court stipulated in *Church of The New Faith v. The Commissioner for Pay-roll Tax*[20] that the criteria of religion were twofold: (1) belief in a supernatural Being, Thing or Principle, and (2) the acceptance of canons of conduct in order to give effect to that belief.[21]

One can appreciate why the Australian High Court has not gone all the way along its American counterpart's path of rejecting the content-based definitions. In general, the subjectivist-functional definition may be said to suffer from three important defects. First, it seems to be tautological: in order to know whether certain beliefs "play the role of religion", we need to know what the religion is in the first place, but this is precisely what the subjectivist-functionalist test refuses to tell us. Second, any set of beliefs, even those commonly seen as non-religious or anti-religious, may be seen as "playing the role of religion" in a person's own scheme of things, so treating them as "religious" has the effect of diluting the meaningfulness of the word "religion", and cannot account for the privileged status of religion in constitutional texts. If beliefs generally viewed as non-religious obtain protection under constitutionally entrenched rights, why did these constitutions mention "religion" specifically, rather than protecting an individual conscience or individual beliefs in general? Thirdly, the subjectivist-functionalist test, in order to disqualify claims which are not serious but merely a hoax (a danger inherent in a situation where the characterization of a belief as religious is beyond the competence of anyone other than the adherent) must inquire into the sincerity with which given beliefs are held by a person or a group, but sincerity is notoriously difficult to prove or to disprove before a court.

I will argue later that the first two "defects" are really the sources of strength of the subjectivist-functionalist definition, and that they can be justified by the overall pattern of freedom of religion moulded, as it is, by the principle of neutrality. About the third defect, it is perhaps sufficient to say that the inquiry into sincerity of religious beliefs is not qualitatively different from any other judicial scrutiny of the individual state of mind, such as in the examination of criminal *mens rea*, or legislative intent in statutory interpretation. That this cannot be a serious objection against the subjectivist test of religion is perhaps indicated by the fact that even the critics of this definition rarely raise this particular objection. After all, there are a number of methods of measuring the sincerity of a claim for religious exemption: the conformity of this claim with the written or empirically verifiable traditions and proscriptions of the religion or the cult, congruence between the professed religious tenets and one's actions, the willingness to undertake alternative duties and burdens, equally onerous but neutral from the point of view of that religion's proscriptions, etc.

Let us however grant, *arguendo*, that the first two defects mentioned above are real, and that a substantive definition of religion is necessary. From this point of view, the effort of the High Court of Australia seems to deserve some applause: its substantive definition is arguably so general and non-discriminatory that it seems to successfully avoid the perceived danger of so defining religion "as to exclude from its ambit minority religions out of the main streams of religious thought".[22] On closer reflection, however, this becomes less obvious. The key operative word in the Court's substantive definition of religion is "supernatural": in order to be religious, the belief must be in a supernatural Being, Thing, or Principle. What exactly "the supernatural" means for the judges is not absolutely clear. True, a judicial opinion is not a philosophical or a theological treatise. And yet, so much hinges upon the concept of "supernatural" in the *Church of the New Faith*, as *the* test for discriminating between religious and non-religious beliefs, that we must have some degree of clarity about what it means, and how it can be used to avoid the Scylla of too narrow definitions (and hence, biased against minorities) and the Charybdis of too broad (and hence, according to the Court, useless) definitions.

A closer reading of the *Church of the New Faith* suggests that the judges' concept of the "supernatural" encompasses two related philosophical notions: a metaphysical concept of the transcendental order, transcending the bounds of individuals and of the physical world, and an epistemological concept of non-empirical (or extra-empirical) cognition, available to humans by means other than through the mediation of our senses and reason. But then it is not clear how useful the notion of "supernatural" (as the transcendental order and cognition) can be in defining the scope of "religion". For one thing, some modern Protestant theologians have called for the rejection, in the name of authentic Christianity, of the ideas of transcendence and of associated Christian metaphysical statements. John A. T. Robinson, Bishop of Woodwich, gives in his book an explicitly negative answer to a dramatic question: "Must Christianity be 'Supranaturalist'?"[23] and the general thrust of his book is to reject emphatically the notion of a God "out there" and replace it with a view of religion as "ground[ing] all reality ultimately in personal freedom — in Love"[24]. True, this view was criticized by the mainstream Christian writers, but surely the High Court does not want to get embroiled in a theological dispute about the ontological status of God.

The main thesis of one of the leading modern progressive theologians, Paul Tillich, is that the essence of religious phenomena is in the matters of "the ultimate concern" for an individual: the test of "religiousness" lies therefore, for Tillich, not in the substance of a given experience but in the superior ranking that religious experiences have over all other concerns.[25] For this reason, according to Tillich, every person experiences "the presence of the divine" and "the relation to the holy"[26] and "even he who denies God as a matter of ultimate concern affirms God, because he affirms ultimacy in his concern".[27] Clearly, whether or not these "concerns" relate to what the Australian judges would characterize as "supernatural", is of no importance for this theory.

The above remarks suggest that even the superficially innocuous demand that religions appeal to the supernatural may be under-inclusive and may leave some "religions" outside the limits of judicial protection. But, at the same time, it may prove over-inclusive. The idea of the supernatural, if reducible to the twin components of a transcendental reality and a non-empirical cognition, is present in a great number of philosophical and ideological traditions which are not generally viewed as religious, or which are even openly anti-religious. Significantly, some theologians lament that the notion of transcendence has been captured by the agnostic or atheistic ideologies, thus weakening the position of religion. A leading Lutheran theologian in the United States, M. E. Marty, deplores the rise of "unbelief" in the forms of nationalism, Fascism and Communism, which "supplant[] the God of Christian faith" with their own "pantheisms and paganisms of history and power" as new foci of transcendence in a world without God.[28]

Now a possible defence of the High Court's definition against the charge of over-inclusiveness could be that the Court quite deliberately avoided the conventional notions of "religion" and therefore we should not be worried about the inclusion of various traditions of thought and movements which are *not usually thought of* as religious into the judicial definition of religion: the aim is to avoid the majoritarian bias inherent in conventional definitions. Suppose that the Court would be willing to recognize as religious any theory which sincerely contains the ideas of transcendental order and non-empirical cognition. But if the Court were prepared to extend the ambit of its definition as broadly as that, then its superiority over the subjectivist-functional definition would all but vanish. The notion of religion would be very importantly diluted in comparison with conventional notions of religiousness. At the same time, the problems with under-inclusiveness, as pointed out earlier, would remain: religions which do not rely on the notion of the supernatural would remain beyond the ambit of constitutional protection.

At this point one can anticipate the protest that we demand the impossible: a definition which is sufficiently narrow (in order to be meaningful) and at the same time broad enough (in order to avoid the bias against unconventional religions). Surely no single definition can satisfy these two conditions. Some writers conclude from this that the quest for a definition of religion (*any* definition) is misconceived, and that religious systems, as we know them, have nothing in common that distinguishes them from all other belief systems: hence "religion" cannot be defined at all.[29] But if this is the case, how can a court decide in real-life cases, which raise the free exercise or non-establishment challenges, whether a given belief, group or purpose is "religious" or not?

A solution advocated in this Chapter lies in an appeal to the concept of neutrality between substantive conceptions of the moral good, including between moral conceptions. Within this unifying scheme, the Free Exercise Principle and the Non-Establishment Principle have equally important but distinct functions. They both serve the aim of securing an equal moral agency of every individual with respect to religious matters, beliefs and conduct. The principle of neutrality means that no legal burden or privilege can attach to an individual's choice, change and pursuit of religious ideals (nor to the choice of non-religious morality). This is the supreme value of a liberal legal order. In a substantiation of this general ideal, the Free Exercise Principle defines a sphere of individual rights (which must not be affected by one's choice of a religion or of non-religious beliefs) and the Non-Establishment Principle describes the institutional structure within which the state disengages itself from religious bodies and groups in order to secure equal moral agency of its citizens. Neither of the two principles need to prevail over the other because they both serve, in their distinct spheres of application and in their own specific ways, the overall ideal of legal neutrality.

Consider the consequences of these propositions for the definition of religion under the two principles. What matters under the Non-Establishment Principle is the non-interference of the state in the actions of religious bodies and institutions, and making sure that the government-regulated sphere of public life in uncontaminated by religious (or anti-religious) considerations. The principal insight here is that religion must remain a private matter for every individual, and that social life (in this sphere in which it is governmentally regulated) must remain unaffected by religious or anti-religious motivations of the policy-makers and legislators. Consequently, the public decision-makers must know clearly and precisely what is to count as "religion", and how to demarcate the non-religious concerns, in order to screen off the religion-conscious considerations from their decisions. The main evil that the Non-Establishment Principle attacks is a non-neutral merger of secular regulatory concerns and the religious motives.

But the evil identified by the Free Exercise Principle is quite different: this principle seeks to eliminate not institutional favouritism but rather the coercive pressure imposed upon an individual who is in pursuit of his or her moral (including religious) choices. From this point of view, the distinction between a religion (or what is usually considered religion) and *other moral* beliefs is of no importance, because the wrong committed through illegitimate state coercion consists in restricting one's moral choice. While religious choices constitute an important sub-class of moral choices, the boundaries between them and non-religious moral choices are irrelevant because all these moral choices have to be respected by the government, as long as they are harmless. Once we appreciate this, we need find no contradiction in a somewhat bizarre labelling, in *Torcaso*,[30] of "Secular Humanism" as one of the religious beliefs, for the purposes of the Free Exercise Principle, because from the point of view of this principle the boundaries between secularism and religiosity simply do not matter. In contrast, the Non-Establishment Principle deals only indirectly with coercion applied against individuals — its main goal is to eliminate institutional favouritism of the state.

This explains why there is no inconsistency in adopting a broad definition of religion for the purposes of the Free Exercise Principle and a narrow one for the purposes of the Non-Establishment Principle. To test this conception, consider the costs involved in adopting a too broad (or, in contrast, too narrow) definition of religion under either of the principles. Under the Free Exercise Principle, as we have seen, the costs of erring on the side of narrowness are that some religions (which, due to the definitional bias will not be recognized as such) will not receive legal protection which other, more mainstream religions receive. The danger of erring on the side of broadness is rather trivial: it is that some groups will successfully make fraudulent claims for exemptions from burdens. We mentioned that law has at its disposal some means of minimizing such a risk (imposing alternative burdens on persons seeking religious exemptions, etc). On the other hand, under the Non-Establishment Principle, the consequences of adopting an unduly broad conception of religion are that some legitimate government activities will be delegitimized by virtue of their allegedly "religious" character: a very real and grave danger. But what are the consequences of erring on the side of narrowness? It is that some activities will receive governmental support (thanks to an under-inclusive definition of "religion") although in fact they are religious in character. Now consider how unlikely it is that such a situation will occur, for it has to be remembered that only these cases of governmental involvement with religion can be said to result from a narrowness of the definition which can be attributed to the lawmaker's ignorance about a particular body of thought being a religion. But typical cases under the Non-Establishment Clause have a totally different character: the lawmakers well know what beliefs are religious, but they claim that the activity in question has a secular purpose or effect. Typical examples of the state's illegitimate entanglement with religion do not stem from the mistake of perceiving some religions as being non-religions, but from disagreement about whether secular purposes or effects in a given action prevail over the religious ones. The case of illegitimate favouritism attributable to an excessively narrow definition of religion would occur in the unlikely situation that the legislators had not known that the program they run favours a religion of which they happen to be ignorant (or which they mistakenly take to be something other than a religion). By the very nature of such a scenario, the (putatively unfair) benefits in question would have to be conferred upon some small, unknown or unorthodox religious groups, and for this reason the governmental support given (by mistake) to such religions obviously cannot have any significant consequences. The real threat perceived by the Non-

Establishment Principle is that a powerful group will press the policy-makers to support their religion, or that the policy-makers will attempt to favour their own religion, but in these cases it would be nonsensical to attribute such a favouritism to a mistake stemming from too narrow a range of "religions" included in the official definition of the word.

There is therefore no parallelism in the evils targeted by the two principles, and in the costs of over-broad or under-inclusive definitions of "religion" under the two clauses. In consequence, there is nothing unusual about postulating a "bifurcated" definition of religion.[31] Legal definitions are devices which serve the purpose of an as adequate as possible attainment of certain substantive values and ideals which a given legal rule is supposed to protect. They do not describe an objective reality but form a part of the normative language in which the legally protected values are cast. The specific purpose of any given rule is best captured by describing the special problem that the rule is intended to attack: if a refinement of an accepted meaning of a particular word or a phrase will help us tailor the rule better to attack this evil, then this refined meaning should be adopted. Once we decide that the functions of the two principles regulating the state and religion relationship are equally important but operate differently within a uniform scheme of state neutrality, then there is nothing odd or improper in reading the same word differently in the two different clauses.

In the light of these considerations, the stipulation of the meaning of "religion" by the United States Supreme Court in *Seeger* and *Welsh* exhibits a deep wisdom, and the possible objections which we mentioned earlier (about "tautology" and "dilution") lose their validity. Whether the person's beliefs "play the role of religion" and whether they "function as a religion in the [person's] life"[32] is all we need to know before we decide about the presumptive protection of these beliefs against state-imposed burdens (presumptive, because they still have to pass the balancing test). The "circularity" of this definition is illusory, for it is not a definition at all: we do not need to draw the line between religion and non-religion for the purposes of this particular clause. And the objection about "dilution" of the specificity of religion is for the same reason irrelevant: both religious and non-religious beliefs, if held sincerely by an individual as the motivating grounds of his or her actions, call for legal protection in a liberal and secular state.

3. REAL-LIFE CONFLICTS OF FREE EXERCISE AND NON-ESTABLISHMENT

Here is a simple working criterion to distinguish "easy cases" from "hard cases" with respect to the operation of legal principles governing the state/religion relationship. "Easy cases" are those which generate a challenge based upon only one of the two major principles (i.e., the Non-Establishment Principle and Free Exercise Principle) *or* (as is more often the case) where both principles point in the same direction. In contrast, "hard cases" imply the conflicting claims triggered by the two principles.

Consider, as contrasting background, some "easy cases" first. In the flagrant examples of religious oppression and denials of religious freedom, such as when people are terrorized against worshipping, when churches and holy scriptures are destroyed by officially sanctioned actions, when people are discriminated against in their access to public offices, education etc., because of their religious background, there is no apparent conflict between the Non-Establishment Principle and the Free Exercise Principle because both argue against such practices. Denial of the right to freely exercise one's religious beliefs, and the establishment of the official orthodoxy in matters of faith, are two sides of the same coin. Some of these "easy cases" lend themselves better to the argument based on the Non-Establishment Clause (e.g. the imposition of religious tests in selecting candidates for public appointments, where arguably the freedom of non-favoured religions to profess their faith is not restricted), other cases generate more obviously the arguments based on the Free Exercise Principle, but the question of characterisation is not crucial because no conflicting demands issue from the other principle in these cases.

In contrast, "hard cases" give rise to conflicting claims based on the two fundamental principles: of free exercise of religion and of non-establishment. Such "hard cases" most typically (though not necessarily) involve a state practice which is demanded on the basis of the Free Exercise Principle (calling for a religious recognition, support, accommodation, or exemption) but which falls foul of the Non-Establishment Clause. The problem to be resolved then is how to reconcile the duties and limitations of the state under the Establishment Clause and the rights of the individuals under the Free Exercise Clause: untrammelled protection of "free exercise" would naturally lead to the "establishment" of religion. Consider some typical examples of practices generating such conflicting responses from the two principles:

(1) Voluntary school prayer in public (State) schools.

(2) State financial assistance to denominational schools.

(3) The content of school curricula, with regard e.g. to teaching "creationism" on an equal basis with the evolution theory.

(4) Military chaplaincy in the army (and state paid priests in the prisons).

(5) Religion-based exemptions from military service, from compulsory schooling, and from other burdens and duties.

The question of the voluntary, organized prayer in public schools provokes widespread emotions in the United States. An argument of the proponents of organized school prayer has a deceptive air of neutrality: by stressing the voluntary nature of such a practice, these proponents suggest that it is the only way of protecting the religious child's free exercise rights without at the same time infringing on the rights of non-believers. The only "neutral" course of action, they claim, is neither to prohibit nor to order public prayer, but merely to permit it.

The critics usually point out that the voluntary nature of organized prayer in a sensitive school setting is largely illusory; that given children's impressionability and need to conform, the pressure upon the non-religious children would be very strong; that those who would not conform, would stand out from the rest and run a risk of being stigmatized and labelled as outsiders; that, finally, where a teacher leads school prayer, then notwithstanding its formally voluntary character, the practice would be seen by children as a norm, promoted and encouraged by a school, and hence that public schools would get involved in promoting purely devotional activity.

While accepting these arguments as valid and convincing, I would like to raise an issue of neutrality with regard to voluntary school prayer. The argument of the proponents of voluntary school prayer that the prohibition is non-neutral with respect to the religious expression of the believers, must be taken seriously. But to see why this argument has no force in this case, compare voluntary school prayer with another issue from our list of "hard cases": the one of military chaplaincy, funded by the government. The latter seems at first even more problematic, since it requires very substantive funding from the public purse, and a high degree of state involvement (entanglement) with religious bodies and structures, occasioned by governmental monitoring and administration of the military chaplaincy system. And yet the program seems to fare better on a scale of "neutrality" than a cost-free and non-entangling practice of voluntary school prayer.

The reason is this. As already indicated in Chapter 4.2, to describe a practice as neutral, with respect to conflicting moral (and religious) conceptions, we must imagine a baseline of action (or non-action) by a neutral agent (here: the government) which establishes, as it were, a normal situation, by reference to which all departures from the baseline may be judged as non-neutral. Consider a position of an agent N who wants to be neutral between two warring parties: A and B. Imagine further (similarly to Raz's example discussed earlier in Chapter 4.2) that before the conflict broke, the agent N was supplying one of the parties, A, with a resource R which may now be helpful in ending the conflict to the benefit of A. Will N behave neutrally by continuing the supply of R, or by withholding it from A at the moment of the beginning of the conflict?

The answer, I submit, depends on our views about the "normalcy" of the N supplying A with R in a pre-conflict situation. If A, B and N are three neighbouring states, and R is wheat (and it happens, for the sake of argument, that A cannot easily find another supplier), then by terminating its export to B, N weakens A economically, threatens it with starvation of the population and the loss of efficiency of its army. Hence withholding of R would be non-neutral: it would be a departure from the baseline set by our views about "normalcy" in international relations. But if, in contrast, R is an enriched uranium with which A can complete building its own nuclear bomb, then to continue to supply R with it puts the country N in the position of taking sides, while withholding its export would be a more neutral course of action. The reason for this is that we do not consider the export of commodities which are so threatening to international peace and security as something "normal" but rather as something very problematic, calling for some special justification, and operating only between allies, with respect to whom the question of "neutrality" does not arise at all. That is why a possible complaint by A that, by terminating the export of uranium N behaves non-neutrally, cannot have any force because the export was tainted with non-neutrality from the very beginning. It couldn't have established a baseline of normalcy but rather constituted a departure from it.

Now back to voluntary school prayer and military chaplaincy. The baseline in the latter example is established by the usual religious needs of individuals which include, quite typically, attendance at masses in the church, access from time to time to a minister (e.g., for confessional purposes, for advice in personal crisis situations, etc). By removing a person from his or her normal environment, and by putting them in a (more or less) closed institution, the government deprives a person of what are his or her usual religious needs. The consideration of "neutrality" is established by a baseline of normalcy, the departure from which calls for a redressing action by that very government which caused the disturbance in the first place. (Note, incidentally, that the argument in its "pure" version works well with respect to compulsory institutionalization, hence with respect to prison chaplains or military chaplains in a system of compulsory draft. With respect to voluntary military service, the chaplaincy must be defended by a derivative argument, with the extra support of the incentive considerations: the absence of military chaplains in a relatively closed (though voluntary) institution, would be a powerful counter-incentive against joining the army, and thus would work against the nation's needs.)

But an analogous argument cannot be made with respect to state schools: while compulsory schooling disturbs the daily routine of a pre-school period of a child, it would be impossible to argue that there is a baseline of "normal" religious needs which is so disturbed by a schooling duty that a prayer has to be introduced in the school as a redressing measure. School prayer is seen by its proponents not as a substitute for another collective prayer which would occur were if not for the compulsory presence of a child in a public school; it is rather seen as an additional religious activity in a public forum, added to those already existing in private. The forum of a school establishes the value of a collective prayer, in the eyes of the proponents of school prayer. Such prayer would, therefore, be non-neutral between religious and non-religious students, because it would be a move in the direction of religious beliefs and practices, as compared to a baseline of a "normalcy" of religious needs outside the school forum.

This type of reasoning helps also to explain why the neutrality of a "moment of silence" (as opposed to a moment of prayer) in a public school is illusory. It has been argued that such a moment of silence would allow both the non-religious persons to meditate or reflect and the religious ones to pray, and that it merely "provide[s] the opportunity for those inclined to pray to do so" without the school's endorsement of prayer as a favoured practice.[33] Indeed, one might perhaps argue that there is no possibility of creating any feeling of opprobrium on the part of the non-religious, because one could not distinguish between those who pray and those who merely meditate. But, again, this measure does not meet the condition of neutrality as indicated by a baseline of normalcy disturbed (in this case) by compulsory schooling. It is not a normal, usual practice for non-religious people to "meditate" collectively and regularly in public fora, except under most extraordinary circumstances (e.g., when mourning the death of a friend, or of some great public figure). The school "moment of silence" does not therefore restore any initial practice, hindered by school. In contrast, collective and regular praying (in silence or otherwise) is a religious practice. The moment of silence does not resemble to non-religious students any usual ritual of their own life, but it does appear as something very familiar to religious students, evoking an unmistakable analogy with their church services. The moment of silence is, therefore, non-neutral; it is simply an attempt to smuggle in prayer to public schools under a more palatable guise.

Another issue which generates a great deal of controversy is state aid to religiously affiliated schools. The question of whether it is a forbidden "establishment of religion" for the government to provide some assistance to religious schools has been given different answers in Australia and in the United States. In Australia, the High Court announced (by a 6:1 majority) that federal financial assistance to denominational schools did not constitute the "establishment of a religion", and did not contravene the Constitution.[34] In the United States, the argument has been set within a complex scheme of the Establishment Clause analysis established in *Lemon v. Kurtzman*,[35] a decision which invalidated state statutes paying the salaries of teachers in non-public schools or reimbursing such schools for teachers' salaries, textbooks and other instructional materials. Under this scheme, the scrutiny of state aid focuses on three issues: whether it has "a secular legislative purpose", whether its "principal or primary effect" is one that "neither advances nor inhibits religion", and whether it does not foster "an excessive government entanglement with religion".[36]

Consider the postulate of neutrality in the context of state aid to religious schools. The proponents of aid argue that a denial of such aid is non-neutral because it disfavours those parents who send their children to private schools pursuant to their religious duties, as compared to other believing and non-believing parents. The former have to carry a double burden: as taxpayers who contribute to the support of the public school system, and then as parents who pay tuition for their children. For the government to assist them (by tax subsidies directly to them, or by various forms of funding religious schools which would result in a reduction of tuition costs) would simply relieve them of this extra burden, not incurred by those whose religious beliefs do not require sending their children to religiously affiliated schools. State aid to religious schools may therefore be seen as an equalizing measure assisting those parents who are "compelled to support public school services unused by them and to pay for their own children's education",[37] and recognizing in practice that these parents "are rendering the State a service by decreasing the cost of public education and by physically relieving an already overburdened public school system".[38] In the context of the state-parent relationship, state aid may be therefore seen as effectuating a compensation for this "service", or for the costs incurred; in the context of the state-school relationship, state aid amounts to the payment for services provided by a private school, which the state would have to provide anyway.

Does this argument pass the muster of the neutrality test? Consider the following reply by a parent (let us call her "Parent A") who does not send her children to a religious school. "As a tax-payer, I support the funding by the government of a certain number of essential services which are available to all the citizens on a free or on a subsidized basis. Typically, those services are free when they are made compulsory and there is no possibility for the beneficiaries to opt out (e.g., primary education), and those services are subsidized when they are addressed to such important needs of individuals that it would be unfair to supply them at the market price (public transport). These state-funded (or state-subsidized) services provide a basic level of satisfaction of the needs in a given field, according to collective, politically formed judgments in our community about what constitutes such a minimum. Everyone is free to purchase extra services at the market price, but one has no claim for a state subsidy (even in an indirect way, say through tax deductions) because it would amount to taxpayers' supporting extra tastes or unusual requirements of some of the citizens. It would be a non-neutral policy because it would give extra support to some substantive preferences, over and above what others receive.

"Imagine (our hypothetical Parent A could continue) a claim by a private car owner for a special subsidy. Paraphrasing Justice Rehnquist's dissent,[39] he might well say: 'I am not using public transport services, I am helping to reduce the costs of public transport and I am physically relieving an already overburdened public transport: why should I support public transport unused by me *and* pay fully for my own car, fuel etc.? Financial aid granted to me would merely equalize the cost of transport borne by those who travel by private cars.' Obviously, (Parent A would conclude) these claims have no weight because it would be unfair to burden a tax-payer with the cost of subsidizing extra or special tastes. Likewise, it is unfair to make me pay for the special preferences of some parents for the private, religious upbringing of their children".

Now superficially there is a defect in Parent A's reply: the analogy between a private-car owner and the religious parent is not proper because religious beliefs are not like "tastes": they constitute a much more important part of one's spiritual identity, and therefore for the community to attach costs to exercising them is not like attaching costs to private-car use. A private-car user can still (when hard pressed) travel by public bus without any special detriment to his personal integrity, while a parent unable (for financial reasons) to send a child to a religious school is deprived of a very important part of his spiritual identity.

But is this reply really satisfactory? For one thing, remember that we are dealing not so much with the claims of absolute deprivation (that is with a situation where, in the absence of state aid, a parent will not be able to send her children to a religious school at all — let us assume, *arguendo*, that a system of private scholarships will handle such situations) but rather with a claim of fairness, that is when a parent who can afford to send her child to a private school anyway complains about the "non-neutrality" of what she sees as double payment: once as a tax-payer, and second as a parent. The issue of the loss to personal integrity is therefore, in these cases, largely absent.

More importantly, however, one surely cannot accept a general rule that a community has a duty to subsidize "extra" requirements (i.e. above the minimum already provided in a given field) when they are moulded by the consideration of religion. Would an Orthodox Jew have the right to claim a tax subsidy for his regular travel to another city where the nearest kosher butcher is located? Would a Muslim be able to claim for aid towards the costs of flying to Mecca? If not, then it is hard to see any principled basis for a Catholic's claim for the state support of her children's religious schooling, even if these needs are sincerely felt as essential to her religious duties.

Incidentally, one could also question the premise of an argument just considered, namely that religious beliefs and tastes (such as for private transport) are non-analogous. Indeed, why non-analogous? If it is because of the importance of the former as opposed to the relative triviality of the latter, then this judgment in itself is based on the non-neutral assessment of the moral worth of non-harmful preferences: the sort of assessment that a liberal state is prohibited from enforcing. If it is, in turn, on the basis that religious beliefs are much less controllable by a person than consumption tastes, in the sense that one more or less "chooses" ones consumption tastes but not one's religious beliefs, then we face a dual dilemma. For one thing, it is often untrue: there may well be consumption tastes largely independent of one's volition (resulting, say, from socialization process in which a particular lifestyle is considered natural and essential, or from addiction) and, on the other hand, a religious affiliation can be freely chosen by a person (a convert from another cult, or a former non-believer). For another thing, if indeed "immutability" (in the sense of a characteristic being beyond one's conscious control) is what distinguishes religion from consumption tastes, then religious requirements become analogous to an affliction or a handicap. The community's duty to help meet one's religious needs acquires then a status similar to the community's duty to satisfy a handicapped person's special needs. Quite apart from the anticipated protest by religious people against such an analogy, the problem with it is that in the case of special needs there are always at least two morally justified courses of action: to satisfy them or (even better) to eliminate their source. But surely it would be non-neutral for the state to try to eliminate those religious beliefs which give rise to special schooling needs.

The analogy between religious parents and the private-car owners is therefore vindicated. As long as there is a minimum service provided by the state, those who wish to acquire something extra cannot complain about the unfairness of the system in which they have to contribute to the support of the basic level. In a landmark case about state funding of school transportation (which would benefit the religious schools' children), Justice Rutledge in his dissent made this reply to a charge that "failure to provide it [bus transportation] would make the state unneutral in religious matters, discriminating against or hampering such children [i.e., parochial school children] concerning public benefits all others receive":[40] "Of course discrimination in the legal sense does not exist. The child attending the religious school has the same right as any other to attend the public school".[41] The neutrality of the state in matters of religion (just as in matters of special consumption tastes) requires abstention from the recognition of special preferences and requirements which admit claims to subsidies at the taxpayer's expense, as long as a minimum level of satisfaction of given needs is met.

But *is* it really met in our examples? Consider the claim of a religious parent that her choice between the public (secular) and a private, religiously-affiliated school for her children is not a matter of choosing between a school providing an educational minimum and, on the other hand, a school which provides that minimum plus something extra (namely, a religious content) but rather it is a choice between a totally inappropriate inculcation of secularity (which she rejects, for religious reasons) and an environment inculcating in her children proper religious and moral beliefs. In this case, a public school is not a proper baseline of comparison (by relation to which we may decide about what tastes and preferences are "extra") but rather it is one of two conflicting substantive moral options between which the state must be neutral.

In replying to this argument, Parent A must appeal to a factual demonstration that public schools do not inculcate anti-religious beliefs but are neutral on the questions of faith. If such an argument cannot be made, then religious parents have a point. But if it has a firm empirical basis, and the state in question does not promote atheism through its public schools, then these public schools are religion-neutral. In this situation, the policy of neutrality itself cannot be neutral between a neutral and a non-neutral option: public schools and private religious schools are not two options to be compared for the purpose of the neutrality analysis, but rather the former constitute a baseline, the departure from which is non-neutral and therefore should not be subsidized by the state.

The question is, of course, whether it is at all conceivable that non-religious schools can be neutral on matters of faith, even if they do not actively propagate atheism. Can one be religiously neutral when one, for instance, teaches evolutionism and ignores, or dismisses, creationism? This leads us to our next area of "hard cases". The question of the content of the curriculum, in particular as far as the scientific explanation of the origin of the human race is concerned, has been in a number of countries, including the United States and Australia, an object of political controversy raised mainly by those fundamentalist Christian groups which are offended by the perceived growing secularization of public education. Having, in the past, lost battles to relegate Darwinism from public schools, or to explicitly favour the creationist view of evolution, the current line of the attack is to say that secular education is non-neutral because it promotes anti-religious views of evolution and does not accord proper attention to alternative hypotheses.[42] The consequent demand is either to expurgate public teaching of all these themes which contradict particular religious teachings, or to introduce religious precepts and interpretations (in particular, so-called "creation science") into the curriculum along with Darwinian evolutionism.

While the former option is clearly impracticable (to eliminate all these themes which are not in line with any particular faith's precept would leave virtually nothing left to teach, considering the variety of religious creeds and beliefs), the latter solution has some initial air of "neutrality". Indeed, some writers (not necessarily the fundamentalists themselves) criticise the current doctrine of the Supreme Court (which rejects the constitutionality of the "balanced treatment" or "equal time" statutes) from the standpoint of neutrality.[43]

To see why legislative attempts to limit the exclusive teaching of evolution as the explanation of human origins, and to require that equal time be devoted to creation-based accounts, are non-neutral, it is important to understand the nature of the fundamentalist challenge. The mystification involved in this challenge is to present those values, norms and interpretations which are at variance with certain religious precepts as "anti-religious". There is a double confusion here: first, the teachings which are inconsistent with the precepts of *some* religions may be acceptable to the adherents of other faiths (hence any accommodation of teaching in public schools to the sensitivities of adherents to one religion would favour this particular religion over the others); second, not everything that is non-religious is *eo ipso* anti-religious. Interpretations of human origins which fall foul of some religious precepts do not themselves express hostility toward religion, nor do they necessarily advocate atheism, though they may form a basis upon which a student might wish to reconsider her or his religious commitments and choices. But these reconsiderations need not lead to a rejection of one's religious affiliation (for one may wish to draw a line between matters of faith and matters of knowledge); much less to a rejection of religion as such.

In a recent article, critical of the liberal neutrality approach to school curricula, S.L. Carter asks: "[W]hy is it that contemporary liberalism, which proclaims the freedom of individual conscience, values conscience less when an individual chooses to discover the world through faith rather than through reason? What is it about religious belief that liberalism so fears?"[44] The answer is, I suppose, that liberalism cannot, without running into hopeless contradiction, allow itself to be neutral between neutral accounts (motivated by non-religious considerations, even if in conflict with *some* precepts of *some* religions) and those articles of faith which themselves implicate a rejection of neutrality as the main part of a liberal vision of political values. The fundamentalist challenge to secular education is grounded in a cluster of values which reject respect for value pluralism, toleration for diverse moral views, open attitude to the potentialities of human reason, and the equal moral agency of all individuals, regardless of their substantive moral conceptions. These values underlie the constitutional order of a liberal state; their rejection cannot be mandated by liberal neutrality. It does not follow that "religious faith" as such is dangerous for a liberal order, but rather that it can coexist with a liberal order when kept in a private dimension of social interaction. If given political support through state and law, it threatens those very values upon which liberal neutrality (including the toleration for diverse religious beliefs themselves) is erected.

It is therefore unnecessary, for this debate, to enter into a controversy about whether "creationism" is as "scientific" as Darwinism, or whether it is scientific at all. The critics of the present position of the Supreme Court have a point when they argue that the Court has no constitutional mandate to protect "science" against "non-scientific" approaches.[45] But, more importantly, the effect of bringing creationism into the classroom (and I have in mind here "teaching creationism", rather than "teaching *about* creationism) would be to introduce an account based ultimately on an article of faith, forming an integral part of a sectarian cluster of values, exclusionary of other beliefs (both religious and non-religious) and contrary to the very values which are served by liberal neutrality.

The problem of religion-based exemptions from various duties and burdens raises a different set of *legal* problems, as the exemptions are always claimed under the Free Exercise Clause, and therefore raise the difficult question of comparing the importance of the objector's dilemma with the importance of state regulation, as applied uniformly to all. The comparison, according to the current American doctrine, should be measured on the scale of strict scrutiny, which calls for showing that the state interest is "compelling" and that the regulation uses the least restrictive means available — hence a scrutiny which immediately puts a claimant in a privileged position. In contrast to the Establishment Clause analysis, the test under which the Free Exercise claims are measured is therefore rather unfavourable to the injunction of neutrality.

But, this legal technicality notwithstanding, the question of neutrality arises very clearly with respect to religion-based exemptions. There is no basis, in an ideology of a liberal and secular state, to draw the line between the religiously motivated and other deep moral beliefs, with respect to bearing common burdens and fulfilling societal duties. It does not follow that conscientious objection must necessarily be disallowed, but rather that it should be measured by the sincerity and intensity of moral reluctance to engage in a certain activity, and not by whether this reluctance has religious rather than secular grounds.[46] The fact that an objector derives his or her moral complaint from participation in an organized and recognized religion may be one of the indicia of judging the sincerity of the claim, but it must not be conclusive evidence nor a prerequisite for recognizing it as valid.

Very significantly, this consequence has been achieved, *sans le dire*, by the United States Supreme Court with respect to military service. This result (on which religious and secular objections have been virtually put on a par) has been reached by a broadening of the definition of "religion", as mentioned in Part 2 of this Chapter. Recall that in *United States v. Seeger* a *religious* conscientious objection (restricted by the law to those conscientiously opposed to participation in war "by reason of religious training and belief") has been recognized in a person who admitted that he did not believe in God but whose sincere and meaningful beliefs, according to the Court, "occupie[d] a place ... parallel to that filled by the orthodox belief God...".[47] Subsequently, in *Welsh v. United States* the exemption has been expanded upon all "deeply held moral, ethical, *or* religious beliefs",[48] as opposed to consideration of mere "policy, pragmatism, or expediency". Thus, for all practical purposes, the religious/secular distinction ceased to be operative.

This extension of the coverage provided by religious exemptions to non-religious military objectors is very significant from the point of view of the problem of religious exemptions in general. It suggests how anachronistic the distinction remains in a secular society where the state wants to be neutral between religion and non-religion. The Court, while feeling bound to pay lip service to the constitutional mandate (which, after all, puts "religion" in a preferred position vis-a-vis other forms of conscience), at the same time avoids discrimination against non-religious moralities by extending the concept of "religion".

Interestingly, it does not always happen this way. In another case of conscientious objection, decided shortly after *Seeger* and *Welsh*, the Supreme Court quite explicitly confined the Free Exercise protection to religious beliefs, as distinct from other, secular, beliefs. In *Wisconsin v. Yoder*[49] the Court went to some length to stress that exemption from compulsory school attendance would not be accorded to anyone for "purely secular considerations".[50] In what seems like a clear departure from the expansive, functional concept of religion under *Seeger* and *Welsh*, the Court said:

> [T]o have the protection of the Religion Clauses, the claims must be rooted in religious belief. ... Thus, if the Amish asserted their claims [for exemptions] because of their subjective evaluation and rejection of contemporary secular values accepted by the majority, ... their claims would not rest on a religious basis. ... [S]uch belief [which is based on "philosophical and personal rather than religious" choice] does not rise to the demands of the Religion Clauses.[51]

How can this strange inconsistency between *Seeger* and *Welsh* on the one hand and *Yoder* on the other be explained? The only explanation which seems plausible is that the nature of moral duties, from which the Court grants exemptions to objectors in these cases, is so different that it justifies application of different standards of judicial scrutiny. In *Seeger* and *Welsh* the subject matter is military service: a duty which imposes a very significant burden on the moral objector's conscience, whatever its nature (religious or otherwise) might be. This is amplified by the fact that the war in question was largely unpopular in the United States, and that it was not a defensive war fought on the territory of one's own country. Due to the problematic character of this political and moral duty, the Court applied a very relaxed scrutiny of the objector's claims, resulting in an expanded category of "religious" objection. But in *Yoder* the situation was different for a number of reasons. First, the duty in question (i.e., the duty to send one's children to school until a certain age) is largely unproblematic, or in any event, it is not as dramatic as the duty of military service. Compulsory schooling is widely seen not as a burden and a restriction of one's liberty, but rather as an essential prerequisite of one's conscious citizenship. Second, the Amish protested not on their own behalf but on behalf of their children. It is always much more suspect when one wants to avoid public benefits (and elementary schooling, while a duty, is also a benefit) on conscientious grounds for someone else. There must be some limits to the parental values-imposition upon their children, and the court should be concerned about the danger of parental oppression, or of parental bigotry, producing disadvantageous results to the children, and masquerading under the guise of parental rights. While the *Yoder* Court upheld parents' rights to shape their children's religious beliefs and to control their education, we may speculate that by virtue of the reasons just given, the Court's scrutiny was much more stringent, resulting in a narrow definition of "religion" for the purposes of Free Exercise claims. And while one may disagree with the substantive result, one can see that what really distinguished *Yoder* from *Welsh* was not the different nature of "religiousness" in both cases but the different weight of the moral claim for exemption. But if this is the case, then it confirms our general suggestion that the Free Exercise exemptions should be considered on general moral grounds irrespective of their religious or secular character) and that it is only the stringency of the moral weight of objections which should solely determine the level of judicial scrutiny of an exemption.

There is yet another important lesson to be learnt from *Yoder*, as confronted with military duty objections. If we agree that the objectors' case in *Yoder* is relatively weak (for reasons given above), then the Court's surprising (because inconsistent with *Seeger* and *Welsh*) insistence on the duty to show a *par excellence* religious character of an objection may be explained by an attempt to limit the reach of the exemption about which the Court feels uneasy. At the same time, this confinement of the exemption to religious objections does very little damage here, in terms of possible discrimination against other beliefs, because it is based on very idiosyncratic beliefs of a minoritarian, fringe group. There is a very low likelihood that a number of members of other groups (religious or otherwise) will attempt to release their children from compulsory school attendance. Here we reach a justification for a heightened judicial scrutiny of minorities discussed earlier in Chapter 5: while it is reasonable to expect that mainstream religious groups will be protected, in their Free Exercise rights, through ordinary legislation, groups such as the Amish may fear that their beliefs will be disregarded due to the legislators' prejudice, hostility or ignorance. In conclusion, the indicium of "religion" should still remain operative in the interpretation of the Free Exercise of Religion principle, but only when it is justified by the need to assure (through a judicial process) that the members of small, idiosyncratic minorities will be treated equally with those adherents to mainstream religions who can rely on the political process. Beyond this rationale, however, a differential protection of "religious" and "secular" beliefs is non-neutral, and disadvantageous to the latter.

4. THE IMPORTANCE OF NEUTRALITY

While the policy of neutrality between different religions is probably compatible with the strategy of accommodating religious beliefs in the law, through the policy of non-preferential aid (though there is a latent danger of bias in favour of mainstream, orthodox religions), it is impossible to preserve neutrality between religious and non-religious beliefs while accommodating religions' claims for special protection and recognition. Our survey has suggested that only strict separation of law and religion, and non-recognition of religious classifications as relevant to legally imposed burdens and benefits, may guarantee neutrality between religious and non-religious beliefs, and between religions themselves. It is inherently non-neutral to provide a higher level of protection to religious beliefs than to deeply held and ethically argued secular moral views, in granting exemptions from shared burdens and duties in a society. It is also non-neutral to fund, subsidize and otherwise support religious bodies, including religiously affiliated schools, thus advancing the position of a particular religious denomination. It is only in these unusual circumstances when the state itself deprives a person of the normal, free exercise of her religion (as is the case of such closed institutions as the army or prisons), that the state has a duty to provide her with the opportunities and resources necessary to restore a situation which would have existed without the deprivation.

The strategy of strict separation is, of course, easier to argue for under the Non-Establishment Clause than under the Free Exercise Clause. But if one rejects a principle of separation, then one runs into the problems of inevitable discrimination and favouritism in awarding privileges granted under the Free

Exercise Clause. The way out of this riddle: interpreting even "Secular Humanism" as a religion and then treating it on a par with other religions[52] may be the most palatable solution under a constitutional regime which reserves a special place for the free exercise of *religion*, and yet it indicates the inherent dangers of the rejection of strict separationism. The unattractive dilemma: either favour religions to the detriment of non-religious beliefs, or interpret genuinely secular beliefs as "religious", can be avoided by adopting the policy of strict neutrality: no aid and no disadvantage is to be triggered by a description of a certain belief or activity as "religious".

A usual reaction of the critics of "strict separation" is that it leads to "hostility to religion".[53] This is a sweeping charge. By refusing to recognize religious claims to special treatment, the law is no more "hostile" to religions than it is to anti-religious "atheism" when it refuses to endorse officially atheistic positions. The policy of secularism is critical of allowing a favoured role of religion in the public forum which may be used by religion to impose sectarian religious views upon other cults, or upon the non-religious people. But secularism is not hostile to religious beliefs and observances as the *private* matters of individuals; indeed, it is motivated by a liberal desire to leave private the lives of individuals beyond the scope of governmental regulation.

Contrary to the claims of critics, such a confinement of religion to the private sphere does not inhibit religious exercise. They point out, for instance, that absolute neutrality is impossible, and that often neutrality must be, to use an ironic formula, against or in favour of religion.[54] Discussing the controversy about the "release time" for religious teaching in public schools, one writer claims that any solution would inevitably be non-neutral: to dismiss some students (the religious ones) earlier would be for the school to encourage religious instruction, but, on the other hand, "religious instruction will be discouraged by government to the extent that religious students must wait until after regular school hours to attend religious instruction".[55] It is hard to see why the latter option is seen as "non-neutral", and as hostile to religious instruction. The fact that students who want to attend out-of-school foreign language classes are not released earlier but have to wait until after regular school hours is not a discouragement of language courses — as long as there is reasonable time left after the classes. That such a nonpreferential school policy triggers the accusations of hostility, suggests that the critics of neutrality see "hostility" as departures from the baseline of traditional practices, in which religion had a favoured place in public life, rather than from the baseline of a neutral attitude.

It has sometimes been argued that "neutrality" in general (i.e. not specifically with respect to state-religion relations) may be understood in at least two ways: as requiring non-intervention (or non-involvement) or impartiality (or equal promotion of conflicting interests).[56] In other words, the party who wants to be neutral between two competing parties must either disengage itself from the conflict altogether, or try to affect the interests of the parties to an equal degree. (As applied to the area of state-religion relationship, these two conceptions yield the strategies of strict separation and of equal accommodation, respectively.) In abstract terms, both conceptions can be supported by *prima facie* convincing arguments, though initially the former seems to be theoretically more attractive. Consider Leszek Kolakowski's argument against the "equal promotion"-type definition of neutrality by Alan Montefiore. Montefiore defines neutrality as "do[ing] one's best to help or hinder the various parties concerned in an equal degree".[57] Kolakowski responds that this produces the bizarre consequence of describing as "neutral" a certain state which sells arms to both of two states at war with each other, for example because it is interested in the prolongation of the war and in weakening both parties. For himself, Kolakowski suggests that neutrality in a particular situation of conflict means a purposeful behaviour in such a way as not to influence its outcome.[58] Nevertheless, there seems to be a good linguistic case for understanding impartiality (including impartial promotion of two competing interests) as *a* possible interpretation of neutrality, especially when we do our best to promote all the conflicting parties equally, and try not to influence the conflict between them, but merely elevate the conflict, so to say, to a higher level. However, when we move to a more specific area of the state-religion relationship, and translate the two interpretations of neutrality into the "no aid" versus "equal aid" controversy, the plausibility of the latter conception of neutrality disappears. One *can* apply the equal-promotion theory of neutrality to the impartiality of the state between different religions (trying to accommodate their demands to an equal degree), but it is not possible for the state to equally promote religious and non-religious interests.

In the area of free exercise interpretation, to equally protect religious and non-religious conscientious objections to military service, for example, would in practice mean that the religiousness of the claim has to be ignored — otherwise the impartiality between religion and non-religion is lost. In the area of non-establishment interpretation, to equally promote religious and non-religious interests would mean that whenever a non-religious benefit is conferred, a similar religion-based benefit must be granted. But what is a comparable non-religious unit which may be analogized, say, with religiously affiliated schools? If we answer that it is the secular schooling, then we end up with a claim that whenever a secular benefit is given, an analogous religious benefit must be conferred. This is incoherent, for there is an infinite number of legitimate state actions and services which are secular but not anti-religious: protection of health, protection of environment, public transport etc. A proper unit with which to compare religious beliefs and interests, for the purposes of the Non-Establishment Principle, is not "non-religion" but anti-religion. The state has to be neutral between religion and atheism: it must not establish either as an officially endorsed ideology, nor support either ideology with public means. But it would be absurd to claim that "non-religion", i.e. activities and beliefs irrelevant from the point of view of religious beliefs (and from the point of view of the religion-agnosticism-atheism disputes) must be treated the same as religion. To see the absurdity of this proposition consider a practical implication: under this ideal, when the government supports the opera (an arguably non-religious cultural effort) it would have immediately to support, say, a church as well, in order to give to religion what it has already given to "non-religion". But the comparison is mistaken: you cannot, without running into absurdity, be neutral between *x* and everything that is non-*x*, including those things which are totally irrelevant from the point of view of *x*. In practical terms, it means that the "equal aid" for religion and non-religion is not a viable interpretation of the ideal of neutrality. So the only plausible interpretation of neutrality is along the non-interventionist lines: the state has to remain aloof from religious activities (just as it should not get involved in *anti*-religious, as contrasted to non-religious, activities and beliefs). Only by fully disentangling itself from all religion-related functions, can the law maintain its position of complete neutrality.

POSTSCRIPT

It has been the argument of this book that the concept of neutrality of the law towards competing moral conceptions provides the best account of widely felt liberal intuitions about legally protected liberties, and that it forms a comprehensive framework for a liberal model of law. One of the attractions of the image of neutrality is that it already has a well established place in some areas of law. Perhaps international law, with its well developed doctrine of neutrality, comes to one's mind most naturally, but here one must be careful to note obvious differences with the municipal law's attitude toward the individual beliefs of its citizens. For one thing, the general situation in which neutrality occurs in international law is quite different from municipal law: in international law, a party who wishes to remain neutral towards the conflict has no authority or power over the parties to the conflict, while the most significant feature of the liberal-neutrality image is that neutrality is postulated for the agent who both claims authority and has the power of coercion over the competing parties. Second, and more importantly, the justifying reasons for adopting the stance of neutrality are quite different in both cases: in international law, the doctrine of neutrality serves mainly the aim of conflict-management and conflict-reduction, as well as the protection of the interests of parties who want to remain neutral; in municipal law, the main reason for postulating the attitude of neutrality is to safeguard the liberty and self-determination of competing parties, while the interest of the "neutral" party is not a significant factor.

But there are other areas of law where the concept of neutrality lends itself better to analogy with the comprehensive conception of liberal neutrality as postulated here; e.g. the idea of "content neutrality" in laws regulating limits of free expression, and — most significantly — the idea of the law's neutrality toward religion (explored in detail in Chapter 7). This last doctrine is of immediate relevance to our interests, because it is generated by the same problem to which the general idea of neutrality responds: how should the law react to the diverse (and often conflicting) individual beliefs and values of its citizens? A general conception of liberal neutrality can be seen as an extrapolation of the more specific doctrine of state neutrality toward religion.

Is the doctrine of neutrality neutral itself? Earlier, in Chapter 4, we considered an objection by some writers to the liberal conception of "equality of concern and respect" that it does not equally support all moral conceptions of the good, and in particular that it is biased against those conceptions which, in order to be meaningfully implemented, call for enforcement of individual preferences about how other people should behave (e.g. moralistic or paternalistic preferences). In a slightly different context, in Chapter 7 we considered arguments by those who complain about the bias of the "neutrality of state toward religion" conception against those whose pursuit of religious ideals requires active support, and public endorsement, by the state. In all these cases we found the objections unfounded, and now we can generalize the reasons for this response. The doctrine of neutrality is non-neutral itself in the sense that it is adopted for a substantive moral reason: call this the value of tolerance, or of respect for diverse moral beliefs, or (most appropriately perhaps) the value of individual self-determination about the sort of life one wishes to pursue. The main point of Chapter 4 was to indicate that the ideas of neutrality and of "equal moral agency" provide the best account of a set of moral intuitions related to the Harm Principle — an arguably substantive moral ground. It would therefore defeat this substantive purpose of adopting the concept of neutrality in the first place if we tried to search for a "neutral" accommodation of those interests which respect these underlying moral values and those which call for an imposition of some sectarian moral or religious beliefs upon others. While some degree of compromise may be compatible with the idea of neutrality (as we argued in the context of the legal regulation of visually "offensive" images), nevertheless respect for non-harmful preferences concerning one's own life establishes an absolute limit upon the terrain of such compromise. In a word, the concept of neutrality does not have to strike a balance between those ideals which respect its underlying moral grounds (of respect for self-determination, etc) and those which reject these moral grounds, because that would undermine the reasons for adopting the principle of neutrality in the first place. It would be self-defeating to claim that neutrality (or rather the cluster of values which underlies the image of neutrality) has to compete on a neutral basis with non-neutral clusters of values for legislators' support.

The question may arise, therefore, about the benefit of adopting the image of neutrality if it is derivative of some other, more fundamental values? Would it not be simpler to appeal to these values directly? In particular, does it add anything new to what we can already say by stating the harm principle? True, the Harm Principle has its serious equivocations and ambiguities, as a number of writers have been quick to note, but then neither is the principle of neutrality free of equivocations (as suggested by our discussions of "baselines" of neutrality, appealing as they do to substantive moral conceptions of a "normal" or "natural" state of affairs, departures from which are to be counted as non-neutral).

My hope in writing Part II of this book was to suggest that the concept of neutrality indeed adds extra bite to the harm principle. Here I wish to mention two additional reasons for the attractiveness of the conception of liberal "neutrality". The first has to do with the issue of law's legitimacy. The question concerning the grounds of citizens' obligations to obey the law belongs to the one of the traditionally perplexing issues in the philosophy of law area. Common justifications for such a duty appeal to the citizens' consent (explicit or tacit), or to the fairness of complying with generally observed rules, or to the positive consequences of compliance. All these justifications, however, insufficiently focus on what seems to be crucial in actual moral intuitions about the duties of obedience, namely in the substance of the law itself: whether it is seen by a citizen to properly take into account her interests and preferences or not. More recently, a theory has been proposed which postulates that a good faith effort by the rulers, in conjunction with the fact that the enterprise of law in general is better than no law at all, constitutes a sufficient basis for grounding the obligation to obey.[1] Both parts of this proposition are controversial, as far as I am concerned: neither the mere good intentions of rulers seem to me to sufficiently justify the duty to obey the rulers, nor the status of the value of "some law", compared to the alternative of none at all, is clear. But there is a message in this theory which points in the right direction: that the motives of legislators (and also how well these motives are embodied in actual laws) are not irrelevant to the bases of the duty to obey.

It seems that the public perception of authorities as being neutral towards competing factions which they govern may be seen as a sufficient basis for the authorities' legitimacy, and for the factions' duty to obey. This, I suggest, happens in practice in areas such as sport. If we perceive an umpire as strictly neutral, we do not need to worry about whether he had been properly appointed by the relevant sporting bodies, or whether his authority has been properly recognized by the players before the game began, etc. Even if, *ex post*, we realized that some of these latter grounds of his authority are missing, and even if we realized that he was an impostor, if we are fully convinced of his neutrality, we may still be prepared to recognize his rulings. This, I believe, is an important part of our perception of public authorities as legitimate in a morally diverse society. Their neutrality, even if not conclusive in deciding about their legitimacy, goes a long way toward supporting the duty to comply with the laws they have enacted; in turn, a perception of their bias and partiality is, in itself, an important argument for withdrawing their legitimacy to govern.

There is a second reason for believing that the postulate of neutrality adds an extra bite to the harm principle. There is, it seems, an inherent danger in interpreting the "harm principle" in the light of prevailing standards of conventional morality. If one defines harm, for example, as a "wrongful setback to interests",[2] then conventional-morality standards threaten to enter the definition at at least two points: through the interpretation of what setbacks are "wrongful", and through the determination of what interests are "legitimate" in the first place. To be sure, this is perhaps more of a rhetorical than a conceptual danger, and in order to avoid it one can go to some lengths to safeguard the interpretation of the "harm principle" against such moves. But the temptation is there, and if one succumbs to it, then the whole purpose of Mill's harm principle is defeated: after all, it was meant to be protection for an individual not only against the state's coercion, but also (perhaps primarily) against social pressure based on conventional, majoritarian moral rules. The injunction of state neutrality precludes such a collapse of the harm principle into conventional moral standards. It asserts explicitly, and emphatically, that prevailing moral conventions are not to be given effect by state laws if they interfere with individual, harmless moral conceptions of the good life.

NOTES

PREFACE

[1] R. Dworkin, *Taking Rights Seriously* (London: Duckworth 1977), p. 180.
[2] R. Kennedy, "Persuasion and Distrust: A Comment on the Affirmative Action Debate", *Harvard Law Review* 99 (1986) 1327, 1337-45.

CHAPTER 1

[1] As it will become clear later in this Chapter, it is concerned only with the highest courts exercising the power of judicial review, as exemplified here by the United States Supreme Court and the Australian High Court.
[2] *Regents of the University of California v. Bakke*, 438 U.S. 265, 387-402 (1978).
[3] *Id.* at 387.
[4] *Id.* at 387-388.
[5] *Id.* at 408.
[6] *Id.* at 421.
[7] 413 US 49 (1973).
[8] 381 U.S. 479 (1965).
[9] 394 U.S. 557 (1969).
[10] 381 U.S. 479, 484 (Douglas, J.).
[11] See *Roth v. United States*, 354 U.S. 476 (1957)
[12] This is, naturally, not a logical inference but a matter of rhetorical strategy. It does not follow *necessarily* from the protection of pornography at home that pornography outside private home is prohibited. But, from a rhetorical point of view, a judge endorsing the principle of legal protection of pornography in public places has no interest in appealing to the private home/public place distinction.
[13] 413 U.S. 49, 58 (1973).
[14] *Id.* at 58-9.
[15] *Id.* at 61.
[16] *Id.* at 60-62.
[17] *Id.* at 69-70.
[18] *Id.* at 103. This view Brennan J. attributes to Black and Douglas J.J. See also the dissent by Douglas J. at 71-74.
[19] *Id.* at 109-110.
[20] *Id.* at 110.
[21] No conclusive evidence has been established of causal connections between obscenity and antisocial behaviour, see J. Feinberg, *Social Philosophy* (Englewood Cliffs: Prentice-Hall, 1973), p. 42.

[22] 59 A.L.J.R. (1985) 311.
[23] See W. Sadurski, "*Gerhardy v. Brown* v. the Concept of Discrimination: Reflections on the Landmark Case that Wasn't", *Sydney Law Review* 11 (1986): 5-43.
[24] The exception was Dawson J. who said that, since the provision belongs to a category of "special measures" explicitly authorized by the International Convention, it is not necessary to consider whether it involved racial discrimination, *Gerhardy*, *supra* note 22, at 349-50.
[25] *Id.* at 316.
[26] *Id.* at 316.
[27] *Id.* at 316.
[28] *Id.* at 316-317.
[29] *Id.* at 317-318.
[30] *Id.* at 317.
[31] *Id.* at 318.
[32] See note 24 *supra.*
[33] *Id.* at 318.
[34] *Id.* at 318-9.
[35] International Convention on the Elimination of All Forms of Racial Discrimination, Art. 1(4).
[36] *Id.* at 318 (Gibbs, C.J.), 326 (Mason, J.), 330 (Wilson, J.).
[37] *Id.* at 326 (Mason, J.), at 330 (Wilson, J.).
[38] *Id.* at 317 (Gibbs, C.J.).
[39] See Sadurski, *supra* note 23.
[40] See J. Rawls, *A Theory of Justice* (Oxford: Oxford University Press, 1972), p. 20.
[41] A. A. Leff, "Law and", *Yale Law Journal* 87 (1978) 989, 1005, footnote omitted.
[42] For an opposite view, see e.g. J. B. White, "Law as Language: Reading Law and Reading Literature", *Texas Law Review* 60 (1982) 415; P. Bobbitt, *Constitutional Fate* (New York: Oxford University Press, 1982), pp. 244-5.
[43] Ch. Perelman, L. Olbrechts-Tyteca, *The New Rhetoric: A Treatise on Argumentation* (Notre Dame: University of Notre Dame Press, 1969); Ch. Perelman, *The Realm of Rhetoric* (Notre Dame: University of Notre Dame Press, 1982).
[44] Perelman, *The Realm of Rhetoric*, *supra* note 43, at 9.
[45] "[T]here can be no interaction between writer and reader ... unless they hold certain things in common", R.E. Young, A.L. Becker & K.L.Pike, *Rhetoric: Discovery and Change* (New York: Harcourt Brace Jovanovich, 1970), p. 172.
[46] The notion of the court's "clientele" is used here to denote the groups which have higher access to, and influence upon, the court than others. See M. Schapiro, *Law and Politics in the Supreme Court* (New York: Free Press, 1964), pp. 8-9. The proposition that the Supreme Court of the United States and the High Court of Australia have their respective "clienteles" may sound extravagant to those who believe that these Courts are fully neutral arbiters between conflicting social claims and interests, and that they are and always have been only interested in the impartial enforcement of an impartial law. A broader social theory relating the Courts to particular social interests and classes is beyond the aims of this Chapter: I can only refer the reader to documented expositions and defences of the proposition that the highest courts in liberal societies such as the United States and Australia have traditionally favoured the interests and claims linked with upholding established social structures. See, regarding the United States, S.A. Scheingold, *The Politics*

of Rights (New Haven: Yale University Press, 1974); R.A. Dahl, *Democracy in the United States: Promise and Performance* (Rand McNally: Chicago, 1972, 2nd ed.), pp. 187-210.
[47] *Gerhardy, supra* note 22 at 347 (Deane J.)
[48] Australian Value Study Survey, "Australians Agree Aborigines Should Have the Same Rights as Other Australians", conducted by The Roy Morgan Research Centre, mimeographed, p. 4.
[49] *Id.* at 2-3.
[50] Of course there are more than two opinions in *Paris Adult Theater*, for apart from the majority opinion delivered by Chief Justice Burger and the dissent of Justice Brennan, there is also dissent by Justice Douglas. But Douglas's is a case of "straightforward" rhetoric, and we may leave it aside for the purposes of our discussion.
[51] See W. Sadurski, "'It All Comes Out In the End': Judicial Rhetorics and the Strategy of Reassurance", *Oxford Journal of Legal Studies* 7 (1987) 258, 275 n. 59.
[52] See, in particular, L. Festinger, *A Theory of Cognitive Dissonance* (Stanford University Press, 1957); R. E. Lane and D. O. Sears, *Public Opinion* (Englewood Cliffs: Prentice Hall, 1964), chap. 5.
[53] We may, for our purposes, disregard an opposite situation of cognitive dissonance, i.e. when an unpopular source endorses a popular position; both superior appellate tribunals discussed in this paper enjoy a high degree of prestige, see on the U.S. Supreme Court, J. H. Kessel, "Public Perceptions of the Supreme Court" in T. L. Becker, M. M. Feeley (eds.), *The Impact of Supreme Court Decisions* (New York: Oxford University Press 1973), pp. 198-201; on the High Court, L. Zines, *The High Court and the Constitution* (Butterworths: Sydney 1981), p. 319.
[54] Lane and Sears, *supra* note 51, at 47-53.
[55] *Id.* at 50.
[56] H.H. Wellington, "Common Law Rules and Constitutional Double Standards: Some Notes on Adjudication", *Yale Law Journal* 83 (1973) 221, 267.
[57] J. H. Ely, *Democracy and Distrust* (Cambridge, Mass.: Harvard University Press, 1980), pp. 68-69; see also J. H. Choper, *Judicial Review and the National Political Process* (Chicago: University of Chicago Press: 1980), pp. 67-70, 123-127.

CHAPTER 2

[1] J.H. Ely, *Democracy and Distrust*, (Cambridge, Mass.: Harvard University Press, 1980), pp. 68-69, footnote omitted.
[2] *Id.* at 67.
[3] *Furman v. Georgia*, 408 U.S. 238, 383 (Burger C.J., dissenting).
[4] *Id.* at 443 (Powell J., dissenting).
[5] *Cassell & Co. v. Broome*, [1972] A.C. 1027, 1107 (H.L.) (Dilhorne, V.).
[6] See in particular H.H. Wellington, "The Nature of Judicial Review", *Yale Law Journal* 91 (1982) 486, 493-94.
[7] *John F. Kennedy Memorial Hospital v. Heston*, 58 N.J. 576, 279 A.2d 670 (1971).
[8] *Prince v. Massachusetts*, 321 U.S. 158 (1944).
[9] *Griswold v. Connecticut*, 381 U.S. 479 (1965).
[10] Ely, *supra* note 1, at 219 n. 118.

[11] *Brown v. Board of Education*, 347 U.S. 483 (1954).
[12] See H. H. Hyman, P. B. Sheatsley, "Attitudes toward Segregation", *Scientific American* 195 (December 1956) 35, 36.
[13] (1982) 56 A.L.J.R. 625. This proposition can be advanced only tentatively because the moral issue of racial discrimination was clouded by a controversy about the external affairs power of the Commonwealth. But, legal formalities aside, the High Court in effect invalidated the anti-Aboriginal policy of the government of a state in which unfavourable sentiments and traditions toward Aborigines are more prevalent than in Australia as a whole.
[14] Ely, *supra* note 1, at 73-104.
[15] K. Arrow, *Social Choice and Individual Values* (New York: Wiley, 1951).
[16] R. Dahl, *A Preface to Democratic Theory* (Chicago: University of Chicago Press, 1956), p. 125.
[17] See T. Sandalow, "Judicial Protection of Minorities", *Michigan Law Review* 75 (1977) 1162, 1187-88.
[18] [1972] A.C. 877.
[19] *Addie v. Dumbreck* [1929] A.C. 358.
[20] [1972] A.C. at 897.
[21] *Reg. v. Knuller* [1973] A.C. 435, 455.
[22] [1973] A.C. at 455.
[23] *Id.* at 480.
[24] *United States v. Carolene Products Co.*, 304 U.S. 144, 152-153 n. 4 (1938).
[25] See *Prince v. Massachusetts*, 321 U.S. 158 (1944).
[26] For references, see my "Conventional Morality and Judicial Standards", *Virginia Law Review* 73 (1987) 339, 351 nn. 43-48, 352 n. 51.
[27] For references, see *id.* at 352-53, nn. 58, 59, 66.
[28] *Herrington v. British Railways Board* [1971] 1 All ER 897, 902 per Salmon LJ.
[29] *Shaw* [1961] 2 W.L.R. at 938 *per* Lord Morris.
[30] *Id.* at 940 *per* Lord Hodson.
[31] *R. v. Brodie* (1962) 32 D.L.R. (2d) 507, 528 *per* Judson, J.
[32] For references, see Sadurski, *supra* note 26, at 253 nn. 72, 73, 74.
[33] *Moller v. Keimoes School Committee*, 1911 S. Afr. L.R. App. Div. 635, 643-44 *per* Lord de Villiers, C.J. (arguing that school segregation on racial grounds is legally permissible).
[34] See, *e.g.*, *Miller v. California*, 413 U.S. 15 (1973).
[35] *Towne Cinema Theatres*, (1985) 18 D.L.R. (4th) 1, 13.
[36] *Repouille v. United States* 165 F. 2d 152 (2d Cir. 1947).
[37] See, *e.g.*, *Paris Adult Theatre I v. Slaton*, 413 U.S. 49 (1973), discussed in Chapter 1 above.
[38] *Regina v. Dominion News & Gifts (1962) Ltd.*, (1963) 42 W.W.R. 65, 80 (Man. Ct. App.) (Freedman, J.A., dissenting), rev'd, 1964 S.C.R. 251 (Can.).
[39] *United States v. Various Articles of Obscene Merchandise, Schedule No. 2102*, 678 F.2d 433 (2d Cir. 1982).
[40] *Id.* at 434 (quoting unreported District Court opinion).
[41] B. C. Hennessy, *Public Opinion* (Belmont: Wadsworth 1965), p.345.
[42] *Id.* at 345-6.
[43] L. Free and H. Cantril, *The Political Beliefs of Americans: A Study of Public Opinion*

(New Brunswick: Rutgers University Press, 1967), p. 37.
[44] V. O. Key Jr, *Public Opinion and American Democracy* (New York: A. A. Knopf, 1961), pp. 162-177.
[45] *Meyer v. Nebraska*, 262 U.S. 390, 400 (1923).
[46] *Bartels v. Iowa*, 262 U.S. 404, 412 (1923) (Holmes, J., dissenting).
[47] *Geelong Harbor Trust v. Gibbs Bright* [1974] 2 A.L.R. 362, 369, emphasis added.
[48] *Roe v. Wade*, 410 U.S. 113, 174 (1973).
[49] See, e.g., *Towne Cinema Theatres* (1985) D.L.R. at 6, quoting the judgment by the Court of Appeal of Alberta in the same case.
[50] *Louisiana ex rel. Francis v. Resweber*, 329 U.S. 459, 471 (1947) (Frankfurter J., concurring).
[51] For several examples of this judicial attitude, see Sadurski, *supra* note 26, at 361-62.
[52] *Furman v. Georgia*, 408 U.S. 238 (1972).
[53] *Id.* at 332.
[54] *Id.* at 360.
[55] *Id.* at 361, quoting Frank J. in *United States v. Rosenberg*, 195 F.2d 583, 608 (1952), footnote omitted.
[56] *Furman*, at 362, footnote omitted.
[57] *Id.* at 362-9.
[58] *Gregg v. Georgia*, 428 U.S. 153, 232 (1976).
[59] *Id.* at 168-187 (plurality opinion by Justice Stewart).
[60] *Furman*, 408 U.S. at 295, 299, 300, emphases added.
[61] *Id.* at 300.
[62] *Id.* at 296-300.
[63] This is Ely's term, *supra* note 1, at 67.
[64] Wellington, *supra* note 5, at 494, footnote omitted.
[65] H.H. Wellington, "Common Law Rules and Constitutional Double Standards: Some Notes on Adjudication", *Yale Law Journal* 83 (1973) 221, 244, footnote omitted.
[66] *Id.* at 267.
[67] *Id.* at 248.
[68] *Id.* at 244.
[69] Wellington, *supra* note 6, at 493.
[70] *Id.* at 514.
[71] *Id.* at 514.
[72] *Id.* at 516.
[73] *Id.* at 515.
[74] *Id.* at 514 n. 133.
[75] R. Dworkin, *Taking Rights Seriously* (London: Duckworth 1977), pp. 248-253.
[76] M. J. Perry, "Abortion, the Public Morals, and the Police Power: The Ethical Function of Substantive Due Process", *UCLA Law Review* 23 (1976) 689, 735.
[77] *Id.* at 731.
[78] M. J. Perry, "Substantive Due Process Revisited: Reflections on (and Beyond) Recent Cases", *Northwestern Law Review* 71 (1976) 417, 447 n. 189.
[79] *Id.* at 442 n. 164.
[80] *Id.* at 442.
[81] Perry, *supra* note 76 at 729.

[82] *Id.* at 729, emphasis added.
[83] *Id.* at 730.
[84] *Id.* at 730 n. 195.
[85] *Repouille v. United States* 165 F.2d 152, 154 (2d Cir. 1947).
[86] 408 U.S. at 370 n. 163, emphasis added.
[87] E.L. Hartley & R.E. Hartley, *Fundamentals of Social Psychology* (New York: Alfred A. Knopf, 1952), p. 549.
[88] R. T. LaPiere, "Attitudes vs. Actions", *Social Forces* 13 (1934) 233.
[89] See e.g. *Furman*, 408 U.S. at 385 (Burger C.J., dissenting) and at 437 (Powell J., dissenting); *Gregg*, 428 U.S. at 179-181 (plurality opinion by Stewart, J.).
[90] *Roe v. Wade* 410 U.S. 113, 174 (1973) (Rehnquist J., dissenting).
[91] W. Ebenstein, *Today's Isms* (Englewood Cliffs: Prentice Hall 1954), p. 99.
[92] W. Lippmann, *Essays in the Public Philosophy* (Boston: Little, Brown and Co. 1955), p. 100.
[93] J. A. Schumpeter, *Capitalism, Socialism and Democracy* (London: George Allen and Unwin, 1943), p. 296.
[94] Ebenstein, *supra* note 91, at 99.
[95] See E. S. Griffith, J. Plamenatz, J. R. Pennock, "Cultural Prerequisites to a Successfully Functioning Democracy: A Symposium", *American Political Science Review* 50 (1956) 101, 103, 118, 129.
[96] J. W. Prothro & C. M. Grigg, "Fundamental Principles of Democracy: Bases of Agreement and Disagreement", *Journal of Politics* 22 (1960) 276.
[97] *Id.* at 285, table 1.
[98] *Id.* at 283, 285.
[99] See Key, *supra* note 44, at 50.

CHAPTER 3

[1] J. W. Prothro & C. M. Grigg, "Fundamental Principles of Democracy: Bases of Agreement and Disagreement", *Journal of Politics* 22 (1960) 276, 281.
[2] J. Rawls, "Kantian Constructivism in Moral Theory: The Dewey Lectures", *Journal of Philosophy* 77 (1980) 515, 518, emphasis added.
[3] *Id.* at 518.
[4] J. Rawls, "Justice as Fairness: Political not Metaphysical", *Philosophy & Public Affairs* 14 (1985) 223, 229.
[5] J. Rawls, *A Theory of Justice* (Oxford: Oxford University Press, 1972), pp. 19-21.
[6] *Id.* at 19-21, 48-51.
[7] *Id.* at 50.
[8] *Id.* at 20, emphasis added.
[9] *Id.* at 20.
[10] Rawls, *supra* note 2, at 518.
[11] Rawls, *supra* note 4, at 228.
[12] *Id.* at 228.
[13] R. Dworkin, *Taking Rights Seriously* (London: Duckworth, 1977), pp. 248-253.
[14] For a less cursory treatment of these two issues (expository v. justificatory use of

reflective equilibrium; reasonableness v. obligatoriness of a conception of justice) see W. Sadurski, "Contractarianism and Intuition", *Australasian Journal of Philosophy* 61 (1983) 231.

[15] Rawls, *supra* note 2, at 518.

[16] In the context of discussion of the duty to comply with an unjust law, Rawls wrote that injustice may occur when "arrangements ... conform to a society's conception of justice ... but this conception itself may be unreasonable, and in many cases clearly unjust", *supra* note 5, at 352.

[17] In his *Essays on Philosophical Method* (London: Macmillan, 1971), p. 122.

[18] M. Walzer, "Philosophy and Democracy", *Political Theory* 9 (1981) 379.

[19] M. Walzer, *Spheres of Justice* (New York: Basic Books, 1983).

[20] Walzer, *supra* note 18, at 387.

[21] *Id.* at 380.

[22] *Id.* at 380.

[23] *Id.* at 396.

[24] *Id.* at 393.

[25] *Id.* at 381.

[26] Walzer himself draws this parallel, and discusses the dissimilarities, *id.* at 387-397.

[27] Walzer, *supra* note 19, at xiv.

[28] *Id.* at xiv.

[29] *Id.* at 29.

[30] *Id.* at 313.

[31] *Id.* at 26, emphasis added.

[32] *Id.* at 320, emphasis added.

[33] *Id.* at 56-61.

[34] *Id.* at 86-91.

[35] *Id.* at 46-48.

[36] See B. Barry, Book Review, *Columbia Law Review* 84 (1984) 806, 812-814; J. S. Fishkin, Book Review, *Michigan Law Review* (1984) 755, 757-760; R. Dworkin, "What Justice Isn't", *A Matter of Principle* (Cambridge: Harvard University Press, 1985), pp. 214-220.

[37] Walzer, *supra* note 19, at 5.

[38] See W. Sadurski, *Giving Desert Its Due* (Dordrecht: D. Reidel 1985), pp. 144-153.

[39] Walzer, *supra* note 19, in particular at 6-10.

[40] See Barry, *supra* note 36, at 809-810.

[41] Walzer, *supra* note 19, at 8.

[42] *Id.* at 8-9.

[43] *Id.* at 9.

[44] *Id.* at 9.

[45] *Id.* at 9.

[46] *Id.* at 8.

[47] *Id.* at 8.

[48] W. James, *The Principles of Psychology*, vol. 1 (London: Macmillan, 1910), p. 291, emphasis in original.

[49] *Id.*, at 291, emphasis in original.

[50] C.R. Snyder & H.L. Fromkin, *Uniqueness: The Human Pursuit of Difference* (New York: Plenum Press, 1980), p. 108.

[51] See R. Nozick, *Anarchy, State, and Utopia* (New York: Basic Books, 1974).
[52] *Id.*, at 5.
[53] See, in particular, "Relativistic Ethics: Morality as Politics", *Midwest Studies in Philosophy* 3 (1978): 109-21; "What Is Moral Relativism?" in A. I. Goldman & J. Kim (eds), *Values and Morals* (Dordrecht: D. Reidel, 1978); "Moral Relativism Defended" in J. W. Meiland & M. Krausz, eds., *Relativism: Cognitive and Moral* (Notre Dame: University of Notre Dame Press, 1982), reprinted from *Philosophical Review* 84 (1975): 3-22.
[54] Note that Harman's relativistic thesis applies only to "inner judgments", as will be explained later. These judgments, expressed in the "ought to do" propositions, figure more prominently in Harman's ethical theory than all the other moral judgments which are beyond his concern in this context.
[55] "Moral Relativism Defended", *supra* note 53, at 200.
[56] D. Lyons, "Ethical Relativism and the Problem of Incoherence" in Meiland & Krausz, *supra* note 53, at 211-12.
[57] "Moral Relativism Defended", *supra* note 53 at 193.
[58] *Id.* at 190.
[59] *Id.* at 190.
[60] *Id.* at 193.
[61] *Id.* at 190.
[62] *Id.* at 192.
[63] *Id.* at 191.
[64] S. L. Darwall, "Harman and Moral Relativism", *Personalist* 58 (1977): 201-2.
[65] "Relativistic Ethics: Morality as Politics" *supra* note 53, at 111, see also "Moral Relativism Defended" *supra* note 53, at 193-5; "What Is Moral Relativism?" *supra* note 53, at 152-6.
[66] "Moral Relativism Defended" *supra* note 53, at 194.
[67] "Relativistic Ethics: Morality as Politics" *supra* note 53 at 111.
[68] "What Is Moral Relativism?" *supra* note 53, at 153.
[69] "Moral Relativism Defended" *supra* note 53, at 194.
[70] "What Is Moral Relativism?" *supra* note 53, at 153.
[71] "Moral Relativism Defended" *supra* note 53, at 194.
[72] "Relativistic Ethics: Morality as Politics" *supra* note 53, at 112.
[73] "What Is Moral Relativism?" *supra* note 53, at 152.
[74] "Relativistic Ethics: Morality as Politics" *supra* note 53, at 110.
[75] *Id.* at 113.
[76] See B. C. Postow, "Moral Relativism Avoided", *Personalist* 60 (1979) 97.
[77] R. Attfield, "How Not To Be a Moral Relativist", *Monist* 62 (1979) 519.
[78] "Moral Relativism Defended" *supra* note 53, at 196.
[79] See R. Coburn, "Relativism and the Basis of Morality", *Philosophical Review* 85 (1976): 87-92.
[80] R. L. Trammel, "Saving Life and Taking Life", *Journal of Philosophy* 72 (1975): 131-37.
[81] "Relativistic Ethics: Morality as Politics" *supra* note 53, at 115.
[82] *Id.* at 114.
[83] *Id.* at 115.
[84] *Id.* at 115, emphasis added.

CHAPTER 4

[1] *The Moral Limits of the Criminal Law*, vol. I: *Harm to Others* (New York: Oxford University Press, 1984), p. 15.
[2] M. Sandel, "Introduction", in M. Sandel (ed.), *Liberalism and Its Critics* (Oxford: Basil Blackwell, 1984), p. 1.
[3] See R. Dworkin, "Liberalism", *A Matter of Principle* (Cambridge: Harvard University Press, 1985), p. 203; J. Rawls, "The Idea of an Overlapping Consensus", *Oxford Journal of Legal Studies* 7 (1987) 1, 12-15. For an example of a liberal appeal to moral scepticism, see D. W. Brock, "Paternalism and Autonomy", *Ethics* 98 (1988) 550-65.
[4] J. Rawls, *A Theory of Justice* (Oxford: Oxford University Press, 1972), p. 563.
[5] *Id.* at 560-567.
[6] *Id.* at 327-328.
[7] A. Gutmann, *Liberal Equality* (Cambridge: Cambridge University Press, 1980), pp. 18-47.
[8] *Leviathan*, ed. by C.B. Macpherson (Harmondsworth: Penguin Books, 1981), pp.230-31.
[9] H.C. Mansfield, Jr., "Hobbes and the Science of Indirect Government", *American Political Science Review* 65 (1971) 97, 107.
[10] Rawls, *supra* note 4, at 448, both emphases added.
[11] Significantly, Rawls explains one of the aspects of the priority of the right over the good in the following way: "To have a complaint against the conduct and belief of others we must show that their actions injure us, or that the institutions that authorize what they do treat us unjustly", *id* at 450.
[12] Dworkin, *supra* note 3. See also M. Walzer, "Liberalism and the Art of Separation", *Political Theory* 12 (1984) 315, 320-21.
[13] J. Rawls describes this as the expression of the principle that people must see each other "as primarily moral persons with an equal right to choose their mode of life", *supra* note 4, at 563. The relationship in Rawls between the principles of neutrality and moral equality is achieved through the description of the original position, in which the parties "regard moral personality ... as the fundamental aspect of the self", *id.*
[14] That is, preferences concerning the way other people should behave.
[15] J. Finnis, *Natural Law and Natural Rights* (Oxford: Oxford University Press, 1980), p. 222.
[16] Joseph Raz argues that "the libertarian deontologist fashions the state to favor those whose conceptions of the good includes not coercing others in the circumstances where coercion is prohibited by the law. Their conception of the good is in part realized by the state", J. Raz, "Liberalism, Autonomy, and the Politics of Neutral Concern", *Midwest Studies in Philosophy* 7 (1982) 89, 96.
[17] L. B. Schwartz argued along these lines in his well-known essay "Moral Offenses and the Model Penal Code", *Columbia Law Review* 63 (1963) 669. For a different approach to offence, see J. Feinberg, *Offence to Others* (New York: Oxford University Press 1985), pp. 25-49; A. Ellis, "Offence and the Liberal Conception of the Law", *Philosophy & Public Affairs* 13 (1984) 3.
[18] See "On Liberty" in J.S. Mill, *Utilitarianism, On Liberty, Essay on Bentham*, ed. by M. Warnock (London: Collins 1962), pp. 230-231. See also H.L.A. Hart, *Law, Liberty and Morality* (London: Oxford University Press, 1963), pp. 44-48.

[19] See, e.g., T.C. Grey, *The Legal Enforcement of Morality* (New York: Random House 1980), pp. 26-29.
[20] Report of the Committee on Obscenity and Film Censorship, London 1979, discussed by R. Dworkin in "Is There a Right to Pornography?", *Oxford Journal of Legal Studies* 1 (1981) 177-212.
[21] Hart, *supra* note 18, at 47.
[22] Quoted by Dworkin, *supra* note 20, at 186.
[23] See *id.* at 187.
[24] Finnis, *supra* note 15, at 222.
[25] R. M. Smith, "The Constitution and Autonomy", *Texas Law Review* 60 (1982) 175, 193
[26] See E.D. Cohen, "Paternalism That Does Not Restrict Individuality: Criteria and Applications", *Social Theory & Practice* 12 (1986) 309, 312.
[27] This point is made forcefully by Rawls, *supra* note 4, at 447-48.
[28] "Within limits" is an important qualification but it does not undermine the whole construction. These "limits" are determined by the judgement about what "harms" other, and what "harms" others in the want-regarding political philosophy is detectable through the objectively discernible protest of the victims of harm.
[29] J. Raz, *The Morality of Freedom* (Oxford: Clarendon Press, 1986), p. 112, see also pp. 114-15.
[30] *Id.* at 112.
[31] See J. Rawls, "The Priority of Right and Ideas of the Good", *Philosophy & Public Affairs* 17 (1988) 251, 262 and 264-68.
[32] See id. at 265-7.
[33] Raz, *supra* note 29 at 114-15.
[34] See text accompanying footnotes 54-57 of this Chapter.
[35] Raz, *supra* note 29, at 120.
[36] *Id.* at 120-21.
[37] *Id.* at 121, emphasis added.
[38] *Id.* at 121.
[39] *Id.* at 121.
[40] *Id.* at 122.
[41] *Id.* at 124.
[42] *Id.* at 123-24.
[43] *Id.* at 122.
[44] *Id.* at 412-20.
[45] *Id.* at 415: "I would suggest that the [harm] principle is derivable from a morality which regards personal autonomy as an essential ingredient of the good life...".
[46] *Id.* at 417.
[47] *Id.* at 417-18.
[48] See J.M. Finnis, "Legal Enforcement of 'Duties to Oneself': Kant v. Neo-Kantians", *Columbia Law Review* 87 (1987) 433-57.
[49] Elsewhere in his book he describes "independence", understood as the absence of coercion and manipulation, as "a separate dimension of the conditions of personal autonomy", Raz, *supra* note 29, at p. 378. This does not help to answer the question about the moral value of independence in the case of morally repugnant, autonomous actions.
[50] 381 U.S. 479 (1965).

[51] L. H. Farber, *Lying, Despair, Jealousy, Envy, Sex, Suicide, Drugs, and the Good Life* (Basic Books: New York, 1976), p. 114.
[52] *Id.* at 113.
[53] See in particular *Sour Grapes* (Cambridge: Cambridge University Press, 1983).
[54] "Legal Interference with Private Preferences", *University of Chicago Law Review* 53 (1986) 1129.
[55] D. L. Shapiro, "Courts, Legislatures, and Paternalism", *Virginia Law Review* 74 (1988) 519, 549, footnote omitted.
[56] J. Elster, "The Market and the Forum: Three Varieties of Political Theory", in J. Elster & A. Hylland, eds, *Foundations of Social Choice Theory* (Cambridge: Cambridge University Press 1986), p. 110.
[57] *Id.* at 110.
[58] T. M. Scanlon, "Preference and Urgency", *Journal of Philosophy* 72 (1975) 655, 664.
[59] See Note, "An Argument for the Application of Equal Protection Heightened Scrutiny to Classifications Based on Homosexuality", *Southern California Law Review* 57 (1984) 797, 817-821.
[60] Scanlon, *supra* note 58, at 664-66.
[61] D. Regan, "On Preferences and Promises: A Response to Harsanyi", *Ethics* 96 (1985) 56, 57.
[62] J. C. Harsanyi, "On Preferences, Promises, and the Coordination Problem: Reply to Regan", *Ethics* 96 (1985) 68, 69. See similarly R.B. Brandt, *A Theory of the Good and the Right* (Oxford: Clarendon Press, 1979), p. 111.
[63] R. E. Goodin, "Laundering Preferences" in J. Elster & A. Hylland, eds, *Foundations of Social Choice Theory* (Cambridge: Cambridge University Press, 1986), pp. 83-85.
[64] See J. Elster, *Ulysses and the Sirens* (Cambridge: Cambridge University Press 1984, rev'd ed).
[65] Goodin *supra* note 63, at 82.
[66] R. Dworkin, *Taking Rights Seriously* (London: Duckworth 1978), p. 272.
[67] Finnis *supra* note 15, at 222.
[68] *Id.* at 222-223.
[69] See, e.g., R. M. Smith, *Liberalism and American Constitutional Law* (Cambridge, Mass.: Harvard University Press, 1985), pp. 185-197; S.I. Benn, "Egalitarianism and the Equal Consideration of Interests", in H.A. Bedau (ed.), *Justice and Equality* (Englewood Cliffs: Prentice-Hall, 1971), p. 159.
[70] S. Benn, "The Protection and Limitation of Privacy, Part I", *Australian Law Journal* 52 (1978) 601, 605.
[71] Dworkin *supra* note 66, at 272.
[72] 410 U.S. 113 (1973)
[73] G. Calabresi, *Ideals, Beliefs, Attitudes, and the Law* (Syracuse: Syracuse University Press, 1985), p. 97.
[74] *Id.* at 109.
[75] *Id.* at 98.
[76] *Id.* at 109.
[77] See, e.g., J.G. Murphy, "Rationality and Constraints on Democratic Rule", in J. R. Pennock & J. W. Chapman, eds *Justification: Nomos XXVIII* (New York: New York University Press, 1986), p.158.

[78] Calabresi, *supra* note 73, at 117.
[79] See B. Williams, *Ethics and the Limits of Philosophy* (London: Fontana, 1985), pp. 86-7.
[80] Calabresi, *supra* note 73, at 98, emphasis in original.
[81] *Id.* at 113.
[82] See W. Sadurski, *Giving Desert Its Due: Social Justice and Legal Theory* (Dordrecht: D. Reidel, 1985), chap. 5.
[83] Rawls, *supra* note 4, at 100-108.
[84] G.A. Cohen, "Freedom, Justice and Capitalism", *New Left Review* 126 (March-April 1981) 3, 8-11.
[85] See, in particular, M.R. Cohen, "Property and Sovereignty", *Cornell Law Quarterly* 13 (1927) 8, 21-26.
[86] See R. L. Hale, "Coercion and Distribution in a Supposedly Non-Coercive State", *Political Science Quarterly* 38 (1923) 470.
[87] See generally C. Sunstein, "Lochner's Legacy", *Columbia Law Review* 87 (1987) 873.
[88] F.A. Hayek, *The Constitution of Liberty* (Chicago: University of Chicago Press, 1960), pp. 20-21.
[89] See Rawls, *supra* note 4, at 332; R. Dworkin, "Can a Liberal State Support Art?" in *A Matter of Principle* (Harvard University Press 1985), pp. 221-33; D. Richards, "Human Rights and Moral Ideals: An Essay on the Moral Theory of Liberalism", *Social Theory and Practice* 5 (1980) 461, 467-68; S. Shiffrin, "Liberalism, Radicalism, and Legal Scholarship", *UCLA Law Review* 30 (1983) 1103, 1132-33.
[90] See, e.g., M. Walsh, "To Subsidize or Not to Subsidize?", *Time* 14 Nov. 1988 (Internat. Edition) 30-32.
[91] R. B. Stewart, "Regulation in a Liberal State: The Role of Non-Commodity Values", *Yale Law Journal* 92 (1983) 1537, 1570.

CHAPTER 5

[1] Kirby P in *BLF v. Minister for Industrial Relations* (1986) 7 NSWLR 382, 405.
[2] *United States v. Carolene Products*, 304 U.S. 144, 152 (1938).
[3] 198 U.S. 45 (1905) (invalidating New York's maximum hours law for bakers).
[4] 4 Wheat 316 (1819).
[5] 303 U.S. 177, 184 n. 2 (1938).
[6] *McCulloch v. Maryland*, 4 Wheat 316, 428-29 (1819).
[7] *South Carolina v. Barwell Bros*, 303 U.S. 177, 184 n. 2 (1938).
[8] *Minersville School District v. Gobitis*, 310 U.S. 586, 606 (1940).
[9] See, e.g., *Selective Service System v. Minnesota Public Interest Research Group*, 468 U.S. 841 (1983); *Hudson v. Palmer*, 468 U.S. 517, 557 (1984).
[10] *Compare Selective Service System v. Minnesota Public Interest Research Group*, 468 U.S. 841, 878 n. 21 (1983) (Marshall J, dissenting) (suggesting that the young people are so politically powerless as to command special protection from the majoritarian process) *with City of Cleburne v. Cleburne Living Centre*, 53 L.W. 5022, 5032 n. 24 (Marshall J, concurring and dissenting) (suggesting that statutes discriminating against the young need not be feared because the legislators were once themselves young and often interact with minors).

[11] L. F. Powell, Jr, "*Carolene Products* Revisited", *Columbia Law Review* 82 (1982) 1087.
[12] B. A. Ackerman, "Beyond *Carolene Products*", *Harvard Law Review* 98 (1985) 713, 737.
[13] *Id.* at 740.
[14] J. H. Ely, *Democracy and Distrust* (Cambridge, Mass: Harvard University Press, 1980).
[15] Ackerman, *supra* note 12, at 742.
[16] See also L. H. Tribe, "The Puzzling Persistence of Process-Based Constitutional Theories", *Yale Law Journal* 89 (1980) 1063; P. Brest, "The Substance of Process", *Ohio State Law Journal* 42 (1981) 131.
[17] 373 U.S. 526 (1963).
[18] 373 NE 2d 21 (1978).
[19] Superficially, the latter preferences may be represented as the "internal" ones, and so yield a warmer moral treatment: the Skokie people do not want themselves to be exposed to the Nazi manifestations. But this is also the case with the white racists in *Watson*: they themselves do not want to suffer frequent contacts with the Blacks. What matters in the categorization of a preference as "external" is that in its effect it dictates the rules about what other people have to do. In this sense probably all preferences are "external" but the degree of this "externality" may vary, depending on the costs imposed on others for non-compliance.
[20] Because Blacks are not exactly a discrete and *insular* minority.
[21] See R. M. Cover, "The Origins of Judicial Activism in the Protection of Minorities", *Yale Law Journal* 91 (1982) 1287, 1296.
[22] *Carolene Products*, 304 U.S. at 152 n. 4.
[23] Ackerman, *supra* note 12, at 722-31; similarly M. Tushnet, "Darkness on the Edge of Town: The Contributions of John Hart Ely to Constitutional Theory", *Yale Law Journal* 89 (1980) 1037, 1054.
[24] See, further, W. Sadurski, "*Gerhardy v. Brown* v. the Concept of Discrimination: Reflections on the Landmark Case that Wasn't", *Sydney Law Review* 11 (1986) 5, 38-39.
[25] *Carolene Products*, 304 U.S. at 152 n 4.
[26] See, similarly, J. S. Wright, "Judicial Review and the Equal Protection Clause", *Harvard Civil Rights-Civil Liberties Law Review* 15 (1980) 1, 27.
[27] Brest, *supra* note 16, at 136-37, Tribe, supra note 16, at 1075-76.
[28] This argument is supported by sociological definitions and analyses of "minorities", the indicia of which include both objective characteristics (differential and unequal treatment, lower social status, lack of privileges enjoyed by a dominant group) and subjective ones (perception of discrimination), see Ch. Wagley & M. Harris, *Minorities in the New World* (New York: Columbia University Press, 1958), p. 10.
[29] Tribe, *supra* note 16, at 1073; Ely, *supra* note 14, at 150.
[30] "Legislation imposing special disabilities upon groups disfavored *by virtue of circumstances beyond their control* suggests the kind of 'class or caste' treatment that the Fourteenth Amendment was designed to abolish", *Plyler v. Doe*, 457 U.S. 202, 217 n. 14 (1982) (emphasis added); see further W. Sadurski, *Giving Desert Its Due: Social Justice and Legal Theory* (Dordrecht: D. Reidel, 1985), chap. 5.
[31] Similarly Ely, *supra* note 14, at 154.
[32] See Tribe, *supra* note 16, at 1078.
[33] *Id.*
[34] Many reports indicate that no more than approximately one-third of homosexuals who

are highly motivated to change to heterosexuality can do so, see Note, "Developments in the Law — The Constitution and the Family", *Harvard Law Review* 93 (1980) 1156, 1288-9.

[35] This view found recently a powerful support in *Watkins v. United States*, 847 F.2d 1329 (9th Cir. 1988), a decision by the US Court of Appeals for the Ninth Circuit, Norris J said: "it is clear that by 'immutability' the [Supreme] Court has never meant strict immutability in the sense that members of the class must be physically unable to change or mask the trait defining their class. ... At a minimum, ... the Supreme Court is willing to treat a trait as effectively immutable if changing it would involve great difficulty, such as requiring a major physical change or a traumatic change of identity. ... [W]e have no trouble concluding that sexual orientation is immutable for the purposes of equal protection doctrine".

[36] As Professor Hart observed many years ago, "Resistance to the temptation to commit these crimes [of theft, or wounding, or murder] is not often, as the suppression of sexual impulses generally is, something which affects the development or balance of the individual's emotional life, happiness, and personality", H. L. A. Hart, *Law, Liberty and Morality* (London: Oxford University Press, 1963), p. 22.

[37] Tribe, *supra* note 16, at 1076.

[38] See *Regents of the University of California v. Bakke*, 438 U.S. 265, 295-97 (1978) (Powell J); also *Sugarman v. Dougall*, 413 U.S. 634, 657 (1973) (Rehnquist J, dissenting).

[39] See E. J. Erler, "Equal Protection and Personal Rights: The Regime of the 'Discrete and Insular Minority'", *Georgia Law Review* 16 (1982) 407, 440-44.

[40] See A. Bickel, *The Supreme Court and the Idea of Progress* (New Haven: Yale University Press, 1970), p. 83.

[41] For an argument that racial segregation does not necessarily imply inferiority see H. Wechsler, "The Neutral Principles of Constitutional Law", *Harvard Law Review* 73 (1959) 1, 33.

[42] R. K. Merton, "Insiders and Outsiders: A Chapter in the Sociology of Knowledge", *American Journal of Sociology* (1972) 9, 38.

[43] *Sugarman v. Dougall*, 413 US 657 (1973) (Rehnquist J, dissenting).

[44] Powell, *supra* note 11, at 1091.

[45] "One reasonably may doubt the capacity of the courts to distinguish wisely among [different minority groups] or determine which groups — at a given time and place — operate effectively within our politics", id, see also *Sugarman v. Dougall*, 413 US 634, 657 (1973) (Rehnquist J, dissenting).

[46] For this reason, a strategy proposed in this Chapter may be seen as directly opposite to that offered by Ely (who emphasizes the analysis of "prejudice" in terms of flushing out unconstitutional motivations, and considers "discreteness and insularity" to have a derivative significance only, see Ely, *supra* note 14, at 153), though it shares his aspiration of founding the protection of minorities on neutral grounds, rather than on substantive judgments about preferences (see *id.* at 153-54).

[47] *Hunter v. Erickson*, 393 US 385, 391 (1969) (White J).

[48] *Adelaide Company of Jehovah's Witnesses v. The Commonwealth*, [1943] 67 CLR 116, 124 (Latham CJ).

CHAPTER 6

[1] *The Moral Limits of the Criminal Law*, vol. I: *Harm to Others* (New York: Oxford University Press, 1984), pp. 65-70.

[2] *Id.* at 67, emphases in original.

[3] *Id.*

[4] See, *inter alia*, M. Sandel, *Liberalism and the Limits of Justice* (New York: Cambridge University Press, 1982); A. C. MacIntyre, *After Virtue* (Notre Dame: University of Notre Dame Press, 1981); R. M. Smith, *Liberalism and American Constitutional Law* (Cambridge, Mass.: Harvard University Press, 1985).

[5] J. Feinberg, *Doing and Deserving* (Princeton: Princeton University Press, 1970), p. 93, emphasis added.

[6] See, for instance, L. O. Ericsson, *Justice in the Distribution of Economic Resources* (Stockholm: Almqvist & Wiksell, 1976), p. 140.

[7] B. A. Ackerman, *Social Justice in the Liberal State* (New Haven: Yale University Press, 1980), p. 248, emphasis in the original.

[8] H. Morris, "Persons and Punishment", *Monist* 52 (1968) 475.

[9] See J. G. Murphy, *Retribution, Justice, and Therapy* (Dordrecht: D. Reidel, 1979), pp. 77-81; J. Finnis, *Natural Law and Natural Rights* (Oxford: Clarendon Press, 1980), pp. 263-4; G. Sher, *Desert* (Princeton: Princeton University Press, 1987), chap. 5.

[10] The following three paragraphs summarize some points made in W. Sadurski, "Distributive Justice and the Theory of Punishment", *Oxford Journal of Legal Studies* 5 (1985) 47.

[11] G. Fletcher, *Rethinking Criminal Law* (Boston: Little, Brown & Co., 1978), pp. 417-8.

[12] G. Dworkin, "Is More Choice Better than Less?", *Midwest Studies in Philosophy* 7 (1982) 47, 49.

[13] *Id.* at 52.

[14] *Id.* at 54.

[15] *Id.* at 56.

[16] See R. A. Wasserstrom, "Punishment", in *Philosophy and Social Issues* (Notre Dame: University of Notre Dame Press: 1980), p. 145.

[17] That the critics of the "balance of benefits and burdens" model usually identify the "benefits" incurred by the criminal with material goods unlawfully taken is illustrated by the critique by H. Fingarette, who describes the "restoration of the balance" after the theft as the "returning [of] the stolen goods", H. Fingarette, "Punishment and Suffering", *Proceedings and Addresses of the American Philosophical Association* 50 (1977) 499, 502.

[18] A. H. Goldman, "The Paradox of Punishment", *Philosophy & Public Affairs* 9 (1979) 42, 44.

[19] R. W. Burgh, "Do the Guilty Deserve Punishment?", *Journal of Philosophy* 79 (1982) 193, 209.

[20] *Id.* at 209.

[21] M. Davis, "Why Attempts Deserve Less Punishment than Complete Crimes", *Law & Philosophy* 5 (1986) 1.

[22] See e.g. P.J. Fitzgerald, *Criminal Law and Punishment* (Oxford: Oxford University Press, 1962), p. 98.

[23] See e.g. H. Gross, *A Theory of Criminal Justice* (New York: Oxford University Press,

1979), pp. 423-36.
[24] See Note, "The Cultural Defense in the Criminal Law", *Harvard Law Review* 99 (1986) 1293, 1299-1300.
[25] H.L.A. Hart, *Punishment and Responsibility* (Oxford: Oxford University Press, 1968), pp. 180-83.
[26] A. H. Goldman, "Toward a New Theory of Punishment", *Law and Philosophy* 1 (1982) 57, 61; see also H. A. Bedau, "Retribution and the Theory of Punishment", *Journal of Philosophy* 75 (1978) 601, 617.
[27] 104 S.Ct. 3065 (1984).
[28] *Id.* at 3079 n.14.
[29] J. Rawls, *A Theory of Justice* (Oxford: Oxford University Press, 1972), pp. 204-205; N. MacCormick, *Legal Right and Social Democracy* (Oxford: Oxford University Press, 1982), pp. 9-12.
[30] See W. Sadurski, *Giving Desert Its Due: Social Justice and Legal Theory* (Dordrecht: D. Reidel, 1985), pp. 263-5; see also N. Daniels, "Equal Liberty and Unequal Worth of Liberty", in *Reading Rawls*, ed. N. Daniels (Oxford: Basil Blackwell, 1975).
[31] See, e.g., D. L. Bazelon, "The Morality of the Criminal Law", *Southern California Law Review* 49 (1976) 385; R. Delgado, "'Rotten Social Background': Should the Criminal Law Recognize a Defense of Severe Environmental Deprivation?", *Law & Inequality* 3 (1985) 9.
[32] M. Davis, "Harm and Retribution", *Philosophy and Public Affairs* 15 (1986) 236, 248.
[33] *Id.* at 248.
[34] M. M. Falls, "Retribution, Reciprocity, and Respect for Persons", *Law & Philosophy* 6 (1987): 25, 30.
[35] *Id.* at 31.
[36] J. Deigh, "On the Right to Be Punished: Some Doubts", *Ethics* 94 (1984): 191, 203.
[37] Falls, *supra* note 36, at 30-31.

CHAPTER 7

[1] *Roemer v. Board of Public Works*, 426 U.S. 744, 746-7 (1976), footnote omitted.
[2] *Id.* at 747.
[3] "Congress shall make no law respecting an establishment of religion, or prohibiting the free exercise thereof", *U.S. Const.* amend. I.
[4] "The Commonwealth shall not make any law for establishing any religion, or for imposing any religious observance, or for prohibiting the free exercise of any religion, and no religious test shall be required as a qualification for any office or public trust under the Commonwealth", *Aust. Const.* (Cth) s. 116.
[5] 330 U.S. 1 (1947).
[6] *Id.* at 15-16.
[7] 403 U.S. 602 (1971).
[8] *Id.* at 612-13.
[9] 374 U.S. 398 (1963).
[10] 406 U.S. 205 (1972).
[11] See, e.g., J. Choper, "The Religion Clauses of the First Amendment: Reconciling the Conflict", *University of Pittsburgh Law Review* 47 (1980) 673; W.G. Katz, "Freedom of

Religion and State Neutrality", *University of Chicago Law Review* 20 (1953) 426.
[12] *United States v. Ballard*, 322 U.S. 78, 79 (1944).
[13] *Torcaso v. Watkins*, 367 U.S. 488, 495 (1961); *Church of the New Faith v. Commissioner for Pay-roll Tax*, (1983) 57 A.L.J.R. 785, 791.
[14] 380 U.S. 163 (1965).
[15] *Id.* at 176.
[16] 398 U.S. 333 (1970).
[17] *Id.* at 339.
[18] *Id.* at 343.
[19] *Church of the New Faith* (1983) 57 A.L.J.R. 785, 791.
[20] (1983) 57 A.L.J.R. 785.
[21] *Id.* at 789.
[22] *Id.* at 787.
[23] See J.A.T. Robinson, *Honest to God* (London: SCM Press, 1963), p. 29.
[24] *Id.* at 130.
[25] P. Tillich, *Dynamics of Faith* (London: Allen & Unwin: 1957), pp. 1-4.
[26] *Id.* at 13.
[27] *Id.* at 46.
[28] M. Marty, *Varieties of Unbelief* (New York: Doubleday, 1966), p. 122.
[29] G.C. Freeman,"The Misconceived Search for the Constitutional Definition of 'Religion'", *Georgetown Law Journal* 71 (1983) 1519.
[30] 367 U.S. 488, 495 n. 11 (1961).
[31] See L. Tribe, *American Constitutional Law* (Mineola, N.Y.: Foundation Press, 1978), para. 14-6; D.A.J. Richards, *Toleration and the Constitution* (New York: Oxford University Press, 1986) 145-46.
[32] *Welsh v. United States*, 398 U.S. 333, 339 (1970).
[33] A.H. Loewy, "Rethinking Government Neutrality Towards Religion Under the Establishment Clause", *North Carolina Law Review* 64 (1986) 1049, 1068.
[34] *Attorney-General (Vic.) Ex rel Black v. Commonwealth* (1981) 55 A.L.J.R. 155.
[35] 403 U.S. 602 (1971).
[36] *Id.* at 612-13.
[37] *Committee for Public Ed. v. Nyquist*, 413 U.S. 756, 813 (1973) (Rehnquist, J., dissenting)
[38] *Id.* at 813.
[39] *Id.* at 813.
[40] *Everson v. Board of Education*, 330 U.S. 1, 56 (1947).
[41] *Id.* at 58.
[42] For a good survey of these attacks on "secular humanism" in public schools, see Note "Developments in the Law — Religion and the State", *Harvard Law Review* 100 (1987) 1606, 1665-74.
[43] J.T. Valauri, "The Concept of Neutrality in Establishment Clause Doctrine", *University of Pittsburgh Law Review* 48 (1986) 83, 127.
[44] S.L. Carter, "Evolutionism, Creationism, and Treating Religion as a Hobby", *Duke Law Journal* (1987) 977, 985-86.
[45] *Id.* at 984.
[46] For a similar argument, see J. Weiss, "Privilege, Posture and Protection: 'Religion' in the Law", *Yale Law Journal* 73 (1964) 593, 621-23; P. B. Kurland, "Of Church and State and

the Supreme Court", *University of Chicago Law Review* 29 (1961) 1, 22-52.
[47] 380 U.S. 163, 176 (1965).
[48] 398 U.S. 333, 334 (1970) (emphasis added).
[49] 406 U.S. 205 (1972).
[50] *Id.* at 215.
[51] *Id.* at 215-16.
[52] See *Torcaso v. Watkins*, 367 U.S. 488, 495 n. 11 (1961).
[53] See, *e.g.*, W.G. Katz, "Freedom of Religion and State Neutrality", *University of Chicago Law Review* 20 (1953) 426.
[54] Valauri, *supra* note 43, at 120.
[55] *Id.* at 120.
[56] See E. Mack, "Liberalism, Neutralism, and Rights", in J.R. Pennock, J.W. Chapman, eds., *Religion, Morality, and the Law: Nomos XXX* (New York: New York University Press, 1988) 46-70.
[57] A. Montefiore, *Neutrality and Impartiality* (Cambridge: Cambridge University Press, 1975) p. 5, footnote omitted.
[58] L. Kolakowski, "Neutrality and Academic Values", in Montefiore, *supra* note 57, at 72-73.

POSTSCRIPT

[1] P. Soper, *A Theory of Law* (Cambridge, Mass.: Harvard University Press, 1984), chap. 3.
[2] See J. Feinberg, *The Moral Limits of the Criminal Law*, vol. 1: *Harm to Others* (New York: Oxford University Press, 1984), chap. 1.

INDEX

Law and Philosophy Library

Publications:

1. E. Bulygin, J.-L. Gardies and I. Niiniluoto (eds.): *Man, Law and Modern Forms of Life*. With an Introduction by M. D. Bayles. 1985 ISBN 90-277-1869-5
2. W. Sadurski: *Giving Desert Its Due*. Social Justice and Legal Theory. 1985 ISBN 90-277-1941-1
3. N. MacCormick and O. Weinberger: *An Institutional Theory of Law*. New Approaches to Legal Positivism. 1986 ISBN 90-277-2079-7
4. A. Aarnio: *The Rational as Reasonable*. A Treatise on Legal Justification. 1987 ISBN 90-277-2276-5
5. M. D. Bayles: *Principles of Law*. A Normative Analysis. 1987 ISBN Hb: 90-277-2412-1; Pb: 90-277-2413-X
6. A. Soeteman: *Logic in Law*. Remarks on Logic and Rationality in Normative Reasoning, Especially in Law. 1989 ISBN 0-7923-0042-4
7. C. T. Sistare: *Responsibility and Criminal Liability*. 1989 ISBN 0-7923-0396-2
8. A. Peczenik: *On Law and Reason*. 1989 ISBN 0-7923-0444-6
9. W. Sadurski: *Moral Pluralism and Legal Neutrality*. 1990 ISBN 0-7923-0565-5
10. M. D. Bayles: *Procedural Justice*. Allocating to Individuals. 1990 ISBN 0-7923-0567-1
11. P. Nerhot (ed.): *Law, Interpretation and Reality*. Essays in Epistemology, Hermeneutics and Jurisprudence. 1990 ISBN 0-7923-0593-0

KLUWER ACADEMIC PUBLISHERS – DORDRECHT / BOSTON / LONDON